T0318281

The Politics of Punishment

Prisons are everywhere. Yet they are not everywhere alike. How can we explain these differences in cross-national uses of incarceration? *The Politics of Punishment* explores this question by undertaking a comparative sociological analysis of penal politics and imprisonment in Ireland and Scotland.

Using archives and oral history, this book shows that divergences in the uses of imprisonment result from the distinctive features of a nation's political culture: the different political ideas, cultural values and social anxieties that shape prison policymaking. Political culture thus connects large-scale social phenomena to actual carceral outcomes, illuminating the forces that support and perpetuate cross-national penal differences. The work therefore offers a new framework for the comparative study of penality.

This is also an important work of sociology and history. By closely tracking how and why the politics of punishment evolved and adapted over time, we also yield rich and compelling new accounts of both Irish and Scottish penal cultures from 1970 to the 1990s.

The Politics of Punishment will be essential reading for students and academics interested in the sociology of punishment, comparative penology, criminology, penal policymaking, law and social history.

Louise Brangan is a lecturer in Criminology, University of Stirling, UK.

New Advances in Crime and Social Harm

This series seeks to publish original cutting-edge contributions to the fields of criminology, criminal justice and penology. Volumes include discussions of Foucault and 'governmentality'; critical criminology; victims and criminal justice; corporate crime; comparative criminology and women's prisons.

Series Editor: David Nelken
All titles in the series:

For more information about this series, please visit: https://www.routledge.com/New-Advances-in-Crime-and-Social-Harm/book-series/AICSERIES

The Politics of Punishment

A Comparative Study of Imprisonment and Political Culture

Louise Brangan

Routledge
Taylor & Francis Group

LONDON AND NEW YORK

First published 2021
by Routledge
2 Park Square, Milton Park, Abingdon, Oxon OX14 4RN

and by Routledge
52 Vanderbilt Avenue, New York, NY 10017

Routledge is an imprint of the Taylor & Francis Group, an informa business

British Library Cataloguing-in-Publication Data
A catalogue record for this book is available from the British Library

Library of Congress Cataloging-in-Publication Data
Names: Brangan, Louise, author.
Title: The politics of punishment : a comparative study of imprisonment and political culture / Louise Brangan.
Description: Milton Park, Abingdon, Oxon ; New York, NY : Routledge, 2021. | Series: New advances in crime and social harm | Includes bibliographical references and index.
Identifiers: LCCN 2020049751 (print) | LCCN 2020049752 (ebook) | ISBN 9780367900724 (hardback) | ISBN 9781003022398 (ebook)
Subjects: LCSH: Imprisonment–Ireland–History. | Imprisonment–Scotland–History. | Punishment–Political aspects–Ireland. | Punishment–Political aspects–Scotland. | Criminal law–Ireland. | Criminal law–Scotland. | Imprisonment–Political aspects
Classification: LCC KJC8251.I55 B73 2021 (print) | LCC KJC8251.I55 (ebook) | DDC 365/.9411–dc23
LC record available at https://lccn.loc.gov/2020049751
LC ebook record available at https://lccn.loc.gov/2020049752

ISBN: 978-0-367-90072-4 (hbk)
ISBN: 978-0-367-75661-1 (pbk)
ISBN: 978-1-003-02239-8 (ebk)

Typeset in Galliard
by SPi Global, India

For Michael, with whom there is no comparison

Contents

Figures

Tables

Acknowledgements

This research took place over almost ten years and across three countries, with those kinds of distances, making it to the finish-line meant accruing some substantial debts. I can only ever partially repay them, but feel honoured to be able to acknowledge them here.

I am tremendously grateful to Mary Rogan who told me I should, at the very least, think about a PhD. Her encouragement while I was still in Dublin made me think about possible futures that I never would have imagined otherwise. Having eventually made the leap, I have been fortunate to have found an academic home in Scotland, which has proved to be an incredibly fulfilling place to do criminology. The Scottish Centre of Crime and Justice Research has been a genuinely lively, critically engaged and stimulating group to be a part of. I owe a great debt of thanks to my former PhD supervisors at the University of Edinburgh: Richard Sparks and Lesley McAra – I could not have asked for more supportive and encouraging mentors. I am grateful to have since found myself a place in a department as collegiate as the one here at the University of Stirling. It seems increasingly rare to hear of academic departments that give ECRs time to write – finishing this book simply would not have been possible without those conditions of support. During the research, in 2015, I was a visiting Fulbright scholar at the Center for the Study of Law and Society, UC Berkeley. My thanks to Anne Swidler, who welcomed me as a late addition to her cultural sociology graduate course, as well as to Jonathan Simon, Tony Platt and the fellow members of the Carceral Study Group for giving me an intellectual home there. That time and those conversations shaped my thinking about this project in fundamental ways at a critical stage in the analysis.

A number of people generously took the time and trouble to read versions of this work at various stages of its development: Harry Annison, Colette Barry, Lynsey Black, Matt Bowden, Jamie Buchan, David Garland, Cara Jardine, Lesley McAra, Kieran McEvoy, Fergus McNeill, Jonathan Simon, Richard Sparks and Marion Vannier. I am particularly grateful to Claire Hamilton for her sustained encouragement and support with the manuscript. Their criticisms, questions and comments have undoubtedly improved the book's focus and sharpened the precision of the overall argument. I would also like to thank Jim Carnie, Jimmy Martin, Susan Mathieson, Paddy Terry and

Kevin Warner. Each of them helped with access to historical materials that have proved to be utterly essential in writing these histories. My greatest thanks are reserved for my wonderful family and most fervent supporters, Michael, Rua and Connell.

1 Introduction

The prison is everywhere. Yet it is not everywhere alike. For all its apparent universality, the prison continues to display marked, sometimes staggering, divergences in how it operates from one country to the next. What is permitted as a matter of course in one prison system, such as conjugal visits, modern interiors, literal warehousing or extended segregation, are each seen somewhere else as peculiar, utterly inexplicable, even offensive uses of imprisonment. These differences in prison practice and culture are not only regional; a prison system is liable to evolve and change over time. The present imprisonment arrangements in one place may bear little resemblance to how they were organised only a few decades earlier. Why is this? Why does the prison differ and transform as it does? This book sets out to explore these questions by conducting a comparative, historical and sociological study of adult male imprisonment and political culture in Ireland and Scotland from 1970 until the 1990s. I begin from the contention that prisons are social and political institutions. This requires asking: What are the social conditions that give rise to specific penal measures? What cultural values make certain uses of confinement permissible and appropriate while rendering others unacceptable? How does punishment shape social order, reproduce state power and enforce cultural norms? How does the prison relate to other penal, social and welfare institutions (Garland 1991:119)? To understand how exactly social, political and cultural forces find themselves realised in actual prison practices requires a much greater attention to the policymaking that shapes, remakes and maintains prison systems. In exploring these matters, this book aims to recover and compare the meanings, ideas and sensibilities that made Ireland and Scotland's distinctive penal cultures possible at the end of the twentieth century.

Comparative penology: Conceptual challenges

Comparative study adds new depth to how we understand penality. The contrasting light of comparative reflection admonishes the tendency to take for granted, revealing prohibitive moral boundaries, oddities of outlook and characteristics of punishment and penal politics that may have previously gone unremarked.

Conducting our research questions cross-nationally can help further refine how we theorise the relationships between punishment, culture, politics and social structure. However, we need to address what it is we compare, and why, if we are to advance comparative study in new directions that allow it to live up to its empirical and theoretical potential. As it stands, comparative sociology of punishment continues to be hindered by conceptual ambiguity regarding *imprisonment* and *penal politics*.

These conceptual limitations are rooted in the pervasiveness of punitiveness. Contemporary comparative penology developed in the shadow of the punitive turn experienced at the end of twentieth century in the USA and Britain, as well as other nations, evident first in what seemed to be the unravelling of the penal welfare consensus (Feeley and Simon 1992; Garland 2001). Integration practices and individual treatment were displaced in favour of punitive segregation, actuarial techniques, rapidly rising prison populations and the emergence of a more populist and virulent penal politics (Feeley and Simon 1992; Garland 2001; Pratt et al. 2005; Cavadino and Dignan 2006; Wacquant 2009a).[i] The travesty and tragedy of mass incarceration was felt to be totally unanticipated as late as 1970, by which time penal welfarism was seen to have succeeded as the settled and widely accepted penal culture (Garland 2001). The rapidity of this transformation, and the vociferousness with which penal welfare approaches seemed to be actively dismantled, drew considerable academic attention. The subsequent rise and spread of mass incarceration came to occupy a central place in contemporary sociology of punishment (Sparks 2001; Robinson 2016).

In this atmosphere, comparative researchers of punishment found energy and purpose. They have been compelled by the 'importance of understanding the shared pattern of experience in the USA and UK (and by implication, quite likely elsewhere)' (Newburn and Sparks 2004:11) and the study of those exceptional places that avoided the punitive turn (Brangan 2020). There was thus an urgency to comparative scholarship. Cross-national analysis gave scholars a means to more generally theorise what ignited, supported as well as rebuffed this severe penal trend during these crucial decades in the late twentieth century (Downes 1988; Savelsberg 1994; Whitman 2003; Cavadino and Dignan 2006; Green 2008; Lacey 2008; Pratt and Eriksson 2013).

In order to establish differences in penal harshness, studies have tended to favour breadth. Often looking at clusters of countries (Scandinavian, European or Anglophone, for example), they primarily rely on aggregated imprisonment rates and explanatory grand narratives of national heritage and political economy. This has been an especially fecund means of comparison. It has allowed researchers a platform from which to illuminate patterns of significant cross-national difference in how much a given country relies on incarceration to maintain social order. And the analytical frameworks highlight important connections between penal severity and a nation's embedded culture or overarching political inclinations.

Yet, this broad approach to punitive comparisons has also left us with gaps in our understanding of, and explanations for, divergent penal cultures. In the comparative literature we see very few examples that highlight both the precise social contingencies and governmental choices which produce contrasts in penal practice. We have even fewer examples which systematically demonstrate the cross-national differences in how people are imprisoned. These empirical omissions are due to comparative criminology's underlying conceptual limitations. The predominance of punitiveness (and hence abstraction and aggregation) in comparative study has meant that both imprisonment and penal politics remain opaquely and thinly conceptualised.

This book seeks to redress this balance by developing a new agenda for the comparative sociology of punishment. The framework developed and deployed here allows us to undertake fine-grained comparisons of penality. I describe comparative punishment using *imprisonment regimes*, a concept that compares the various ways in which people are housed, categorised, disciplined and monitored across a prison estate. As such, this compares how people are imprisoned, capturing the systematic differences within as well as between national prison systems. The second point of departure is the approach to penal politics. To explain these comparative carceral patterns we need to reconstruct and trace in sharper detail the comparative differences in prison policymaking. Like others, I agree that national culture, social structure, political ideology and historical antecedents are among the essential stuff that creates convergence and divergences in cross-national punishment. However, even 'the more sophisticated studies leave us with something of a black box when it comes to demonstrating how penal law and policies are shaped and how penal decisions are made' (Garland 2013:492). These broad forces and influences will only find themselves realised in the material character of imprisonment regimes when they shape the practical logic, styles of reasoning, values and visions of those actors who are charged with prison policy – what I define here as *political culture*. Hence, we will be equipped to better elucidate exactly how political, social and cultural patterns translate into actual prison practice by generating an insider perspective of penal policymaking (Barker 2009, Jones and Newburn 2005). The theoretical premise and central lesson here is socio-political: that grasping a meaningful understanding of the political ideas and social meanings that shape the routine decisions about how to imprison will help us explain differences in cross-national imprisonment regimes, as well as deepen our understanding of penality in each comparator nation.

Ireland and Scotland: Anglophone punitive exceptions

Comparative research has worked within some theoretical and methodological restrictions of its purpose. This historical penal comparison is sited in Ireland and Scotland arising from the knowledge that the geography of our penal theories and comparative concerns take place in a surprisingly small number of regions (Aas 2012). Prison rates, political economies and enduring historical legacies might help capture and explain dominant aspects of penality in England and the USA, but these discrete punitive patterns have come to prejudice our general comparative questions (Brangan 2020). Examining and comparing penal culture in familiar times but in less places helps us rethink our comparative priorities.

If we should choose our comparator regions for theoretically relevant reasons, then Ireland and Scotland were decided upon precisely because they are both considered outliers within Anglophone penality. Ireland and Scotland, for different reasons, are seen as anomalies, exceptions to the punitive trend. Both nations experienced rising (Ireland) or comparatively high (Scotland) prison numbers from the 1970s, but by and large their carceral developments during this period do not fit with the prevailing historical narrative. In different ways, both Ireland and Scotland are considered to have avoided and mitigated the social drama and political high stakes of mass incarceration and penal populism that otherwise defined that era in this region. In addition, they are both nations that are often omitted in the wider theoretical literature on penality, rarely included in their own geo-political criminological context, despite their cultural, political and physical proximity to England and USA (e.g. Garland 2001; Pratt and Eriksson 2013; Lappi-Seppälä 2008). Barker's (2009) revealing and instructive example demonstrates the theoretical insights that can be gained from comparing penality *within* exceptional and overlooked English-speaking regions. Following this, comparing Ireland and Scotland provides an opportunity to begin the necessary conceptual development to expand the comparative field of vision. Researching in places not considered mass incarcerators nor stalwarts of penal parsimony (but also not considered alike) saves us from the punitive/exceptional distraction.

This study also takes an historical turn. This is because there is an implicit historical dimension to much leading comparative work: how have things come to be so here and not there? Following Loader and Sparks (2004), our contemporary theories would be enriched if we examine 'the contours and conflicts' of penal culture 'in the latter half of the twentieth century *in their own terms*' (Loader and Sparks 2004:15; original emphasis). We will be better able to compare and contrast what happened in Irish and Scottish penality, and better equipped to refine our comparative explanations and concepts, 'when we think seriously about the past' (ibid.).

The historical approach has other advantages. While there have been exemplary works of scholarship that look at penality in both nations at the end of the twentieth century, it certainly still seems that much more could be written about the histories of both Irish and Scottish penal politics. Thus, Ireland and Scotland are recovered and compared as they are historical outliers, appear comparatively obscure and are most often studied at a distance from the main theoretical conversations (Brangan 2020).[ii]

Ireland

Ireland has an emerging reputation as an Anglophone penal exception, described now as 'Hibernian exceptionalism' (Griffin and O'Donnell 2012; Hamilton 2016; Griffin 2018; Rooney 2020). This is partially because as the crisis of rehabilitation was occurring in the USA and England and Wales in the 1970s, Ireland first adopted the term in legislation in the Prisons Act 1970. It is argued by some that this moment of penal change – the formal adoption of rehabilitation – lacked ideological commitment, apparently marking little more than a discursive shift, giving the appearance of penal welfarism without a subsequent systematic or ideational reorientation (Kilcommins et al. 2004:287; Rogan 2011). What we see is that Irish penal history of the late twentieth century is defined by what it is not. Ireland was, it is argued, curiously 'immune to broader pressures' of punitive transformation (Griffin and O'Donnell 2012:613). Instead, Irish penal practice has rarely been 'supported by reference to a set of clear principles' (Kilcommins et al. 2004:292–293), academic influence or other professional expertise. Punishment in Ireland was mostly a neglected area of policy – essentially operating in what is widely described as a 'vacuum' (Rogan 2011; Griffin and O'Donnell 2012). As a result, in lieu of political principles, the dominant terms employed to describe Irish prison policy history before the 1990s are 'stagnation', 'pragmatic' and 'drift' (O'Donnell 2008; Rogan 2011; Griffin and O'Donnell 2012; Hamilton 2014). Even an apparently punitive penal transformation in the 1990s, where prisoner numbers rose, the prison estate expanded and political discourse was engrossed with talk of dangerous criminals, has been explained as 'political opportunism' before a general election, pursued by a particularly vociferous individual opposition politician (O'Donnell and O'Sullivan 2003; Rogan 2011). Thus, it is argued that it was an empowered actor, rather than a change in ideology, structure or culture, who instigated these largely uncoordinated penal changes.

But questions remain. If Irish prisons did not treat or rehabilitate, then in what ways were people imprisoned? What sorts of programmes and regimes were prisoners subject to? What expectations were made of prisoners and prisons? Moreover, no decision is ever merely pragmatic – even the most baldly straightforward choice is a constellation of 'principled positions often unintelligible to their promoters' (Freeden 1996:18). What did civil servants think about prisons, what problems were raised and what solutions did they pursue? These are significant questions that remain to be answered and would yield new theoretical insights if subject to a fuller historical recovery.

Scotland

It is believed that Scotland has equally avoided the punitive trends that otherwise define Anglophone penal transformation. Instead, it is widely accepted that Scotland 'fully embraced penal welfare values' and practices from the 1960s (McAra 2008:489; Mooney et al. 2015). These conditions have been supported by Scotland's distinct national culture (McAra 1999, 2005, 2008; McNeill 2005; Croall 2006; Tata 2010). Yet, despite its established place as an Anglophone punitive exception, there has been scant analytical or historical engagement with this claim. The Scottish case is all the more interesting given that it is not only in the Anglophone region, but is a constituent of the UK. Though it has always had a separate prison and legal system, when the punitive turn was occurring in the 1970s–1990s Scotland was governed by Westminster.

Scotland's distinction is believed to be the progressive character of the penal system (McAra 2005, 2008, 1999; Hamilton 2014) and its relative immunity 'from the populist tendencies that were rapidly infecting its southern neighbour' (Cavadino and Dignan 2006:231). From this comment we see that Scottish exceptionalism has a comparative calling-card, aimed at establishing that Scotland's penal system is believed to have been 'better' than that in England and Wales (Mooney et al. 2015:210). A reader familiarising themselves with the Scottish socio-legal context will also be confronted with claims that the Scottish criminal justice system can be characterised as 'England and Wales it isn't!' (Tata 2010). Discussions of Scotland's penality refer as much to technical differences in the system as they do to something much more essential. The penal system in Scotland, it is argued, reflects Scotland's idiosyncratic civic identity as somewhere with an impregnable collective sense of fairness and communitarian values (McAra 1999; Croall 2006; Hamilton 2014;), which guarded against the negative forces of penal intolerance (Duff and Hutton 1999; Smith and Young 1999; Hamilton 2014).

However, from the mid-1980s Scotland's prison population was large, equivalent in per capita terms to England and Wales (House of Commons 2017), so, if the exceptionlist and punitive claims were ever mainly about numbers, then Scotland was in a precarious position from the outset. Scottish penal parsimony, in relation to the prison at least, is less than clearly established, with McManus (1999:231) suggesting that the impact of welfarism upon imprisonment was only 'piecemeal'. There are clear empirical gaps in our understanding of the historical shape, character and practices of Scottish imprisonment across this period – leaving claims of Scottish penal exceptionalism open to uncertainty.

Comparing penal cultures

If not quite punitive, then what was the nature of their respective penal politics by the end of the twentieth century? How are we to best characterise the respective Irish and Scottish penal developments across the critical decades from 1970 to the 1990s? What distinguishes their prison practices? What sorts of social, political and cultural conditions shaped their penality?.

Underpinning this project are the problems of describing and analysing penality cross-nationally. Comparative studies of punitiveness tend to proceed with the characterisations of penal culture made. What should we compare if we instead wish to begin from a more neutral starting point, seeking to discover how carceral systems vary and why countries make different prison policy choices? To this end, the book aims to move comparative research of punishment beyond the aggregate, abstract and binary parameters that have largely occupied it. Chapter 2 provides a reconsideration of what constitutes politics and imprisonment in light of a reflection about how best to compare them. Chapter 2 first highlights that the comparative study of punishment has become largely detached from the sociology of imprisonment and suggests a reconciliation between these approaches. Rather than thinking statistically in terms prison populations, we need a means to be able to compare how people are imprisoned. I sketch out the concept of imprisonment regimes, which is concerned with precisely this penological quest. Imprisonment regimes encourages a focus on the institutions, prisoner categories, routines and aims that shape the organisational life of a prison estate. As such, it foregrounds the factors that perpetuate the curious cross-national divergences in the uses of imprisonment.

Thereafter, I set out a new conceptual vocabulary for discussing the politics of punishment. To convincingly explain comparative variation, we need to examine imprisonment in a 'substantively political light' (O'Malley 1999:189). To allow this kind of governmental insight I introduce the concept of political culture. This concept illuminates the distinctly political ideas and social meanings that drive policy choices and ultimately provide the ideational scaffolding that supports and legitimises distinctive systems of incarceration. Political culture is not merely a conduit for macro forces, therefore. It is generative, becoming the buffer between what is seen and felt to be permissible and impermissible in uses of imprisonment and the deployment of penal power. Hence, conceived this way, this project requires a grounded approach, which is all too rare in comparative penality. This chapter concludes by highlighting the distinctly ethnographic orientation taken towards historical comparative research. This helps reconstruct the immediacies of the policymaking process and situates this within the specificities of their historical context.

This work is equally comparative and historical. To do justice to these interlocking agendas I forgo ongoing comparisons; instead, the analysis is presented as historical case studies, set out in Sections 1 and 2. The benefit of presenting each nation singly is that a richer contextual history can be more successfully sustained. Additionally, the trajectory of each history is amplified, showing the long-term patterns of penal developments and social change in each case (Pierson 2004; Barker 2009). As Barker proposes, this long-term perspective provides a more thoroughgoing way to research comparative penal politics as 'the work of governance is made up of ongoing activity, small moments: small movements, repetitive and mundane' (2006:7). Taking these penal histories seriously within the remit of their precise social meanings and historical events resulted in the timelines being slightly different. Both begin in 1970 as this is widely seen as the general point in history when new trends began emerging in Anglophone penal policies. Ireland's major penal transformation occurred in the mid–late 1990s, while Scotland's prison system underwent significant redevelopment at the very beginning of the 1990s. Here each comparative account ends when transformations had become domesticated as the relatively settled penal culture. So, Ireland is looked at from 1970 to 1999 while Scotland is presented from 1970 to

1995. Extending Scotland's prison history by four years seemed a pedantry of wanting chronological equilibrium at the expense of comparative and analytical depth. Thus, both accounts end in different years of the same period.

In Chapters 3 through 5 we explore Irish penal culture in depth from 1970-1999. Chapter 3 begins from 1970. During this period the Irish imprisonment regime was remarkable for its moderate practices and humane agenda. This was the product of a zealous pastoral penal culture, which valued collective social morality above all else and as a result gave impetus to supportive and permissive prison policies. In Chapter 4 we see that no matter how deeply held a set of values are, they morph and adapt to fit events and circumstances. We see in this Chapter the slow corrosive impact of challenging social change in Ireland upon the imprisonment regime. Panic and impotence reshaped the policymaking priorities, permitting punitive amendments that were largely not the result of punitive government intent. Chapter 5 concludes this section, explicitly mapping the impact of Ireland's rapid social and political transformation upon the penal culture. By 1999 new punitive desires and political ideas came to drastically revise how prisons and government were organised. The aims of exclusion and political sovereignty came to reshape Irish penal culture, while at the same time Ireland was becoming a more liberal society. These contrasting changes were mutually reinforcing. The Irish prison was repositioned, mirroring and shoring up the new socio-political architecture of modern Irish life at the end of the 1990s.

Section 2 begins in Chapter 6, which introduces the social, cultural and political landscape in Scotland, and shows how this context and the prevailing sensibilities informed the distinctive thinking behind Scottish prison policymaking. It is argued that Scotland's prison system was a dismal and punitive set of routines and programmes, which reflected and buttressed Scotland's social hierarchies and liberal political ideals. Chapter 7 recounts a series of prison riots that left the prison administration shocked and reeling and a sense that the prison system was now suffering chronic disarray. Chapter 8, following this empirical and analytical narrative, reveals how these unsettling events, along with the rise of Thatcherite managerialism and Scottish civic nationalism in the late 1980s, led to a civilising penal transformation in Scotland by the mid 1990s. Prisons and prison management became a technocratic process, reflecting a desire to take firm control of the prison while also, by contrast, appearing progressive.

Across these chapters I establish new theorisations of both Irish and Scottish penal dynamics during this crucial period. My hope is that by taking this longitudinal form the reader is left feeling they come to know something of these places, with a deeper understanding of both Irish and Scottish penal cultures. And as the prison is a social institution, then studying it historically, politically and culturally will enrich our sociological knowledge of both Ireland and Scotland.

Having set out the Irish and Scottish prison policy histories in their own terms, I use these as the basis for comparative and theoretical inferences in the Conclusion in Chapter 9. We see empirical evidence that prison policy condenses diverse conflicts, sensibilities and anxieties. By undertaking a close-up and fine-grained examination of prison policymaking over a longer period, we can see how social, political and cultural changes rendered practical alterations in how prisons and penal power were organised. While penal transformation in both nations differed (expressive punitiveness in Ireland and progressive penality in Scotland), these modifications were not about crime control alone. They were also explicit political statements about state power, as well as reflecting shifting social conditions and authoritatively displaying new cultural sensibilities. What is presented here therefore complicates, extends and augments what we thought we knew about how imprisonment differs, and illuminates why that is the case, tracing the social and political roots of those cross-national divergences.

Why compare? Comparative study is laborious, at the very least you must undertake your research twice in two different nations – doubling the workload of familiarisation, acculturation, reviewing literature and then gathering data, while adding complexities to the analysis. This uniquely demanding endeavour is worthy of devoting so much time and energy because cross-national study yields empirical and theoretical rewards. Viewing penal culture in comparative perspective creates a reciprocal dynamic that illuminates the taken-for-granted and overlooked penal dynamics in each case study. As Nelken wrote, what does someone know of England if they only know England (2010:14)? As a method it provides the proverbial set of fresh eyes. With comparative research we also garner the analytical leverage to refine our theoretical assumptions about how politics shapes imprisonment, and also what it is we mean when we use these terms comparatively. The comparative perspective powerfully displays that there is always a messy contested nature to how prison policymaking is carried out – a dialectic between duty and desire, abstract logic and local know-how, ideals and real-life events. Such contrasting forces find themselves reflected in the variation we see in national uses of confinement. Together, what these comparative case studies so vividly display is that how and why the power to imprison is deployed, even in diverse contexts, is always best understood as a social institution, embedded in the patterns of history, ideology, culture and structure – a cross-national reality not best captured by comparing punitiveness. By refining our comparative theories, we may think differently about the politics of punishment, and come to know it anew.

Notes

i That these penal welfare/punitive turn narratives are presented here on a grand scale is not because it is a convenient shorthand. This reflects the proclivity in these theoretical histories to capture what is seen as the prevailing, and entirely contrasting, epochs of Anglophone penal transformation. For a critical discussion, see Goodman et al. 2017.

ii Though scholars working in both places have made the case for the relevance of Irish and Scottish criminology to wider theoretical debates (Brangan 2019, 2021; Hamilton 2013, 2014; O'Sullivan and O'Donnell 2007; Barry 2020; Buchan 2020; Jardine 2020; McAra 2008; Fraser 2015)

2 Comparative penal culture

Introduction

Why do we punish as we do? And why does that differ between nations? To attempt to answer these questions we need a means to establish empirical differences (1) in how we punish and (2) in the forces that support those penal practices. Undertaking this kind of comparative investigation is impeded, however, given that comparative sociology of punishment scholarship is still considered to be 'at an early stage' of development (Garland 2013, 2017:2; Sparks 2001; Hamilton 2014). Despite the existence of canonical comparative texts, this somewhat fledgling state of affairs is due in part to the conceptual frameworks with which to think about, research and compare penality remaining nascent (Brangan 2020). Addressing that specific shortcoming, this chapter provides readers with a new conceptual vocabulary developed in order to undertake a grounded comparative study of penal culture.

The first of these is a reconceptualisation of imprisonment in particular. When prisons are compared in penology, the complexity of the prison system tends to be eschewed in favour of thin but apparently objective indices such as per capita imprisonment rates (Whitman 2003; Cavadino and Dignan 2006; Lacey 2008; Pratt and Eriksson 2013). This chapter combines the insights from the sociology of imprisonment with the aims of comparative penology to reconceptualise the prison as *imprisonment regimes*. This chapter therefore proceeds beyond the usual metrics for comparing imprisonment asking: in what kinds of prisons were prisoners held? How were people moved through the prison – namely, what kinds of release and segregation were prisoners subject to? What programmes of rehabilitation were prisoners encouraged to engage in? How were prisoners categorised? Deployed as an analytical and descriptive concept, imprisonment regimes reveal the diverse arrangement of strategies and objectives that are pursued by a single prison system. This makes for a more detailed but still consistent cross-national comparison of imprisonment.

The second section argues that a comparative analysis of penal politics requires a new understanding of *political culture*. Our most prominent comparative explanations tend to rely on macro approaches, particularly political economy or national culture. Rather than seeing them as opposing analytical tactics, each of these accounts makes an important contribution to how we understand penal differences. But why certain forms of punishment are seen as acceptable, even desirable, while others are felt to be inappropriate requires a far more grounded and multifaceted conception of political culture. We need to ask: what emotions, cultural meanings and beliefs are embedded in, and shape, penal policymaking? How do these factors relate to their immediate social context and historical patterns? We also need to investigate the political ideologies and visions of society that policy actors draw on to interpret problems, shape solutions and rationalise government intervention. Political culture thus conceived provides the practical logic that is integral to how penal power is conceived and deployed, and thus why imprisonment regimes are organised as they are. As a comparative lens, political culture, as it has been devised here, provides us with a new way to examine and contrast differences in prison policies and hence explain divergences in cross-national imprisonment.

Before the concluding section there is a brief note on methodology. Interested in *how* those broad social forces and cultural currents are translated into penal policy and practice, I used methods from social history and critical archive studies to achieve a fine-grained investigation of government and prison systems. I went to under-researched archives, found previously unread files, memos, minutes and unpublished reports. I spoke to people who were there at the time, for whom government and prison administration were their career. Therefore, given this historical approach, this comparative study will also add to the respective histories of punishment in both Ireland and Scotland.

Comparing imprisonment

What happens to a person once they are imprisoned? What sort of conditions do they live in? What kinds of activities consume their time? What demands and expectations are made of prisoners? In properly considering these seemingly straightforward questions we are confronted with a view of an entire prison system displaying a varied, and sometimes contradictory, set of forms, routines and functions. This presents dizzying challenges for comparative research. How then do we compare imprisonment? What is it we compare and why?

Comparison is rarely straightforward, however, and it requires a degree of abstraction to save it from spiralling into incomparable detailed inventories of local prison differences and regional policy proclivities. Comparative penology, however, provides few conceptual tools that can, first of all, engage with a prison system's variegated routines and practical character and, second, can do so while also rendering imprisonment comparable. This might seem surprising given the variety and richness of comparative penal scholarship. If there was a 'little avalanche of penal comparisons' in the 2000s (Sparks 2001:165), it has become one of criminology's sustained growth industries. Yet, for all its centrality in the comparative study of punishment,[i] the prison is thinly conceptualised in comparative research; it is at once foregrounded in making the case about differences in cross-national penality and yet poorly illuminated.

Most frequently, the prison is primarily represented via statistics and the comparison of commensurate international imprisonment rates. They are used to situate a bigger story about penal comparison, helping to define a nation's fundamental penal 'profile' (Lappi-Seppälä 2011). In comparative research, imprisonment rates have emerged as a proxy for punitiveness or lenience (Cavadino and Dignan 2006; Lacey 2008; Pratt 2008). The merits of aggregate imprisonment rates are that they provide researchers with an even empirical surface for revealing and comparing the penal patterns of countries without necessarily effacing transnational diversity. Imprisonment rates also allow a greater number of countries to be compared. Patterns of commonalities and divergences in imprisonment rates – and thus in penal harshness – have become the puzzle that much comparative penology has set about trying to solve.

But the problems with imprisonment rates are well-rehearsed (Pease 1994; Nelken 2011; Tonry 2007a; Hamilton 2014). The prison is often at the end of a long journey through the myriad institutions that make up the criminal justice system (Hamilton 2014; Cunneen et al. 2018). Imprisonment rates are more easily understood as an insight into policing, legislative and judicial patterns, rather than as a distillation of an entire culture. As Lynch has written, in the case of imprisonment rates 'penal change is legal change' (Lynch 2011:676) – which of course would give rise to its own series of revealing investigations (see, for example, Nelken 2009). Imprisonment rates also reveal very little about what happens to a person when they are imprisoned (Sparks 2001). This is because the routines and systems that organise prison life and order are often omitted from this broad comparative view (Brangan 2020).

The most resilient defence of giving primacy to imprisonment rates is that there is simply something intuitive about them:[ii] countries with higher prison rates don't tend to surprise us upon closer investigation by actually being systematically humane. However, of late, studies of lenient or exceptional prison systems (judged to be so mostly due to their low prison populations) have come to reveal that the pains of imprisonment remain in abundance, albeit less immediately obvious (Ugelvik and Dullum 2012; Reiter et al. 2018; Laursen et al. 2020). To be held in segregation in a country that is considered welfarist would come as little relief to those persons who experience the depths of confinement that limit and deny whatever degree of autonomy and physical movement is usually afforded the general prison population (Barker 2013; Hannah-Moffat 2014; Shammas 2014). And the opposite is also possible: people held in open prisons with strong community links and liberal uses of release may well be experiencing incarceration in a manner that feels disconnected from what academics perceive as that nation's punitiveness (Barker 2009). What this shows us is that even if a prison estate is broadly progressive or comparatively harsh, there remain differences within any prison system as well as between prison systems. If we took this seriously, our comparative concept of imprisonment would be multidimensional – a hybrid of punitive and rehabilitative, exclusionary and integrative.

Without addressing this conceptual issue, some of the debate has instead focused on the primacy of imprisonment rates to tell us anything about comparative punitiveness. It has been eloquently argued by Nelken that the complexity of punitiveness surely requires a more wide-ranging set of measures if it is to be adequately assessed (Nelken 2009). This in/ability to measure penal punitiveness is where much of the debate about comparative work focuses. The suggestion is that the prison has come to takeover and skew our comparative perspective, and hence there is a need to expand the numbers and penal sites we compare (Tonry 2001a; Hamilton 2014; Hucklesby et al. 2020). This approach usefully and importantly diversifies matters and broadens our penological field of vision. Alternatively, I suggest that it would be premature to abandon comparative imprisonment. The tendency in comparative penology to focus (mainly or exclusively) on the rise of mass incarceration and the spread of punitiveness has meant that, ironically, the prison actually remains opaquely conceptualised in much comparative study. This is work that remains to be done if comparative penality is to be further developed.

To conduct comparative study of imprisonment one is left feeling that the texture of a nation's overall prison system could be better articulated if it was unbridled from Anglocentric concerns with imprisonment rates and punitiveness. Despite the increase in cross-national research, and the significant contributions and advances already made in comparative analysis and explanation, the need for refining what exactly we are comparing when we compare imprisonment remains. A comparative perspective on imprisonment is near impossible without first establishing a *terra firma* of prison patterns.

The sociology of imprisonment

The central contention here is that comparative study of punishment is faced by theoretical restrictions regarding how to conceive of imprisonment, and how, thereby, to study the arrangements that constitute its practice. By prioritising something as amorphous as penal punitiveness, comparative study has tended to neglect the development of concepts that are necessary if we are to compare prison systems. I propose that to further the project of comparative penology we ought to concentrate on developing coherent, consistent and precise descriptions of imprisonment.

I want to briefly turn to the contrasting ways we conceive of the prison in the sociology of imprisonment. Rather than seeing the system monolithically via population numbers, in the sociology of imprisonment the diverse practices of incarceration are brought into vivid relief. Nations depend on complex organisations to imprison people, and therefore in practice imprisonment will be incommensurable, differentiated and multifaceted. A prison system is devised and adapted so that it can contain people, deprive them of their liberty, but also contrives to educate, treat, reform, assess, punish and potentially utilise prisoners. Within a single prison system there are different degrees and forms of control, discipline, rehabilitation, management and measurement of prisoners (Simon 1993; McEvoy 2001; Matthews 2009). There are, quite simply, different kinds of prisons, within which the use of physical security, internal regimes and access to privileges, for example, can differ significantly (Cohen and Taylor 1972; Sparks et al. 1996). Therefore, a single prison system can have sites of great depth, as well as places where prisoners possess more liberties, freedom of movement and autonomy (Downes 1988; King and McDermott 1995; Sparks 2002). The variety of carceral institutions in a single prison estate reflects what will be understood as the different needs and threats posed by prisoners, who are themselves assessed and organised by categories (Coyle 1991). Each institution will likely have its own aims and means, exercising power against its prisoner population to seek certain ends (Foucault 1977; Carlen 1983; McEvoy 2001; Crewe 2009), though what those are should not be taken for granted. Prison sociology also shows that it would be a mistake to think of individual prisons like islands, detached from each other. Prisons also involve circulation (Birkbeck 2011), whereby prisoners move in and out (Guiney 2018) as well as around the prison estate, and this can be central to achieving the overall aims of imprisonment (Armstrong 2015). How these release and transfer systems are organised can mean the difference between a prison regime that demands prisoners get through their sentence as opposed to more simply getting out of the prison (Birkbeck 2011:322).

Prison research also shows us that similar policy discourses can obscure significant operational divergences. For example, prison education is important and laudable; in practice it can be designed to support people to develop confidence (Warr 2015), but it can also be used as a narrow means to reduce prisoners' potential for reoffending (Warner 2007). Rehabilitation has a similarly generic meaning, but in practice there are startling programmatic nuances (Robinson 2008). The aims of imprisonment therefore cannot always be easily read as either punitive or lenient, even when policy agendas are stated in clearly progressive or retributive terms (Crewe 2011a, 2011b; Reiter et al. 2018).

Finally, a prison's form is changeable, never truly fixed let alone singular in its ethos. Prisons patterns evolve and adapt over time (Garland 1985, 2001; Page 2011; Robinson 2008). However, when viewed via imprisonment rates or overarching penal culture, important changes in how people are imprisoned are impossible to decipher. Significantly, then, while the size of a national prison estate may expand or retract, we should also pay close attention to how its forms and techniques of intervention alter and change (Feeley and Simon 1992; Hannah-Moffat 2005; Simon 2007).

This overview demonstrates that imprisonment is a constellation of goals, with a diversity of sites and practices. These are cross-national penal patterns calling out for comparative investigation and explanation. If we are to advance the comparative study of penality, we should think of imprisonment as a system, a polymorphous 'regime of practices', those 'sets of calculated, reasoned prescriptions in terms of which institutions are meant to be reorganized, spaces arranged, behaviours regulated' (Foucault 1991a:80). It is those activities and modes of imprisonment which cause human suffering and potentially foster opportunities for personal development within the prison, and thus should concern us as comparative researchers of punishment. However, to do this we must integrate the somewhat disparate areas of sociology of imprisonment with the comparative sociology of punishment.

Imprisonment regimes

The kinds of cross-national differences in the uses of imprisonment that might provide a rich comparative research field are effaced by primarily contrasting punitiveness. The sociology of imprisonment shows us that prisons (and thus prison systems) are heterogeneous and functional places in which people are incarcerated, but also potentially coerced, incentivised, medicalised and disciplined in order to achieve certain social, moral, cultural and political ends (Foucault 1977; Carlen 1983). We require a way of conceiving imprisonment that can capture its complex practical character, while still rendering it comparable.

I take a view of what I shall call the *imprisonment regime*. Drawing on the sociology of imprisonment we can better conceptualise comparative imprisonment, reassembling its core features and practices beyond levels of confinement and punitiveness. Comparing imprisonment regimes allows us to identify what kinds of *places* prisons are, and, by locating those places more securely within the context of the organisations in which they are embedded, we can discern their systems of interventions, categorisations and routines. Looking at the precise functions and routines that shape imprisonment also provides a better platform for comparatively examining the diversities that exist *within* as well as *between* prison systems. Below I outline six dimensions, drawn from the above literature, that will leave us better able to explore one of comparative penology's key questions: how does imprisonment differ between nations?

Begins at the moment of imprisonment. Imprisonment regimes as a researchable comparative concept would begin at the moment of being imprisoned (Carlen 1983). What happens to people once they are imprisoned? Taking this as our starting point re-orientates our comparative focus upon the regimes and routines that someone is subject to upon being incarcerated.

Prison regimes. The concept of imprisonment regimes takes into account the overarching function and agenda of the different prisons, which tend to traverse a wider gamut than punitive or lenient – from open prisons to segregation units, with much else in between, including closed prisons, high-security prisons, but also smaller experimental units (Genders and Player 1995; Sparks et al. 1996; Sparks 2002; Shammas 2014). However, we must keep in mind that what is considered the standard closed or open prison may differ from one context to the next.

Circulation. Prisons are not stand-alone units in which people are held, static and waiting. Prisons exist in networks and systems, through which prisoners circulate as part of the routine of their confinement. By circulation I do not mean the daily timetable of each institution, but the systematic way prisoners migrate around as well as in and out of the prison system. Circulation includes sentence progression, discipline, segregation, and early and temporary release, for example. The way prisoners are moved through their sentence, and through the system, reflects the overarching demands of the regime (Armstrong 2015), be it to discipline, incentivise, train, rehabilitate, etc. As such, how people are moved or distributed inside a system aims to achieve specific competences within prisoners and within the system (Foucault 1977).

Prisoner classification. Prisoner classifications shape the organisation of imprisonment regimes; they are riven with the perceived needs, vulnerabilities, problems and risks of the penal subject (Carlen 1983; McEvoy 2001; Hannah-Moffat 2005; Shalev 2007; Annison 2015). As a consistent organisational feature across penal systems, categories are an important point of comparison, though it is unlikely they will be identical in their application and meanings.

Rehabilitation and reform. Attempts at transforming prisoners are by and large a generic discourse of modern Western prison systems. But this universal concept will vary in meaning and practice across national prison systems (Robinson 2008) and can change over time (Crewe 2011b). What kinds of interventions and experts shape the rehabilitative agenda in a prison? Are they coercive or supportive? What do these programmes seek to achieve: personal development, normalisation, reducing reoffending or discipline?

Responses to changing prison numbers. Empirically mapping imprisonment regimes still includes imprisonment rates, albeit de-centring them. Whether or not they are successful, we must instead examine the direct attempts that are made to expand or reduce the size of the prison estate and thus ultimately alter the imprisonment regime. This is an empirical question about how high or low imprisonment rates are seen, imagined and responded to by government officials (Armstrong 2013). Amendments to the imprisonment regime in response to the size of its population is a process of comparative concern. Small prison systems can be expanded but still maintain relatively low per capita imprisonment rates, for example. Large prison systems can implement systems of furlough and remission intended to reduce the number of people in prison (Nelken 2011:110). Or political actors can respond to demand for prison places by placing more mattresses on the floor of already cramped spaces, creating a queuing system (Laursen et al. 2020) or simply building more prisons.

Moving beyond imprisonment rates and punitiveness as the object of comparison exposes new gaps in our explanatory comparative accounts. What is it that makes the uses of imprisonment meaningful and legitimate in one time and place but unthinkable in another context? How feasibly can paradigms of capitalism, political typologies or embedded foundational cultures elucidate the contours of our variegated systems of incarceration? To explain the plurality inherent in imprisonment regimes we will also have to develop more nuanced explanatory models, which themselves reflect the multifaceted character of imprisonment regimes.

Political culture

Existing explanatory models for comparative penality show important correlations between broad penal styles and national-level political and cultural patterns. But how best to understand imprisonment regimes? How can we explain how two penal systems espouse the same general aims – say, rehabilitation – but attempt to achieve these ends through different penal techniques? Currently, comparative penology is not able to satisfactorily answer these questions.

There are two competing tendencies that dominate the comparative literature. We know that differences in overarching harshness or lenience of the penal system aligns with the political economy. However, evidence also suggests there is a broad affinity between national culture and imprisonment. The benefits and limitations of these approaches are both discussed before a rapprochement is suggested, one that braids the political and cultural together to develop a new multidimensional theorisation of *political culture*. This concept is necessary, first, to develop more fine-grained accounts of the penal politics that also allow for systematic comparison of political dynamics of punishment; and, second, to offer a new framework to explain differences in cross-national imprisonment regimes.

Explaining penal differences: political economy or cultural compulsion?

Politics are central to our understanding of how people are imprisoned (O'Malley 1999; Wacquant 2009a; Rogan 2011; Annison 2015), and it is now well established that the comparative differences in the uses of imprisonment are linked to political economy in particular (Beckett and Western 2001; Sutton 2004; Cavadino and Dignan 2006; Lacey 2008). Countries with a free market approach are less likely to invest in social welfare spending. As a result, these nations rely on criminal justice as the main tactic in addressing social needs and inequality, and thus have higher imprisonment rates than those nations with more inclusive political economies. This political framework has proved particularly useful for comparative research. We see an alignment between political and penal systems in what Nelken has described as 'near perfect matching' (2011:106), convincingly making the case that comparative research must attend to the ideological determinants of penal policies if we are to understand convergence and/or divergence in international patterns of imprisonment.

This framework is not without its weaknesses, however. This account of politics sees government as a 'black box' (Barker 2009); there are no agents, no issues or events that direct thinking on imprisonment (Jones and Newburn 2005; Annison 2018). This is because comparative penal politics tend to be viewed from a high altitude, giving political culture a fixed and immutable quality. Arguably, current accounts of politics in comparative penology tend to overestimate the coherence of a governmental outlook. As a result, this particular comparative framework, while showing correlations between political typologies and high/low imprisonment rates, is simply not equipped to explain continued variation and transformation within cross-national prison (and therefore also political) systems.

With the emphasis on political tactics there is no sense of punishment's meanings, its expressive functions. This is a major oversight that doesn't permit us a proper comparative view of the prison as a social institution. In this vein, others argue that politics is first and foremost situated within a cultural and historical context that gives punishment its social significance (Tonry 2007b; Smith 2008). To understand comparative differences in punishment, we must understand each nation's cultural heritage and emotional temperament. This analytical approach has been highly significant in comparative punishment studies, showing an affinity between culture, history and levels of penal harshness (Melossi 2001; Whitman 2003; Pratt and Eriksson 2013) – issues that are treated as subsidiary in the political economy comparative approach.

This is an advance in the comparative outlook, reminding us of the embedded nature of punishment (Melossi 2001). However, this often moves the dial too far in the other direction. Bound to national cultural ideals, penality is detached from the instrumental and pragmatic governmental processes which produce imprisonment. As Garland has written, '[s]ocial currents may ebb and flow, but they have no penal consequence unless and until they enlist state actors and influence state action' (2013:494). These conceptions of culture can tend towards essentialising. Therefore, they can account for little more than affinity between punishment and culture. As an explanatory framework, culture risks being an inappropriately deterministic approach to comparative penality. While punishment is a social institution and thus must reflect historically developed cultural values and social norms, punishment also remains contingent on the immediate social and political circumstances. In addition, the emphasis on culture as an enduring historical force makes it less capable of explaining changes and transformations in how people are imprisoned.

Without diminishing the serious advances these collective works represent, there remains much left unsaid about some important core features of both the political and cultural currents of penality. The problems of the comparative literature are (1) that it is riven with tension, separating political thinking from cultural meaning, placing them in analytical opposition. (2) However, while positioned as oppositional explanations, both approaches suffer (to a greater or lesser degree) from similar weaknesses of abstract and largely static accounts of politics and culture. (3) Both comparative approaches are curiously insensitive to the empirical detail of prison policymaking. Hence, neither framework offers an account of how either political ideology or cultural meaning finds itself realised in actual penal practices. These limitations undermine our ability to understand and explain differences in how people are imprisoned.

Comparative framework for the politics of punishment

How do we ameliorate these tensions and shortcomings? Certainly, there seems to be something of a stalemate between political and cultural comparative approaches. It is right and correct to focus on politics in particular. But this should not lead us to disregard place-specific cultural meanings; these are also a vital source of difference in penal practices. I suggest we need a new comparative conceptualisation of the politics of punishment, one that bridges the chasm between these two approaches. The tensions between the political and cultural in comparative exposition can be resolved by bringing these analytical principles together to develop a multidimensional analytical framework (Garland 1990a, 1990b). A multidimensional approach sees punishment as

> a cultural as well as a strategic affair; that it is a realm for the expression of social value and emotion as well as a process for asserting control. And that, for all its necessity as an institution, and despite all our attempts to make it positive and useful, it still involves a tragic and futile quality which derives from its contradictory cultural location and which ought to be recognized in analysis
>
> (1990b:4)

Following this thinking, a comparative framework 'for analysing punishment ought thus to be geared towards interpreting the conflicting social values and sentiments which are expressed and evoked in punishment as well as to tracing instrumental strategies of penal control' (ibid.). In this vein, I offer a conceptualisation of *political culture*, designed to provide a new comparative framework for research and analysis. The term political culture is already present in comparative penology (Green 2008; Lacey 2008; Hamilton 2014). These accounts are important because they emphasise that we should compare 'ways of doing politics' if we are to understand differences in penal policy (Green 2007:591). Specifically, however, political culture here is largely used to describe institutional dynamics, based on political science conceptions of 'consensus', 'majoritarian' or 'conflict' political systems. Alternatively, Hamilton looks at matters in a more grounded manner, suggesting that the political is better understood as a set of 'cognitive constraints' (Hamilton 2013). Advancing on this work, below I outline the key dimensions of an alternative interpretive vocabulary for comparative political culture as a generative set of practices. These focus on (1) *cultural sensibilities*, such as crime anxieties and understandings of prisoners; and (2) *political reasoning*, which includes ideological rationalities, a desire to cultivate citizen-subjects and the practical techniques of government.

Cultural sensibilities

Unlike the essentialising or broad concepts of culture that tend to prevail in comparative penology I focus instead upon specific *penal sensibilities* (Garland

1990a; Girling et al. 2000; Smith et al. 2000), namely those distinct beliefs, social sentiments, precise cultural meanings, specific anxieties and values that actually influence penal policymaking. As Garland once argued, sensibilities have a determinative influence on penal policy: 'Penal laws and institutions are always proposed, discussed, legislated and operated within definite cultural codes…which must be interpreted and understood if the social meaning and motivations of punishment are to become intelligible' (1990a:198). Understanding this aspect of prison policy presents a particularly novel and useful way to explain comparative differences in penal politics. These cultural currents shape penal policymaking dispositions towards what is felt to be desirable and acceptable, ultimately inflecting imprisonment regimes with practices that signify wider social meanings.

Theoretically, penal sensibilities follow Durkheim (1984) and Elias (1978) in emphasising the social sentiments that are central to the uses of punishment and the character of social order (Garland 1990b). There is a propensity to portray punishment as shaped mainly by punitive anger (Hartnagel and Templeton 2012), prioritising the negative emotions that limit empathy for prisoners (Canton 2015:63) and the perverse kind of collective solidarity we gain from punishment (Carvalho and Chamberlen 2017; Fassin 2018). Focusing on the worst and most base penal sentiments tends to be exacerbated in comparative study, where lenient penal virtues are contrasted to penal punitiveness (Cavadino and Dignan 2006; Green 2008; Pratt and Eriksson 2013). Penal sensibilities are indeed viscerally charged; that is beyond dispute. But they are laden with a wider range of feelings and moral standpoints than tends to be accounted for in comparative study of either penal culture or penal politics.

Unlike punitiveness or lenience, penal sensibilities are not homogenous; instead, they are inherently ambivalent, inchoate, with a contrasting quality (Garland 1990a; Girling et al. 2000; Loader 2006). Penal sensibilities are an eternal feature of penal reasoning and are embedded in each practical response to crime and punishment. Hence, government decisions may express an emotional maze of optimism and despair, revulsion and sympathy, a seemingly inexplicable desire to exclude offenders but also to help them. These are the affective sentiments that often draw the line between what is permissible and impermissible in the uses of punishment, and therefore they are a vital, and surprisingly untapped, source of insight into comparative differences in penal politics. This conceptualisation does not portray penal culture as just negative aggressions or episodic moral panics – those are simply moments when cultural ire is more visible and penal transformation is especially conscious. This is instead a more pluralistic view of the emotions that simmer beneath prison plans and debates – though it is not so easy to tidy these views into neat 'punitive' or 'lenient' categories.

For the purposes of comparative inquiry, however, I want to extend the kinds of conceptual content of penal sensibilities to achieve greater clarity when contrasting political cultures, allowing us to identify the specific meanings and outlooks that undergird prison policymaking sensibilities and hence shape political culture. Subjecting cultural meaning to careful comparative study necessitates an investigation of the social images and cultural conventions that anchor and pattern primal sensibilities (Schalet 2011). The anxieties that crime generates, the discomfort or passions that are revealed in penal debates are not mere cognitive possessions or individual dispositions, but are connected to cultural meanings, distinct social imagery and layered narrative associations (Girling et al. 2000). In a provocative metaphor about the pervasive and inescapable character of culture, Geertz wrote 'that man is an animal suspended in webs of significance he himself has spun' (Geertz 1973:5). These meanings are what orientate sensibilities, giving crime, punishment and penal politics their social fit. Below I outline specific theoretical dimensions of cultural sensibilities, emphasising the particular value dispositions and complex web of meanings associated with situated narratives of crime and criminality, the penal subject and place.

Crime and criminality. The absence of a clear statistical correspondence between crime rates and imprisonment rates is regularly reiterated in the literature (Tonry, 2009, 2015:507) – what Wacquant calls the crime–punishment disconnect (2009a, 2009b). This claim is established at the statistical level (Lappi-Seppälä 2008), but culturally, socially and politically, understandings of crime and punishment do not operate independently from prison decision-making (Garland 2001).

The perceived problems of crime, its causes and its consequences, contribute to the reasoning that informs how a government uses imprisonment (Matthews 2009). Comparative research on penal politics must interpret the divergent representations of crime that are bound up in the designing, planning and routine decision-making of prison policy. It is essential that we see crime as a meaningful cultural category that is an inseparable and foundational ingredient in the politics of punishment (Cohen 1972; Hall et al. [1978] 2013; Garland 2020). The perceptions of crime held by those actors inside government impact the reliance on imprisonment, regardless of the crime rates (Melossi 1994).

Personhood. Modes of imprisonment are always undertaken in relation to the kind of people prisoners are perceived to be. Melossi has described this as the 'cultural environment' which 'produces a given "knowledge" of the criminal' that shapes comparative penal responses (Melossi 2000:298). Every deployment of the term 'prisoner', each penal dispensation, is an iteration of the prisoner's perceived criminal motivations, social biography, personal needs and degree of blameworthiness. The kinds of interventions and categorisations employed to correct, punish and encourage transgressive citizens are partially founded on this cultural knowledge of the criminal. Prisoners are rarely viewed homogenously, and different categories of prisoners, depending on their perceived social personhood, will amplify or rebuff the punitivity of the carceral response (Douglas 1992:119), helping us explain any inconsistency within an imprisonment regime. Thus, we might inquire: how are prisoners viewed and politically represented in relation to the central social community – as steadfast members or antisocial threat (Wagner-Pacifici and Schwartz 1991; Melossi 2000; Barker 2017)?

Place. Finally, these penal sensibilities are bound by a sense of place (Barker 2009; Hall et al. [1978] 2013). This also concerns meanings of insider/outsidership, but is embedded in collective dispositions towards communities, streets, towns and cities, all of which constitute a fluid and complex vision of the nation or territory being governed. Justifications for punishment and criminal justice interventions often make descriptive recourse to concrete places, maps and communities (Girling et al. 2000; Story 2016). Such narratives summon the attendant 'place-myths' and metaphors (Sparks et al. 2001:888), employing distinct images of crime, civility or order, all of which are tied to the meanings of those locations, their perceived needs and the possible threats they pose. To understand political culture and how it shapes cross-national differences in imprisonment, we must examine how civil servants, ministers and senior administrators make penal decisions using these particular national narratives, regional cultural frames and imagined criminal geographies. How is imprisonment linked to the places that are governed? How are these sites envisioned and enacted through the practice of penal politics?

The work of penal policymaking is always a cultural affair. But comparative culture here is moved from the national level of the grand narrative, and instead grounded in the discrete meanings attached to actual penal policies and stretched to be more varied, complex and mutable rather than abiding and enduring. Cultural sensibilities are part and parcel of prison policymaking, invoking imagery and feelings that help produce forms of punishment that are culturally legitimate, coordinating penal practices so that they align with the sociological imagination that permeates a place and its inhabitants. Culture here is understood as the frameworks which allow government actors to not just systematically assess but intuitively *know*, without deduction, who and where is dangerous, who is an insider and which groups are deviant outsiders, and what punishments are acceptable and which others are considered cruel and unusual. These cultural sensibilities allow governments to construct a legitimate narrative for the use of punishment and produce a prison system that reinforces those social values. Hence, they firmly root the practices of penal politics in their 'precise moment in history' (Foucault 1982:785). Thick description of the overlapping sensibilities of crime, place and personhood will help us generate context-sensitive comparative accounts of penal policymaking in which the incongruities of imprisonment regimes will become more intelligible.

Political reasoning

These more fine-grained interpretive accounts of sensibilities can reveal what is distinctly *cultural* about political culture. But what is *political* about political culture? The politics of punishment are determined not just by meanings and values; they are also contingent upon strategic understanding of what is an appropriate use of government power and visions of what constitutes the good society (Garland 1997; Loader and Sparks 2016). Here I rely on governmentality literature, which allows us to view imprisonment 'in a more substantively political light' (O'Malley 1999:189). The full scope of governmentality's central claims or popular uses are not outlined, defended or critiqued here.[iii] Instead, this section distils the most relevant concepts – *rationalities*, *subjects* and *techniques* – for this comparative study of the politics of imprisonment.

Rationalities. Governing is always conducted within a web of strategic and instrumental rationalities. These are the political principles about the ideal conduct of government, which frame problems and contain a vision of how government should behave in order to achieve its ends (Rose and Miller 2010). In making choices about the most appropriate uses of confinement, policymakers are also always making decisions about the appropriate uses of government authority. We must ask: 'how have governing authorities understood their powers and what rationalities of governing are implicit in their practices?' (Garland 1997:176). Without suggesting that these are fixed typologies, following Dean (2010), I will identify and outline some themes which form different styles of political reasoning, their governing traits and social agendas.[iv]

Liberalism is shaped and informed by a vision of a society inhabited by rational and unencumbered individuals who exercise self-denial, reason, responsibility and personal initiative. While seeking to inculcate these traits in citizens, liberal political rationalities prohibit government agencies from overzealous intervention, instead promoting wise restraint (Donzelot 1980; Garland 1997). Within this political composition, governments must avoid trespassing upon a citizen's sense of individual responsibility, supporting rather than intruding on the autonomy of civil society (Joyce 2003).

This is just one potential form in which the art of government is deployed. Alternatively, a neoliberal rationality envisions citizens as self-regulating and enterprising entrepreneurs, responsible for their own fortunes, prudent in their decision-making and increasingly guided by calculations of risk (Rose 1989). Governments will therefore 'govern-at-a-distance', allowing the market to fill the regulatory vacuum left by the state.

Dean describes an authoritarian rationality (2010). As a non-liberal view, it seeks to engender obedience in subjects and temper any opposition to official authority. A government with an authoritarian mentality will go to almost any lengths – e.g. eugenics, prison camps and death – to suppress and extinguish threats to governmental power and social order.

A government that is motivated to support or inculcate 'membership of traditional collectives such as the family, the community, or the nation' (O'Malley 1999:186) reflects a conservative set of political rationalities. Such governments will indulge overtly moral reasoning, favouring caution over innovation, indulging practical common sense over abstract reasoning (Loader 2020). This kind of thinking privileges central state power and social authoritarianism, displacing freedom, that key tenet of liberal rationality, to a more subordinate agenda.

We may also observe a pastoral rationality, in which the condition of 'the flock' is paramount. This set of objectives inspires the government to behave as pastor or shepherd, looking after each individual as a member of a community (Foucault 1982:783). Concerned with the morality of individuals rather than the legality of the system, the government agent-as-pastor is animated by the desire for care, control and salvation of the individual. The aim is to ensure that subjects are brought back into the fold, while also seeking to achieve their total obedience (Golder 2007:167; Foucault 1981, 1982:783). In many ways, modern nations exhibit some form of pastoral power, such as the welfare state (Foucault 1981, 1982), though whether pastoral reasoning favours traditions and families or the protection of individuals and their rights will depend on whether it has hybridised with a variant of conservative or liberal rationality.

Each of these positions has a different vision of society and distinct ideas about the conduct of government, and thus have divergent claims about the role of incarceration, in constituting that social order. The prison's aims are always organised in such a way that it may reinforce the character of the state (Foucault 1981). So, comparative divergences and convergences in penal politics and imprisonment are also the outworking of the political order, be it conservative, liberal or neoliberal, etc. Punishment is always political (O'Malley 1999), and these 'mentalities of government' imbue imprisonment regimes with a distinctly political motivation.

Subjects. These political ideas are exercised towards the behaviour of its subjects (Foucault 1991b:92; Rose and Miller 2010:277). Governments, in other words, are concerned with shaping the conduct of citizens. Guided by a particular set of norms, governing bodies aim to direct and align people's behaviour, aspirations and subjectivities with their governing objectives (Garland 1997:175; Dean 2010:18). The prison, then, is a tool of social engineering, with routines and programmes that are intended to instil certain traits in prisoners.

This provides an important distinction about the nature of penal power as it is conceived here. Governments are not necessarily punishing to solely inflict pain or express censure, but are imprisoning citizens in ways which may also serve particular political rationalities. Penal power is not just negative and prohibitory, but also productive and inciting (Foucault 1981:253; O'Malley 1992:506; Rose and Miller 2010:272). As Foucault (1977:23) wrote, punishment is a 'political tactic' that is designed to have 'positive effects'. Government action is motivated by a sense of how the society, and all it encompasses, should be (Rose and Miller 2010; O'Malley 2010:38); their prison policies are also an attempt to cultivate the desired personal dispositions in prisoners via the prison.

Techniques. Competing political rationalities are eventually realised through techniques, which are the mechanisms and tools governments use to identify and govern social problems, populations and subjects. We can more fully understand the nature of penal politics by examining differences in techniques, namely how government power is exercised and how prisons are understood.

Techniques include the organisational infrastructure, such as use of agencies, devolving power, creating additional layers of management oversight, inspectorates, working groups and boards. Techniques also include the systems of paperwork, oversight, report writing, accountability audits, evaluations and bureaucratic hierarchies, incentives, audits, line management and reallocation of budget resources (Barrett 2015). Techniques are therefore an important conduit for institutionalising political culture. They impose political styles of reasoning upon the working routines of civil servants, binding the government to certain behaviours and prohibiting others that defy the ideological bias (Sauder and Espeland 2009).

Techniques are important also because they render the prison population 'visible both as an object and as an end of government' (Gunn 2006:709), shaping how prison policy is made. Decisions of prison design, planning and administration are taken using governmental techniques, such as statistics, individual and expert discretion, budget audits, dossiers, performance measures, independent reviews, prisoner demographics, census information and prison population forecasts. This is how prisoners as subjects are identified and how their social identities are constituted in the eyes of government (Franko Aas 2004) These provide governments with the workable knowledge for decision-making and inform the format through which punishment is communicated, be it informal and narrative structure, or pro forma, wherein the 'circumstances of interest are prescribed in advance' (ibid.:382).

Some differences in how prisons are organised will reflect the different techniques a government uses to manage a prison system, which in turn reflect the governing rationality (Rose 1993:290). How this information technology differs between prison administrations will illuminate their underlying political rationalities, and these techniques will help identify contrasts in the respective political cultures.

In sum, the political dynamic refers to the strategic and distinctly political 'ways of thinking and styles of reasoning' embodied in penal policymaking (Garland 1997:184). O'Malley (2010:13) writes that governmentality is 'rather hostile' to grand narratives, 'preferring to focus on contingent and specific turns of history and politics, as opposed to unfolding historical logics of modernity, and therefore has the capacity for ambiguity and uncertainty'. This grounded approach helps avoid reductionist analysis of governing activity,[v] which clears the way to think about political culture as inflected with instrumental governmental aims, not only animated by abstract punitive demands or cultural norms. Rationalities provide the lens to identify the comparative political ideational forces that shape how government agents make choices and take penal actions.

Political culture – a logic of practice

This conceptualisation of political culture differs from those that prevail in comparative study. Here it is 'instrumental and rhetorical, archaic sometimes and advanced, culturally embedded and politically tactical' (Sparks 2001:169). In many ways, governing mentalities, with their rational character, are opposed to the non-calculative values expressed by cultural sensibilities. Each framework proposes a different analytical and empirical agenda – one concerned with control, the other with meanings. However, following a programmatic agenda set out by Garland's earlier works (1990a, 1990b), the cultural and the strategic are reconnected here, understood as 'twinned' dynamics (Garland 1997:203). Political culture is thus determinative, shaping how prison and social order are seen and understood, and providing the borders for what action is desirable, legitimate and strategically acceptable. These give the politics of punishment its operational fault lines and creative tensions, and will allow us to examine and compare imprisonment between nations and across time, exposing the sources and counterforces of the prisons' contradictory policies. Departing from Garland's example, however, I suggest we instead focus on the inner workings of the prison policy world, examining those sites where actual decisions are made and imprisonment regimes decided upon (Rogan 2011; Annison 2015). Certainly, some of the most illuminating comparative penality has taken this grounded approach to the politics of punishment (Jones and Newburn 2005; Barker 2009).

This framework aims to capture some of the messy reality of penal policy, highlighting that actions are taken and policies are made in response to particular problems and struggles as they are encountered in reality (Bourdieu 1990:86). This kind of 'practical logic' means that a government 'never ceases to sacrifice the concern for coherence to the pursuit of efficiency' (Bourdieu 1990:262). As governments attempt to tame the social world, political culture 'is continually producing, altering or adapting its governing practices and institutions' (O'Malley et al. 1997). In desperate situations 'the threshold of logical requirements [is] lowered even further so as to exploit all the available resources' (Bourdieu 1990:262).[vi] Each problem, dependent on its context and object, will invoke different ideas about what is culturally and strategically appropriate, meaning a policy portfolio may only loosely cohere.[vii]

Political culture is not merely habits of tradition, determined by ideology or regulated by institutions. It is the terrain of ideas and feelings upon which substantive penal agendas are mobilised, governmental struggles are bound and problems are resolved, albeit within the existing remit of power and resources (Sewell 1996). The work of penal politics, then, is not a pure expression of political culture upon the world. It is the logic enacted and embedded in government conduct, responses and inactions as they attempt to negotiate populations and places and enact their social visions.

We should not overstress political culture's grip and ubiquity. Many people come to work in prison policy departments, like any occupation, and do what is required. Some colleagues will commit to the modus operandi of prison policymaking; others will not agree entirely with the institutional ethos but do their work in accordance with it anyway. Instead, we must see political culture as the 'bounded rationality' (Vaughan 1996, 2004) that provides the everyday vocabulary of ideas and meanings in which the social and political demands of imprisonment can be identified, made intelligible and legitimately acted upon. The point is that political culture as I have set it out is not necessarily something every co-worker shares on a deeply committed emotional level. As an explanation of action this verges on the tautological – someone's actions are of course shaped by someone's feelings and ideas – and should not be misunderstood as such. Political culture is the set of predominant ideas, cultural codes, political visions and social meanings that shape the *context* in which this work is conducted (Swidler 2001). Akin to Bourdieu's *habitus*, this is a 'feel for the game' (Bourdieu 1990:66); political culture is the prevailing common sense about what is a right and fair use of government and punishment. This is how political culture shapes action most successfully: by becoming the way in which work is done rather than necessarily winning over the hearts and minds of every employee of a prison administration. This also means that there is always room for people to take actions that do not align with the political culture's prevailing values of how matters ought to be conducted (Swidler 1986). This dynamic is what makes political culture generative as well as mutable. Because political culture is never settled, it is always vulnerable to wider social issues, and this is why the meanings of imprisonment can quickly become subject to heated internal debate, resulting in sometimes dramatic policy and organisational transformation. This advances comparative work in necessary new directions, examining how cultural norms, historical events and political thinking shape divergent prison policies (Hamilton 2013).

Finally, I favour the term 'political culture' because it denotes that there is a way of doing government work, a 'practical consciousness' (Williams 1964), that is framed by political ideals and cultural meanings. Importantly, the term 'political culture' is never here used to refer to '*the* political culture' of the entire body politic or government. Of course, political culture is common in the literature and has a colloquial familiarity, though these uses tend to reinforce a broad or generalising view of a single political culture that I wish to avoid here. Prisons and penal policy have their own practical logic. Vague values and broad principles are shaped into political culture with material consequence through their practical usage. So while the political culture that governs penality will be scaffolded upon the dominant moral framework that generally informs government work, in practice broad norms and values will be refined by the particular demands of imprisonment – thus imbuing the political culture that governs imprisonment regimes with distinctive contours of meaning and practical aspirations. Readers should bear in mind that political culture as it appears throughout this book refers only to the specific ideational and cultural views, as they were practiced, in relation to the prison.

Comparing politics and imprisonment

How does the concept of imprisonment regimes support a new phase in comparative research? And why might comparative sociology of punishment require a conception of penal politics that is dynamic, relational, pragmatic and built upon the inter-subjective fault lines of political instrumentality and cultural sensibilities? First, *imprisonment regimes* allow us to:

(1) focus on differences in how people are imprisoned;
(2) capture diversity within as well as between national prison systems; and
(3) comparatively highlight patterns of change beyond severity and lenience.

Second, the potential of *political culture* conceived here overcomes gaps in current comparative frameworks as it:

(1) provides a pluralistic understanding of penal politics;
(2) avoids the more essentialising and enduring depictions of comparative culture;
(3) has a defamiliarising effect upon our understanding of governmental actions; and
(4) allows us to illuminate the reasoning behind imprisonment regimes, and thus explain cross-national differences in the use of imprisonment.

Imprisonment regimes move us beyond the limited comparative view of imprisonment rates and punitive versus lenience. Imprisonment regimes do not operate at the aerial view of prison populations; this moves our attention away from how many bodies are imprisoned and allows us to 'establish the phenomenon' (Merton 1987) of cross-national prison systems. The prison is repositioned so that we can compare how it contains people, what demands a prison system makes of prisoners, what processes they are put through and what opportunities they are offered. Taking this view will show the network of prisons and programmes that constitute a prison system. In so doing we may also reveal the significance of more mundane penal practices that tend to go unremarked in comparative study, see important new patterns in imprisonment and ultimately illustrate a fuller picture of the characteristic forms and functions of each national prison system.

The imprisonment regime is also a fluid concept, giving us points from which to monitor how forms and functions of imprisonment evolve, therefore benefiting the comparative study of penal transformation. What new prison programmes are developed or disbanded? What kinds of prisons are built? We can observe how circulation and prisoner categories are (or are not) modified. These transformations and events themselves become points of comparative concern. This gives us a basis from which to comparatively examine the continuous changes in uses of prison and its relation to the prevailing social, political and culture values.

Similarly, the inherently pluralistic view of political culture counters the abstract, or 'skimpy' (Sparks 2001), view of the penal politics that can appear in comparative penology (Nelken 2009; Garland 2017). This allows us to look at who is involved in prison decision-making, and what ideational, cultural and emotional factors inform their thinking process. Unlike current concepts of comparative penal politics, political culture is rooted in the routine administering, designing and managing of prison systems, and these practices are contingent and mutable. Political culture has the dimensions that can show how and why governments create penal systems that simultaneously make use of diverse strategies, such as segregation and progressive welfare programmes, for example.

This is a grounded approach to comparative politics of imprisonment, forcing us to confront the precise meanings embedded in otherwise generic penal terminology (Nelken 2009), a matter often overlooked in comparative studies of punitiveness (Brangan 2020). While they are still broadly comprehensible, we cannot disregard their distinct local usage; seemingly objective terminology of prison programmes – such as education, parole, labour, training and rehabilitation – are deprived of some of their general meaning as we begin to look at *how* they are deployed (to educate? to make employable? to aid? to exclude? to normalise? to discipline?). As Williams wrote, we may use the same words, but 'each group is speaking its native language, but its uses are significantly different, and especially when strong feelings or important ideas are in question' (Williams 1976:11). Comparative study is particularly illuminating in this respect, allowing us to unpack seemingly objective terminology and taken-for-granted familiarity, revealing the context of their definitions (Biernacki 1995; Schalet 2011).

Here we see that explaining differences in imprisonment regimes requires an understanding of the political culture that governs them. A generic term such as 'prisoners' now must be understood as having condensed within it a diffuse array of culturally and politically appropriate ideas, visions and meanings. For example: an implicit cultural and social biography that is invoked every time the term 'prisoner' is stated, with a related moral and emotional quality, feelings of fear and/or sympathy, an implied understanding of criminality, varying degrees of tolerance of these acts and the people who commit them, and an express view on the nature of social disorder. The prison is then also fine-tuned to engender particular political traits in the transgressive subject. But it can only attempt to achieve these ends within the limits of government, be they demarcated by conservative, liberal or pastoral rationalities, and with a knowledge of the penal pains that are permissible to achieve those goals. It is this array of political cultural resources that government actors employ each time they identify a problem, propose a penal mode of redress or suggest an adjustment to penal sanctioning. As a result, a nation's imprisonment regime reflects political intuition of social hierarchies, feelings about what is appropriate and understandings of social problems. Both the prison and penal politics, then, should not be compared as a means to an end, namely to confine, but understood first as social institutions, riven with a density of meanings, political objectives and structural ideas.

In undertaking a comparative study of the political culture governing prisons, it will be impossible to avoid tracing our way back to the wider social stratifications and structural forms ordering everyday life. While cultural sensibilities and political mentalities encourage a fine-grained study of the politics of punishment, we must also look at the wider field of relations in which each respective penal culture exists and of which it bears the specific hallmarks. It should be clear by now that political culture as it is conceived here is relational and cannot be cabined away from its precise 'social ground' (Geertz 1973:9). These political visions of prisons, prisoners, government, place, citizenship, order/disorder and crime are inescapably entangled with other social norms, such as family, community, nationality, gender, race, poverty, class and so on. Political culture is always produced within a 'larger societal set of stories, conflicts, troubles and insecurities' (Sparks et al. 2001:889), and these forces are mediated into imprisonment regimes. As Mills wrote, every imputation of reason each of us gives is not itself without a social reason (Mills 1940a:904).

The prison is a social institution; understanding this is central to solving the puzzle of why prison systems differ. The prison is designed to achieve certain ends with prisoners, to punish, to transform, to exclude. And, in so doing, the prison seeks to make social contributions, such as emphasising cultural norms, upholding lines of moral worthiness, deepening solidarities or demonstrating state sovereignty. That is why we need to fully grasp the political cultures that shape incarceration. By its nature, political culture mediates social distinctions, transforming them into concrete government actions, while reproducing political norms and social sensibilities of what is worthy, valuable, troublesome, distasteful and repugnant. Imprisonment regimes, then, are the physical and material realisation (in the architecture, rules, prisoner classifications, organisation of prison space, programmes, etc.) of these competing social, political and cultural frameworks.

Taken together, this has ramifications for the comparative analysis – denying this study the neatness that comparative penality tends to produce. This to me seems to be an advance for comparative study, where we can describe and explain why the politics of punishment differs from one place to the next and why it changes over time, even between countries that appear otherwise culturally and politically similar. A contribution of this book is that it demonstrates that properly conceptualised and grounded comparative case studies can illuminate the complex nature of penal politics more thoroughly and offer an explanation for the differences we see in cross-national imprisonment.

A methodological note

There are methodological tactics that result from the concerns set out here. Generating the material for this kind of comparative project required oral, archival and social history, as well as an analysis of documents that focused on their discourse as well as their materiality.

Oral histories

To undertake a comparative study of political culture as '*as a category of thought and affect*' (Loader and Mulcahy 2003:39; original emphasis), we must focus on the different thinking driving penal policymaking (Jones and Newburn 2005; Barker 2009), as such, looking at penal politics '*from the inside*' (Loader 2006 original emphasis) with an anthropological sensibility (Vaughan 2004). This meant focusing on the 'leadership elites that direct and control' imprisonment (Garland 2013:495). Political culture is thus looked at here on a small scale in the specific locations from which prisons were governed and administered. In order to reconstruct governmental dispositions, I conducted interviews with a variety of prison and criminal justice civil servants, senior prison governors who had policy influence, and one politician. The interview material used in the chapters on Ireland relied on the stories and recollections of Jim, Liam, Niall, Gerard, Seamus, Pádraig, Eamon and John; the section on Scotland draws on the memories and reflections of Douglas, Adam, William, Derek, Euan, Ken and Alistair.[viii]

As Thompson has written, oral history 'provides a more realistic and fair reconstruction of the past, a challenge to the established account' (1988:6). This generosity should not be mistaken as 'indulgence'. This more appreciative sociological approach allows for a fuller historical reconstruction and provides a stronger grounding from which to build both critique and comparison (Bourdieu 2000:61). It is a humane and qualitative way to recover the past, to think about penal politics and political culture and what it is we mean when we draw on these terms in criminology.

Archival research

The understanding of Irish and Scottish political culture was deepened by an analysis of the available prison related materials, such as Annual Prison Reports, policy papers and visiting committee and Parole Board reports, as well as archival material, such as prison administration circulars, letters, memos, internal policy positions, meeting minutes, press releases, unpublished working group reports, inter-departmental communications, standing orders, pertinent marginalia, research trip reports, organisational maps, and prison design and regime plans. There were also a number of valuable unpublished research reports and notes, several of which have not been analysed before as far as I am aware.[ix] Taken together, these reveal the 'scrupulously planned utopias' (Stoler 2009:21) that the prison system was bound up in, along with the considerations and concerns that moulded this vision.

This material also allowed me to map imprisonment regimes, as well as to track how these routines altered over time. This means not merely mining this material for numbers but to discern, and then follow, the changing dynamics of how people were imprisoned. As Stoler writes, to read the archival material 'is to pause at, rather than bypass, its conventions, those practices that make up its unspoken order, its rubrics of organization, its rules of placement and reference' (Stoler 2002:103).

Focusing on the key features of how prisoners are managed and disciplined tells the comparative story of the prison organisationally rather than ethnographically. There is much to be added to the comparative canon by undertaking an internal and close-up study of imprisonment (e.g. Downes 1988; Crewe 2020), but that approach tends to focus upon particular prisons, specific groups, the impact of imprisonment, prisoner or staff subjectivities and the texture of prison life, all of which adds a much-needed richness to the comparative study of prison life. However, as a result it is more impressionistic of the system as a whole. The concept of imprisonment regimes instead affords us an improved comparative perspective on the logic of cross-national prison systems, which is absent from the literature.

Reading the material culture of documents

Annual reports and policy papers also serve political as well as penal ends: they make law and penal power 'visible' (Latour 2010). The historical perspective reveals the necessity for a further interpretive angle on the formal document, one that views 'documents *as* things – and that we see the object in relationship to its own past' (Biber 2019:5). This means attending to a document's character (Freeman and Maybin 2011; West 2020): 'the tactility of the object – its shape, form, substance, and size' (Downes et al. 2018:3).

The policy document imparts information, but in a way that also serves to construct and enforce an image of the state within social life (or at least attempts to do so). The policy report may be a relatively standard feature of modern governments, but how it looks and the order it takes has not been static across the twentieth century. Reports and policy documents are sites of political cultural production and should be seen as government attempts to express and thus entrench political power. To paraphrase Godson, ordinary material items that represent power can propagate, disseminate and standardise new understandings of political authority (2015:1). Conducting that kind of analysis of documents longitudinally helps in reassembling the changing character of the political culture as we can interrogate the changing techniques of political knowledge production. In sum, documents are 'monuments of states as well as sites of state ethnography' (Stoler 2002:90).

When looking at these publications across a longer period of time and between two different political contexts, changes and contrasts in the 'culture of documentation' (Stoler 2009:88) physically displayed transformation and differences in the political culture. This added important empirical support to the reconstruction of political practice. Political culture is communicated, it is in public dialogue, it must be represented. Extending our analytical eye to include new and changing material forms of the policy document can deepen our understanding of the history of penal politics and penal transformation.

Contingent social field of relations

A history of the kind proposed above must be grounded in evidence, but must also succeed in going beyond mere description of the themes and fully analyse the data in its wider social and cultural context (Braun and Clarke 2006:94). Following Bourdieu's incitement to empirical recovery, research must seek out 'the deepest logic of the social world', which can be recovered 'only if one plunges into the particularity of an empirical reality, historically located and dated' (Bourdieu 1998:2). Here we must make a scale shift, situating micro-political dynamics of penality within the social conditions which supported and conditioned it. Hall et al. employed this perspective to powerful critical, insightful and empirical effect. They wrote that if we want to recover and know a social world, we may begin by 'reading masses of secondary material in the form of books, articles and commentaries', which, while not participant observation, is still informed by an ethnographic sensibility (Hall et al. [1978] 2013: xi–xii; see also Vaughan 2004:321). We should research 'concrete events, practices, relationships and cultures' by also 'locating them in the histories taking place behind all our backs' (Hall et al. [1978] 2013: xi–xii). This sociological perspective shows that 'crises in penality do not arise primarily from the internal problems of punishing offenders but from transformations in social and political structures' (Simon 1993:5). Comparatively, it will further explicate differences penality.

W\scriptsize{HY}\normalsize{ } do we imprison as we do? And why do penal politics differ between nations? In comparative penology the tendency is to broadly generalise the nature of imprisonment and to then explain these carceral differences by using abstract political and cultural frameworks, though these frameworks have analytical and empirical gaps that are now widely acknowledged. In this chapter I have suggested that to attempt to answer these seemingly simple questions requires a reworking and a refinement of our concepts of imprisonment and penal politics. Rather than looking at *how many* people are imprisoned, we should compare *how* people are imprisoned. And instead of mapping national cultural tropes and political economic typologies, we should take a grounded sociological view of political culture.

The conceptual framework is intended to emphasise the heterogeneity and multiplicity of both prison systems and penal policy. This means the findings will be able to identify links between political, cultural and social forces and the uses of imprisonment. However, this limits the study's capacity to alight upon neat typologies or home in on a key determinative variable. Yet, it seems to me that one of the limitations of the comparative penality literature is that it only rarely manages to deepen or expand the realms of scholarship that constitute the study of punishment. Prison sociologists rarely utilise comparative punishment work; those interested in prison policy tend to lament the absence of empirical character in comparative studies of penal politics, and scholars often actively write against their national depictions in comparative research. By taking a grounded and pluralistic approach to comparing punishment, it is hoped that this framework can help us understand how and why Irish and Scottish penal culture differed.

Notes

i And indeed, in how we think about and theorise punishment more generally, the prison has dominated our research, potentially limiting our grasp of a nation's 'dispersal of discipline' (Cohen 1985; Phelps 2017; Robinson 2016; Barker 2017).

ii Which is likely why they are the *modus operandi* not just for academics, but also for activists and politicians, informing popular debates on penal policy (Pease 1994).

iii Governmentality can seem to have an established and fixed methodology. However, Foucault encouraged this kind of permissive use of his conceptual outputs, stating that 'if one or two of these "gadgets" of method or approach I've tried to employ…can be of service to you, then I shall be delighted. If you find the need to transform my tools or use others then show me what they are because it may be of benefit to me' (1980:66). For a useful and more committed overview of governmentality's central claims, see Dean (2010), O'Malley (2010), Barry et al. (1993) and Rose (1989). In studies of penality, Garland (1997) provides a comprehensive overview and sociological critique and O'Malley (1999) provides a good example of how to put a governmentality methodology to work.

iv This is not intended as an exhaustive list; one could also look at the specific styles of rule that make-up social democracy, neoconservatism and communitarianism. But for our purposes here, I highlight the political reasoning that will allow us to understand comparative differences between Ireland and Scotland.

v While governmentality is interested in the 'programmers', namely those making policy, these agents are implied rather than researched explicitly. Governmentality studies usually avoid the 'familiar, realist, sociological terrain' of government (O'Malley 2010:193), instead separating programmes and textual analysis from the 'messy actualities' (Barry et al. 1993) in which government work actually happens. Leading figures in governmentality are candid in the claims that governmentality is not a sociological endeavour, interested in neither the 'simple empirical activity of governing' (Dean 2010:28), nor creating descriptive accounts 'of how various people or agents in positions of authority rule. Distancing governmentality from sociology has been critiqued by Garland (1997) and O'Malley et al. (1997). Garland (1997) emphasises the amenability of governmentality to sociological inquiry, and provides an instructive criticism about how historically reassembling the character of mentalities and technologies should not be analysed as distinct from 'the pragmatics of use' (ibid.:199).

vi See also Sewell (1996) on 'emotional ruptures' and Vaughan (1996) on normalisation of organisational deviance.

vii This is what Bourdieu means when he describes, in typical Bourdieusian paradoxical prose, how the logic of practice is not the logic of the logician. It is coherent in a fuzzy way but realised when deployed in relation to practical problems (1990).

viii I held seven interviews in Scotland and eight interviews in Ireland. The small number of interviewees reflects the scale of the Irish and Scottish prison systems. Interviews lasted between two and three hours. All interviews were recorded and fully transcribed. All names are pseudonyms.

ix I had intended to spend summer 2020 conducting additional archival research in both Ireland and Scotland. Particularly since the initial archive research was completed in 2015, Irish governmental archival files for 1986–1989, which now fall outside the Irish government's 30 year rule, would have been deposited at the National Archives in Dublin. However, a summer of lockdown due to the COVID-19 pandemic meant the archives in Scotland remained closed and Ireland was inaccessible. It will thus be up to future archival researchers to extend and validate the claims made here, particularly regarding the later period of Irish penal culture.

Section 1

Irish imprisonment regimes and political culture, 1970–1999

3 Pastoral penality

Addressing the pains of imprisonment

The Republic of Ireland is said to be an exception within Anglophone penal history, whereby it resisted the punitive turn of the 1970s and a more pragmatic and dispassionate penal politics prevailed. In this respect, Irish prison policy was informed by not much at all, and instead tended to drift. In Chapter 2 it was suggested that prison systems always reflect the cultural, emotional and ideational currents of the political culture that governs them, arguing that political culture, in turn, is orientated towards the wider field of social relations. If we want to understand Irish imprisonment regimes, then we must discern the ideas, visions and feelings embedded in the prison policies devised at this time. Using this methodological agenda, this chapter reveals a counter-narrative of an intentional and highly principled penal transformation led by Irish prison policymakers during the 1970s. Who those policymakers believed the prisoner to be, what they blamed as the causes of crime and disorder, and what they understood as the main aims of government all converged to give Ireland's imprisonment regime a humane and empathetic approach – one less interested in transforming and reforming prisoners and more concerned with mitigating the pains of imprisonment. This unusual carceral logic reflects the pastoral political culture that dominated Ireland's Prison Division. We begin, however, by setting the scene and tracing the social and cultural dynamics of 1970s Ireland.

Political, social and cultural background

Ireland became an independent state in 1922. From its inception as a nation, Irish cultural, political and social life was dominated by the Catholic Church,[i] a colossal power bloc (Inglis 1998) whose interests were reflected in legislation, policy and the machinery of social control (ibid.; Fahey and McLaughlin 1999). In Ireland in the first half of the twentieth century the Church and government often supported each other, a relationship Inglis (1998:77) characterises as 'peaceful coexistence' (see also Larkin 1975). From its formation the state had yielded the power of social services to usually religious organisations within the principle of 'subsidiarity' (McNally 2007; Healy and Kennifick 2019). The Church held considerable authority as a result, seeing itself as 'responsible for the moral well-being of the nation'

(Larkin 1975:1274).[ii] Subsequently, the Church resisted state intervention in its perceived realm of authority, often advocating anti-statist views on matters of social and moral life. Thus, there was a 'catholicization of the public sphere' (Patterson 2006:14–15), reflected in much of the contemporary political legislation, particularly on health and education (Whyte 1980; Inglis 1998; Fahey and McLaughlin 1999; McDonnell and Allison 2006). The Church was against schemes which threatened to contravene its sovereignty over these matters. For example, the Catholic Hierarchy opposed what it felt were overly intrusive welfare programmes such as free access to health care, which would have reduced their remit.[iii] They contributed to the alternative 1953 Health Act; they supported the implementation of ongoing censorship with their prominent presence on the Vigilance Committee, a small group responsible for banning what was considered to be morally improper books, films and magazines and investigating 'non-Catholic activity' (Cooney 1999). Their power also extended into the everyday running of Irish schools, hospitals and welfare systems, which were all largely controlled and staffed by nuns, brothers and priests (Whyte 1980; Chubb 1992; Inglis 1998; McDonnell and Allison 2006).

Religious regulation was most pervasive and censorious when it came to the family unit (Whyte 1980; Fahey and McLaughlin 1999; Canavan 2012; Mohr 2017), which was considered the rudiment of a strong Irish Catholic society. It is widely argued that 'no society in Europe so exalted the ideal of the family in its official rhetoric' as the Irish (Lee and O'Tuathaigh 1982:15). The 1937 Irish Constitution – its creation a joint enterprise between the government and the Irish Catholic Hierarchy – made explicit that the family unit was central to Irish social order: 'The State recognises the Family as the natural primary and fundamental unit group of Society, and as a moral institution possessing inalienable and imprescriptible rights, antecedent and superior to all positive law' (Article 41.1.2). It went on: 'The State, therefore, guarantees to protect the Family in its constitution and authority, as the necessary basis of social order.'

Families were not entirely autonomous units, however: they existed in community networks. Irish class relations were largely communitarian and far less rigidly hierarchal than those in Britain (Coakely 1999:50–51). Ireland's general 'absence of class based cleavages' (Chubb 1992:33) allowed a national 'culture of community' (Hazelkorn and Patterson 1994:52) to prevail. As a result, Irish identity and social life had a deeply embedded ethos shaped by a sense of 'community, kinship and mutual aid' (O'Dowd 1987:44).

Catholic cultural forces and conservative social influence also significantly affected Ireland's austere field of social control. In an important work of historical recovery, O'Sullivan and O'Donnell (2007) have illustrated the novelty of imprisonment in modern Ireland. They demonstrate Ireland's staggering use of 'coercive confinement', such as Mother and Baby Homes, Industrial and Reformatory Schools, Borstals, Magdalene Laundries and state-run asylums. While crime was statistically low, with Ireland described as a 'policeman's paradise' (Brady 1974:240), and the prison had a per capita use of 16.5 per 100,000 in 1951, it is conservatively estimated that 1% of the Irish population (more than 1,000 per 100,000 people) were confined in one of these other institutions. These sites were employed to confine those considered deviant, as well as the urban poor and unemployed. The monopoly on legitimate violence was therefore not entirely controlled by the democratic state; instead, the penal culture prior to 1970 (and especially until the 1950s) had cohered around matters of morality and deviance which empowered non-state actors. In line with conservative political thinking, then, social problems and the capacity to punish, chastise, stigmatise and control deviant Irish populations were felt to be better addressed by traditional social units and institutions, such as communities, families and the Church.

Arguably, the Irish government's sovereign power was underdeveloped in comparison to other Western democracies. The Catholic church operated as a shadow authority structure in Ireland, and 'while the rest of Europe secularized its institutions and culture the Irish commitment to religion was sustained and even intensified' (Girvin 1986:62). Rather than the rational, science-based reasoning of Western modernism (as prevailed in the UK and USA, for example), Christian morality and conservative politics shaped the political and policy character of modern Ireland.

These socio-political relations existed in a context of abiding poverty and emigration, described as the phenomena of 'the vanishing Irish' (O'Brien 1953). Mass emigration shaped and regulated Irish life (Delaney 2000), and this remained the case until the 1970s. It is argued that migration functioned as an additional, if somewhat inadvertent form of social control, 'sweeping social problems aside' (Fanning 2007:1), such as unemployed young males, and maintaining the quotidian image of Irish purity as homogenous, Catholic and family focused. Following this argument, Brewer et al. (1999:177) suggest that emigration served to subdue crime rates as young adults left Ireland. It has been found that in the 1960s English prisons actually held twice as many Irish-born men as Irish prisons (O'Donnell et al. 2005:166).

The 1970s brought dangers and insurrection too as the Troubles erupted in Northern Ireland. In 1972, 13 peaceful Catholic protesters were killed in Derry by British forces, an episode known as Bloody Sunday or the Bogside Massacre. This was seen as brutal evidence that the British were persecuting Northern Ireland's Irish Catholic minority. The anger resonating from the incident was felt throughout the Republic, and the Taoiseach made a public call for the 'cessation of the harassment of the [Catholic] minority in the North' by British troops and policies (RTÉ 1972a). A public protest held in Dublin on 2 February 1972 concluded dramatically with the burning of the British Embassy (RTÉ 1972b). At the same time, the Irish government had an ongoing legal case against the UK regarding the torture of Republicans interned and interrogated in Northern Ireland – the first inter-state case to appear before the European Court of Human Rights.[iv] There was thus an ambiguity in the Irish position, exemplified by the Arms Crisis. In 1970, a sum of government money intended for the development of aid in

Northern Ireland was surreptitiously siphoned off by a number of officials, including sitting ministers, for the purchase of arms from German dealers for Republican groups in Northern Ireland. Legal action was taken against the ministers, which met with considerable public and political protest (Ferriter 2012:141–151). It seems the Troubles had reignited a pronounced nationalist and anti-British sentiment in the Republic among the public and the political classes. Ireland was suddenly the site of what was known as 'subversive' activities. This included a bombing campaign, the murders of members of the public, political figures and Gardaí (the Irish police), as well as the assassination of the British Ambassador in 1976. Ireland found itself in a state of 'emergency'.

At the end of the 1960s/early 1970s there was a short-lived improvement in Ireland's economic fortunes, however. In the face of chronic poverty and industrial and economic stagnation, in the 1960s the Irish government began to assume a greater responsibility for the health and well-being of its citizens and for the first time introduced welfare provisions (Cousins 1995; Fahey and McLaughlin 1999). These new welfare ideals coalesced with the existing Catholic and conservative culture within government, however. Even as the welfare state emerged, the integrity of the family remained a central relay for government activity, with state welfare being used to maintain the stability and status of the family unit (McGowan 2016:9).

In sum, by 1970 Ireland was distinct within the North Atlantic nations. Mass emigration and mass confinement contributed to the international image of a nation unperturbed by crime (e.g. Adler 1983). Rather than being a liberal democracy interested in perpetuating individual rights, the obligations and ethos of government were informed by conservative values, making religion and morality its 'mainstay' (Freeden 2003). Ireland was a nation also defined by its communitarian Catholic culture, where the moral verities of family life were paramount to the national order. By the 1970s there had also been a shift, supported by new financial gains: the state tentatively began to develop welfare to protect and improve the essential social values of community and family security, signalling the slightest separation of Church and State. There was also the burgeoning sectarian conflict in Northern Ireland and rising nationalist political tensions. It was in this political, social and cultural context that Ireland's delayed progressive prison transformation took place.

Prison developments

While the 1960s had seen the signs of new ideas creeping into Irish prison policy (Rogan 2011), it was the 1970s that came to be the period with the most extensive developments in Irish penal practices to date. The 1970s was a decade defined by first-of-its-kind penal developments in Ireland.

Prisons were managed by the Prison Division, a small centralised group of civil servants based inside the Department of Justice in Dublin. They were responsible for a relatively small number of prisoners – 749 in total

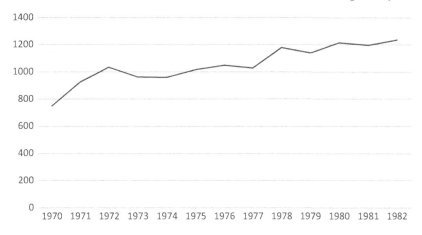

Figure 3.1 Daily average adult prison population 1970–1982.
Source: Annual reports 1970s, various years

(almost entirely male), with men prisoners held across three prisons: Mountjoy, Portlaoise and Limerick. Prisoners were only organised into two categories, the large majority being 'ordinary' prisoners, named to distinguish them from 'subversives': those prisoners whose crimes were related to the Troubles in Northern Ireland. While Irish prison populations had been low, they began to increase in the 1970s, leading to serious concern for the Division, who sought to tackle the new phenomenon of prison overcrowding (JUS/2002/2/66). For the first time since the formation of the State, the Irish government began expanding the prison system. Like other Western and Anglophone nations, the Irish prison population began to rise (see Figure 3.1), and within a few years the prison estate expanded to seven adult prisons. But a focus upon prison expansion alone is limiting: we must examine how people were imprisoned.

'Ordinary' imprisonment

During this period, senior Division officials undertook evidence-gathering trips to Scotland and Denmark to explore modern prison design (DFA/2009/120/200). Two new closed prisons, Cork and Arbour Hill, were opened in 1972 and 1975 respectively, both of which were former military detention barracks adapted to hold a modest 90 prisoners each. While these two closed prisons were converted buildings, the Division also embarked on a much more ambitious project: The Training Unit, housing between 90 and 96 prisoners. This was a highly significant development. Ireland had inherited its prison infrastructure from the British; 50 years after independence, the Training Unit was Ireland's first purpose-built prison and was developed with a distinct set of criteria. The Division was explicit: the aims of the Training Unit were to improve the employment prospects of prisoners at a time of economic prosperity via nationally accredited courses (Department of Justice 1981a:3). The Training Unit was further distinguished because it operated an open ethos that was intended to be less incapacitative and confining. Many at the Training Unit went out to work during the day and returned at night. Internally the regime was designed to mimic normal working, living and domestic routines, with prisoners allowed to wear their own clothes and permitted to move around the prison without supervision.

The fourth adult prison opened in 1975 was Shelton Abbey, Ireland's first open prison, with an average of 35 adult prisoners. Shelton Abbey was a grand country manor, and was referred to as the 'big house' within the Division.[v] The annual reports proudly stated that the institution was 'in beautiful condition and the improvements [were] in keeping with such a lovely building' (*Annual Report 1979*: 50). These new prisons were described, in Jim's words, as 'very progressive in terms of penal policy'. John recalled these times as being marked by enthusiasm: 'This was maybe going to be the Brave New World of the prisons…this could be the way the system could go, so that was an exciting time.'

The modernising zeal was also steadily reshaping the public presentation of the prison system. By 1976 the annual reports began to include pictures (which had not previously been the case). The images showcased the renovated units and improved conditions: homely bedrooms, a modern dental surgery, men playing on glossy badminton courts, men at work, corridors with glistening floors, new industrial training workshops, etc. They explicitly sought to display the grandeur of Shelton Abbey, its impressive common spaces with high ceilings and chandeliers, the stateliness of the building's exterior and the extensive grounds. Based on these images, one is left feeling these institutions were hardly like prisons at all, with very little evidence of standard prison iconography, such as barriers, bars and cells (Figures 3.2 to 3.4).[vi]

The motivation was to give the public 'some idea of the present-day conditions' within prisons (*Annual Report 1977*:6). They wrote that the prisons: 'may still look much the same from the outside but inside things are different' (ibid.). The Division was explicitly demonstrating to the public that the *thinking* within the Department, what they aspired to, was embedded in the new imprisonment regimes.

In line with these progressive regime developments, the Division also created a new array of prison professionals. For the first 40 years or so of the state, welfare support inside prisons was mainly provided by the chaplains. In 1972–1973 the first Directors of Probation, Education and Co-ordinator of Work and Training were appointed, and four full-time psychologists were hired (*Annual Report 1973*), allowing the Division to engage with prisoners with what they described as a 'more individual and personal approach' (Department of Justice 1984a:2).

Figure 3.2 Recreation hall, the training unit

Figure 3.3 Exterior image, Shelton Abbey, open prison

Incarceration in Ireland saw another hugely significant development during this time: the use of temporary release, which was established in the 1960s (Rogan 2011) but enthusiastically expanded during the 1970s. Prisoners were increasingly released for either short periods during their sentence, or fully released before their sentence was complete. There were also mass releases for events such as the visit of the Pope in 1979

Figure 3.4 Interior image, Shelton Abbey, open prison

(O'Donnell and Jewkes 2011) as well as regular amnesties at Christmas and Easter across the prison estate. There was no Parole Board, however. While the Minister of Justice was formally charged with the responsibility for granting each release, in reality Prison Division officials were authorised to grant release (*Annual Report 1976*; Department of Justice 1981). The release decision-making process was shaped by informality, pragmatic need and personal discretion. All prisoners were eligible for some kind of parole; prisoners did not have to serve a certain percentage of their sentence to be considered for it, and internal decision-making documents discussing release reveal that there were few crimes which excluded a prisoner from temporary release (Department of Justice 1984a:1–6); it was reported that 'there was no set pattern in the granting of TR as each case was considered on its own merits' (*Annual Report 1979*:46).

According to the Minister, organising parole this way allowed 'unfettered discretion', which ensured individual cases could be addressed in a 'flexible and relatively unbureaucratic' manner.[vii] Discretionary and individualistic decision-making was a key feature of Irish imprisonment, and perceived to be among the system's core strengths. After attending an international prison conference, officials reported that overcrowding had become an international problem, but no other country used prisoner release quite as liberally as Ireland. It was proudly felt that internationally the Irish release system 'compared favourably' and 'was particularly sound' (Treatment of Offenders Minutes, 3 October 1979). Temporary release was understood as central to the Irish style of imprisonment. In fact, it was positively described as having seen a 'noteworthy increase' and they expected, and eagerly hoped, it would grow further still in use and 'variety' (*Annual Report 1977*: 7). Of course, the community setting can be used for extensive penal control, release from the prison should not be presumed as benevolent control (Phelps 2017; Cohen 1985). However, in 1970s Ireland when someone was released they were rarely subject to the kind of onerous supervisory measures which are now familiar (Healy and Kennifick 2019). In an inversion of the principles of incapacitation, it was during this time that release was among the most central aspects of the work of managing prisoners and imprisonment.

Rather than stagnation or pragmatism, we see that in the 1970s Irish penal expansion was informed by innovation. Both the Training Unit and Shelton Abbey presented a less total kind of social exclusion, but all prisons were being made less tight, incapacitative and confining thanks to temporary release, creating a highly permeable mode of imprisonment. The 1977 Annual Report captures this new progressive confidence, opening with a strong statement of achievement and a self-assured public pronouncement: 'Over the past decade there has been a quiet, relatively unpublicised, transformation in the Prison System', revealing what they described as 'a quite revolutionary approach to the handling of those in custody' (pp. 5–6).

These prisons were only for 'ordinary' prisoners, however. Ordinary was a formal category within the penal administration. Informally, they were sometimes light-heartedly referred to as 'ODCs' (ordinary decent criminals). The category emerged to set them apart from 'subversives': those prisoners linked to dissident activities in Northern Ireland.

'Subversive' imprisonment

As mentioned at the outset, the Troubles were an incredibly tumultuous time in Irish and UK history. The Irish government took firm and swift steps to contain the dissident activities that were occurring in the Republic and hastily mobilised a series of authoritarian criminal justice responses. In 1972, a non-jury Special Criminal Court was established to hear cases of dissident crime.[viii] The government also passed the Offences Against the State Act and Emergency Powers Act (1976), emergency legislation that increased the amount of time a suspect could be detained without charge from 48 hours to seven days. Shortly thereafter, Ireland formally declared a state of emergency and derogated from the European Human Rights Act (Mulcahy 2002:284–285; Ferriter 2012:345). As subversives found their way into the prison system, the Prison Division was now faced with a new task: upholding state security. The Republican prisoner population grew during the 1970s, and was formally categorised as 'subversives'.[ix] Osborough described them as presenting 'an array of daunting problems: difficult to house, awkward to handle, not simple to occupy, not cheap to guard' (1985:187, quoted in Mulcahy 2002:290).

The government denied subversives the status of political prisoners, and in response Republican prisoners undertook ongoing hunger strikes (Ferriter 2012). The political protest inside Mountjoy escalated and a major riot organised by Republican prisoners occurred in May 1972. The riot 'lasted almost six hours during which several prison officers were held hostage' (Rogan 2011:138). The new dentist surgery, the plumbing, new cooking equipment, bedding, the school and the library were all damaged. The Division was beset by panic; one civil servant wrote of the time:

> Fires had been started, the doors of cells had been ripped off, toilets were being wrecked and some highly dangerous prisoners were roaming the prison and terrifying the ODCs (ordinary decent criminals), it was what felt like a 'life or death' situation.
>
> (Terry 2012:212)

The Division was also disheartened and felt frustrated by the subversives – their disruption tactics were stymying prison developments (*Annual Report 1973*:9) and the construction of the Training Unit was briefly discontinued for 'accommodation and security reasons' (*Annual Report 1972*:9):

> The work programme of modernising the prison and providing new amenities which was in progress for some years was brought to a halt and much work already completed was destroyed. The efforts of the trades staff were concentrated for the rest of the year on repairing the damage caused.
>
> (ibid.)

Mountjoy's capacity was now significantly reduced, and roughly 200 prisoners had to be dispersed throughout the system (Rogan 2011:138). Up to 40 prisoners, largely drawn from the 'subversives', were transferred to the Curragh (which already held a small number of paramilitary prisoners), a military barracks that was operated by the Department of Defence and therefore outwith the remit of the Prison Division (Mulcahy 2002). The use of the Curragh was a quick response by administrators in the Prison Division and was given formal footing via the hastily passed Prison Bill of 1972. This failed to tame matters. In 1972, soon after prisoners were relocated there, seven subversives tunnelled out of the Curragh. Even more dramatically, soon thereafter three Republicans escaped from Mountjoy prison yard via a hijacked helicopter which landed in the prison yard (ibid; Lonergan 2010).

To those in the Division, the escapes and riots were possible because prisons were designed for ordinary prisoners: 'It has all along been the view of those in the Department of Justice concerned with the prisons that civil prisons are unsuitable for holding members of the IRA' (Department of Justice 1973:1–2). With national security at stake, the Division was faced with the daunting task of ensuring that escapes, hunger strikes and destruction did not become a recurrent feature of Irish imprisonment. A new penal prescription was required for subversive prisoners. What developed was a 'two-tier' prison system (Lonergan 2010), which deployed 'reactive' military imprisonment for subversive prisoners (McEvoy 2001).

With the urgent need to tighten control over the paramilitary prisoners, Portlaoise prison – where the regime was largely focused on farm work – was redesignated in November 1973 as the 'Security Prison' for up to 175 subversive prisoners and 40 ordinary prisoners (Department of Justice 1981a, 1984b; Mulcahy 2002:290). The walls of the prison had to be impenetrable to escape *and* invasion and, in a startling move, the Irish army were appointed to guard the walls of the prison (Lonergan 2010:114) and the Gardaí often supported prison officers inside the prison.

When Portlaoise became the subversive prison, it was reported to be beset by tension, agitation, assaults and numerous escape attempts (*Annual Report 1973*; *Annual Report 1976*:7; *Annual Report 1975*; Behan 2018). During this period, Portlaoise and not Mountjoy came into focus as what was described as the 'the centre of gravity of the prison service' (Liam). Subversives protested against strip-searching, and staff brutality was alleged to be a regular feature of Portlaoise prison life. In 1978, 19 prisoners escaped when the perimeter gates were blown up. Reportedly, the escapees wore imitation prison service uniforms (*Annual Report 1978*:29, see also RTÉ 1974). Prison authorities discovered four ounces of explosive plastic gelatine during a search, and more explosives were found in the heels of shoes sent in for prisoners. On another occasion, a dramatic escape was attempted when a bomb exploded at the outer door of the recreation hall and a steel tank rammed into an outside gate (*Annual Report 1978*). Bombs were found beneath the governor's car, and tragically one prison officer, Brian Stack, was murdered by paramilitaries (Mulcahy 2002:291). In many ways, the frontline of this war was, in the Republic at least, concentrated on the paramilitary imprisonment of Portlaoise.

But behind the austere exterior of Portlaoise a more peculiar set of officially sanctioned, but surreptitious compromises (ensuring their political deniability) evolved after this initially fractious period. Subversives gained privileges that were denied to ordinary prisoners (Lonergan 2010:118). For example, they were allowed wear their own clothes. Trivial enough, perhaps, but certainly a matter of serious contention for subversives who wanted to distinguish themselves from 'ordinary' criminals. In 1978 two Republican prisoners, Rose Dugdale and Eddie Gallagher, who had a child together, were allowed to marry – becoming the first prisoners to do so in the history of the state (Ferriter 2012). Reportedly, Portlaoise prisoners were allowed to order take-away food, which the prison staff would collect. And those 40 ordinary prisoners who were also resident at Portlaoise played a special support role within the regime: housed in a totally separate building, they were known as the Portlaoise Work Party. They undertook the sorts of housekeeping chores that the Republicans were not allowed to do due to security considerations, or simply were unwilling to do – ordinary prison work was the preserve of ordinary prisoners (*Annual Report 1976*; Mulcahy 2002; Lonergan 2010).[x]

That they were indeed not ordinary prisoners is evident in the fact that Republican groups were also allowed to maintain their military structure inside the prison (Behan 2018). This was integral to Portlaoise's prison regime. Within Portlaoise subversives were permitted to act as soldiers, apparently holding military parades in the yard to mark the Easter Rising.[xi] They were also granted fiefdoms, in which each Republican faction was allowed to colonise separate spaces. A designated Commanding Officer, the 'OC' (reflecting the Irish: Oifigeach Ceannais), was in charge of the subversive faction inside Portlaoise, and was recognised and treated accordingly by the governor.

Committed to escape and driven by a radical political purpose, subversives had proved that even within the prison they posed a genuine threat to state security. This makes it all the more remarkable to discover that subversives were also granted temporary release. John Lonergan, a former governor of Portlaoise and Mountjoy, maintains that subversives were in fact more likely to receive temporary release than ordinary prisoners. This was done slightly differently, however, using a system known as 'The Guarantee'. The Guarantee was an oral agreement of trust between the governor (and thus the Prison Division) and the OC, who would 'give their word' that a prisoner would adhere to the stipulations of their release, and once given it was known that 'they always honoured it' (Lonergan 2010:119). The subversive dynamic of the Irish imprisonment regime reflected a paradox wherein these prisoners were subject to both authoritarian control and liberal release.

Political culture

What made these new prison practices permissible, even something to be proud of? The motivations driving Irish prison practices emerges when we examine the political culture – the assumptions, values and beliefs – that informed the power to imprison.

The prisoner of poverty

Crime was statistically low in Ireland, and that may help explain why such permissive and progressive prison regimes developed. In the archives, reports and interviews, crime rarely invoked rebuke or blame; it was often dealt with lightly, particularly in cases being considered for release. Niall, amongst others, described how many offenders could be a 'dreadful nuisance' but they were released 'because their offences they committed were not so grave'. Similarly, Jim recalled, with considerable amusement, those prisoners released early who they felt would likely re-offend: 'They'd say: "that guy is like a Fiat 127, he'll be fine for two months and then he'll break down again!"'

There was a certain feeling of tolerance around crime, but this was not just a reflection of statistical patterns. When we think of prison in terms of sensibilities, we see that in the Irish case, understandings of criminality had a direct impact on decision-making. The more lenient uses of imprisonment in Ireland were predicated on a view that people imprisoned were not inherently criminal: the prisoner tended to be defined first by Ireland's endemic poverty rather than a criminal pathology. Many respondents emphasised the tragic and unfortunate backgrounds of prisoners, generally seeing them as victims of chronic economic deprivation. John recalled being explicitly informed of this cultural ethos on his first day in the Division:

> I remember talking to the Principal Officer and he emphasised a few principles to me, which stood to me. Which was the people you will be dealing with…they're from generally underprivileged backgrounds, they're people who haven't had the chances in life you had. And you know, you should bear that in mind in how you approach this work.

This kind of compassionate and patient sentiment seemed typical. Jim too stated that 'the concept of the person in prison was a humane view of the person, an awareness of their social background being very deprived'. Similarly, Liam emphasised the importance of 'the prisoner, their narrative, their history and the notion of socio-economic disadvantage' when conducting his work during this period.

Many interviewees' tolerant sentiments were partially shaped by their own sense of identification with the difficulties of forging a successful and stable life in a country riven by poverty. Ireland was poor, and prisoners were seen as victims of circumstance: forces of chance and poverty some civil servants understood all too well (Healy and Kennifick 2019). Several of the interviewees discussed getting a job in the civil service as a lucky break, as it meant they no longer needed to work in a factory; it gave them a chance to return to Ireland after working abroad. Others had wanted to go to university, but lacked the financial means to do so, the civil service was an interesting alternative with a regular salary. The precariousness of poverty was therefore also part of many of these stories as well. Pádraig best illustrated these concerns in pithy and explicit terms:

LB: What drew you to the civil service?
Pádraig: Well, God bless your innocence! What drew me into the service was that I needed a job and that was the only job.

In Ireland, prison policy was partially shaped by an empathy with the prisoners' personal and social circumstances, circumventing the limited view of prisoners as inherently or pathologically criminal.

Sanctity of the flock

However, this social view of criminality alone does not fully account for Ireland's prison practices. Absolutely central to Irish penal culture were the ever-present Irish Catholic conservative virtues of the stable family and the traditions of community, so prevalent in other forms of legislation and social policy. This rationale was the most predominant justification given for temporary release, which had been developed in such a manner as to maintain the sanctity of the Irish family unit. Here is a typical general explanation for temporary release from the annual reports:

> Outings for important family occasions such as baptisms, weddings, etc. are a regular feature as are outings on compassionate grounds in the event of the death or serious illness of a close relative…The temporary release system ensures that an offender can return to the family at intervals during his sentence.
>
> (*Annual Report 1979*:22)

Release for short periods was thus 'authorised regularly on compassionate grounds or for very important family occasions' (*Annual Report 1976*:13), or if a prisoner's 'presence in the home' was required (ibid.:8). Similarly, the practice of offering amnesties for Easter and Christmas recognised that these were major occasions in Catholic Ireland when the entire family usually reunited – and in Ireland that could still include family members who were imprisoned.

Crucially, we see that prisoners were understood to remain members of society; their social identities were not overturned. In going about the business of releasing, building and refining the imprisonment regime, there was an underlying recognition of the importance of family, and the prison's routines of mobility were adjusted in ways that preserved community ties and familial obligations. Therefore, we can ascertain that the ad hoc and 'unbureaucratic' form of release allowed, by design, Ireland's Catholic and conservative ethos to shape decisions, rather than objective pro-forma indicators set down by experts who might overlook the social and personal nuances in a prisoner's case.

For Jim, among others, the Department had many flaws (too conservative and not ambitious enough being foremost among them), but he was adamant that these prison developments were progressive because they prioritised Ireland's broader social goals above penological objectives:

> the attitude to the prisoners was that we need to help these guys, not address their offending behaviour, not that narrow objective, we've just got to help them. What did we mean by rehabilitation? Maybe they're just better with their family.

The rationale within the Division favoured the power of the community and the collective as a means to put prisoners back on the right path. However, this statement illuminates an additional characteristic of Irish penal culture: that rehabilitation had a very particular connotation and practical implication in 1970s Ireland.

Rehabilitation: an 'approach to living'

An internal report outlined the new concept of prison rehabilitation, which was entering the Irish prison discourse, but with a clear acknowledgement that in the English-speaking world it was simultaneously coming in for criticism as a failed paternal strategy. Rehabilitation was presented as broadly laudable, but its basic aims needed to be made compatible with its aspirations of improving and supporting family and community life:

> While 'rehabilitation' is not the primary objective of imprisonment it is nevertheless an important and valid objective. It is intrinsically good and should not be abandoned simply because evidence does not prove that it is 'successful'. What is to be the measure of success? Is it to be that the prisoner never again engage in criminal activity, or is never again caught, or is never convicted again, or is not convicted again within a certain length of time, or engages in criminal activity less serious in nature than his original offence? What about the qualitative improvement in the prisoner's *approach to living*, his relationships with family and friends, his involvement in community activities, his willingness to help and support others, his physical and mental well-being?.
>
> (Department of Justice 1981a:7–8, emphasis added)

In this extended quote, rehabilitation as reducing crime was perceived to undermine the more important goal of cultivating and reinforcing social morality in prisoners. Instead, the best prison interventions were not limited to the singular demands of reducing recidivism:

> [the aim is] to equip the offender with educational, technical and social skills which will help him to turn away from a life of crime, if he so wishes. However, even if the offender on release does not turn away from a life of crime, those services can be regarded as having achieved some success if they bring about an improvement in the offender's awareness of his responsibilities to himself, his family and the community.
>
> (*Annual Report 1982*:29)

An improved 'approach to living' was also felt to be best achieved within the community, among family and back at home. Release was therefore justified, according to the Minister for Justice, because it gave priority to the utility of the family:

> [it] obviates the need for rehabilitation programmes and lengthy schemes, which sometimes have low enough success rates for reintegrating prisoners into the community, because here the people are not in prison in the first place. They live at home.
>
> (Dáil Debates, 11 June 1985)

The integrity of the collective loomed large in the prison policy rationale. But this pragmatic insight reveals something else irregular about this conception of rehabilitation: a distinctly suspicious view of the prison, whereby it was seen as a destructive social institution. The prison was what disintegrated a prisoner's social and personal bonds; it was that from which prisoners required reintegrative support. Shortening and softening the use of the prison reduced the need for reintegration and maintained the sanctity of family and community life.

Humanitarian sensibilities: shepherding the prisoner through the pains of imprisonment

Those in the Division often exhibited scepticism about the prison's positive claims and they were concerned by its damaging effects. The Minister for Justice proclaimed the prison environment was 'basically unsuitable for encouraging individuals to become adequate and responsible members of normal society' (Dáil Debates, 26 May 1970). This was more than generic rhetoric, but reflective of a specific humanitarian penal ethos. Humanitarian penal sensibilities are a distinct outlook that seek to reduce the pains of imprisonment, motivated by empathy and a respect for prisoners as people (Garland 2010). This was certainly evident in the form and narrative of the annual reports. Presented in lengthy, diarised, narrative style, the annual reports give a sense that there was something missionary in how the Division went about their work. Year in, year out, it was reported that some prisons and prisoners had good years, others had struggles. This was a linear narrative (Franko Aas 2004) with an emotional tempo; the tone was more intimate and humanising, which exalted the personal success of prisoners and commiserated with tough times.

A penal culture motivated by a humanitarian view will therefore be more suspicious of the negative impact of the prison rather than the negative characteristics of the prisoners. Motivated by their humanitarian ethos, the Division worked to improve and modernise Irish imprisonment regimes, but in ways which sought to reduce the destructive and dehumanising aspects of prison sentences where possible, and this contributed significantly to the shape of Ireland's penal transformation. For example, when temporary release was first introduced the Minister for Justice declared that it would prevent 'the institutionalisation, psychological deterioration and disruption to family and individual life consequent on imprisonment' – better to have the prisoner 'in his own milieu' (quoted in Rogan 2011:109). This thinking was particularly evident in the aims of the new support services such as psychology and probation, which were designed to help prisoners *cope* with the pains of imprisonment. They were 'trying to assist them [prisoners] through counselling to cope with their problems, some of which may arise from imprisonment itself' (*Annual Report 1982*:38). Education's objectives included: 'helping prisoners cope with their sentences ...[as] one element which might compensate for, or modify the deprivations of prison life' (Department of Justice 1984b:5; original emphasis). Even psychology, that power-knowledge instrument so closely associated with prisoner reform, was described in terms of coping, focusing on counselling prisoners so as to 'assist them in coming to terms with their imprisonment and with life in the community after release' (Department of Justice 1981a:10). Instead of attempting to regulate prisoners' criminality, services supported prisoners in overcoming the pains of their imprisonment. Describing these prison professionals at the time, looking back Niall likened psychology to chaplaincy, a humane and pastoral cushion to soften the blow of imprisonment rather than to 'fix' people: 'meeting prisoners, discussing their problems, psychological stuff, you know psychologists play a big role, as do chaplains in the human relationships with prisoners.'

According to Liam, psychological services used discursive rather than curative techniques: 'in the early days the last thing you would talk about was the crime. It was the well-being, how were they getting on?' They were intent on shepherding the prisoner through his imprisonment.

The politics of Irish imprisonment operated as it did because it recognised the 'destructive agency' of the prison (Armstrong 2017) and, where possible, sought to curtail it. As Jim described it: 'prisoners have these needs, so let's make life in prison bearable, it's nothing to do with rehabilitation'. This humanitarian penal philosophy was not entirely taken for granted. It was often passed onto to staff as part of the informal orientation – a way of thinking that should guide their actions:

> I think in those days there was a more liberal approach than there was in more recent times. I told you at the outset about the guiding philosophy given to me… it was all about prison was necessary as a sanction under the criminal law, within that then we should be trying to the best we can…[that was the] guiding philosophy.
>
> (John)

As a result, others, such as Liam, also stressed that there had been a 'humanity about the system' in this period. And reflecting on his colleagues' approach to their work in this period, a later staff member, Gerard, thought that there had been a peculiar 'distaste for the whole business' of imprisonment in the 1970s into 1980s. As such, Irish prison practices reflected a desire to address the problems of the prison, not the problems of the prisoner.

Nationalism

Within this modernising context and embedded humanitarian and conservative culture was the development of an altogether more authoritarian kind of imprisonment, one that expressed the total power of incarceration. For authoritarian political rationality to be realised in practice, it must be seen as a legitimate form of reasoning within the minds of actors who occupy the penal state. But it will inevitably merge with other aspects of prevailing political and social culture, giving imprisonment regimes their often paradoxical character. In Ireland in the early 1970s, the development of Portlaoise was contingent on the state of emergency and the urgency to prevent conflict and disorder. The Department worried about the IRA's strategic capacity and destructive capabilities (Department of Justice 1973:1–2). This anxiety created what has been described as a 'siege' mentality inside the Division (Rogan 2011). John, for one, was reluctant to discuss this time at all, and gave this short anecdote encapsulating his anxieties:

> I never felt fearful, just, you know, wouldn't be advertising where I worked. Close friends knew, but I wouldn't be advertising it. If I was in a taxi and I was asked where I worked, I would have said the Department of Agriculture.

The image of the armed prison was a visual display that dissident prisoners were in the 'deep end' (Sparks 2002) of the Irish imprisonment regime. But the covert compromises resemble policies animated by emotional states other than fear; the shape of their imprisonment regime also clearly demonstrates the privileged political status of subversives (Mulcahy 2002:291). As Pádraig recalled: 'there was no such thing as a political prisoner, they were ordinary criminals who had committed a criminal offence. Anyway, they were political prisoners!'.

Imprisonment regimes will generally have contradictory practices and strategies in simultaneous operation, reflecting the contradictory and ambivalent currents that constitute political culture, social relations and penal problems. The presence of the Irish army was a means by which to take control of a difficult prison population and publicly demonstrate severity; surreptitiously, however, other sentiments and ideas came into play. The trust given to subversives bespeaks the 'cultural resonance' and 'emotional supports' which shaped prison practices in less rational ways (Garland 1990b:1). Republican prisoners seemed to hold a place in the people's imagination, one that was not wholly condemnatory, based on long-standing claims over the North but also more immediate concerns regarding the Troubles.

The cultural sentiments that also shaped the practice of paramilitary imprisonment – with its high-security measures and discreet system of privileges – was the distinct, historically embedded, though certainly not full-throated, nationalism. This was evident in the de facto recognition of the IRA as an army. Pádraig explained the relationship with the OC in straightforward, pragmatic and realistic terms: 'You had a Commander, a general, or whoever he happened to be, and everything was communicated through him. He ran the show really. That was the only common sense way not to have too much trouble.'

These easy feelings of common sense were also evident in this extended recollection from Niall:

> [The IRA] ran their own system, that's where we differed from the Brits. They took a view over in England, and we said this to them, these are not tales out of school, we said all of this to them. They took a view that you had to maintain control, basically…that they had to conform to prison rules. That it was wrong to allow effectively the military command structure to survive inside prisons, and that they should wear certain clothing and all that sort of thing. We took a totally different view on all of that.

We took the view that if they stayed inside the wall we don't care if they wear civilian clothes we don't care or if they march around. With the IRA prisoners you dealt with an OC, with all other prisoners you go and talk to prisoners. But with the IRA prisoners you dealt with the Officer Commanders, they maintained the structure inside, and as far as we were concerned that was fine. The Irish took a totally different view on that.

To Niall's mind, imposing total imprisonment upon the subversives wasn't good for prison order, but it also seemed unnecessarily heavy-handed, drawing an important comparison with how the British imprisoned the IRA:

I think it was that we felt it was not, it was not as damaging as the British thought it was. The British I think felt it was like cocking their noses up at authority, that it was a bad thing to let them behave like an army. We just took a different view, so what?…I mean, what does it matter if the IRA are marching around inside and having parades on Easter Sunday inside? Once they were inside and not outside, and we took that view. We also kept something that I don't think they had in the British prisons and that was the army on the wall. So it was very clear, if you stay inside then we don't have a problem with you, but if you try to go out we do.

(Niall)

Niall thought the British worked against the IRA, using the prison to 'defeat terrorism' (McEvoy 2001). The Irish, in contrast, worked with the subversives, engaging them as an army. Prison is always being modified to reflect the perceived character of the prisoner and the wider cultural and political norms. The peculiarity of subversive imprisonment was positioned along two key axes: authoritarian mentality and implicit respect. This was a kind of parliament-style negotiation of sensibilities and rationalities – as demonstrated by Jim when recalling the Portlaoise regime:

The mentality was, even with security, they saw that these guys had the best brains in Europe and that made them a challenge and the challenge was to keep them in, and above all else we have to keep them in – because there were some escape attempts – but if you can provide something, great, then do it. But security was above all, but if we can do anything for them you should, and that we should modify imprisonment as such.

Descriptions of the subversive prisoners were couched in narratives which shared a general set of army motifs: civil servants understood the IRA in relation to their order, their organisation, their discipline, their aims. Although the subversives were undertaking violent campaigns during this most turbulent era of the Troubles, they were accorded a subtle dignity and were, consequently, subject to a regime that pragmatically evolved to reflect precisely these seemingly contradictory sensibilities. Those aspects of the IRA that unnerved the Department – their strategic capacities and unfaltering political motivations

– were also what inspired a degree of recognition. The IRA were not criminals. Their rebellion and protests were not wild and impulsive, but strategic, formally authorised by the IRA hierarchy, and thus conforming to their army structure (Terry 2012). That sense that subversives lived by an established order yielded a practice of trust, evident in the guarantee scheme. As Niall said:

> The Officer Commander came and said so and so's mother is dying, he needs 24 hours and we'll guarantee he'll be back. In fact, a guy was left outside the gate one night, pissed drunk, because he had to make his time. They [Republicans] brought him back [laughs] and rang the bell.
>
> LB: That's a lot of trust.
>
> Niall: Oh, oh well you could, because they had a different system, a personnel system.

Another important reference point was the IRA Army Council Code, a written document by which the IRA maintained its hierarchy, its order and its unity as an army. Prison Division officials often knew the code and quoted it; for example, they knew the IRA would not turn a weapon on a member of the army or Gardaí, and they had been able to 'trust' that the IRA would stand by this code (Department of Justice 1973; Pádraig; Niall; Terry 2012).

This was a time when the nationalist future the IRA was fighting for, the reunification of Ireland, had been embraced by many people across the political and social spectrum in Ireland right up until the 1970s.[xii] The government certainly did not support the IRA or their tactics; the state acquiesced to them for the sake of social, political and penal order. But to treat them as such was not entirely pragmatic: there was also tacit acceptance of the 'political character' (McEvoy 1998) of the subversives' identity and activity. Their treatment of subversives, even the very use of 'subversive' as a distinct prisoner categorisation, was 'a mirror to the state's view of the conflict' (ibid.:1574).

Moreover, rather than work against the subversives' political identity, that they used the IRA identity as soldiers to develop a trust-based system to give subversives access to temporary release underscores the importance of release in this period of Irish prison development. Subversives posed real risks. But within that state security context, the Prison Division were still concerned with preserving subversives' identities as members of families and communities. Pádraig described giving parole to one subversive prisoner, an example which draws out the interlocking visions of the family man and political actor:

> He was a solider and he was fighting and the last thing he wanted to do was look for an extension of parole, but his wife was sick and he had six children and the neighbours were pressing him. Anyway, he was in and he got his extension.

The Department of Justice wrote that these '"concessions"…ease the effects' of deep imprisonment, and that 'This is in line with the policy of successive Governments, namely to provide, as far as practicable a humane and well-balanced prison regime in all our prisons' (Department of Justice 1983:3). Contrary to the literature on Irish penal history, this was a period of progressive, as well as authoritarian, penal transformation, driven by explicit and implicit intentions, feelings and ideas. Ostensibly, prison practices were being modernised. In making imprisonment more permeable the Prison Division were doing more than reducing the prison population: Irish prisons were being adapted in a manner that reinforced the conservative heritage, cumulative social norms and values of the traditional Irish nation.

Pastoral penality

We see that ideas such as justice and rehabilitation are 'more malleable and multifaceted than is often recognized' (Goodman 2012:439), and that these penal ideas morph and evolve depending on the wider social order (Super 2011; Barker 2009, 2017). Certainly, Ireland's prison developments mirrored those of the penal welfare developments that had occurred in the USA and the UK (Garland 1985, 2001). The Irish imprisonment regime was intended to be less retributive, and these new prison strategies were occurring simultaneously with the flowering of the Irish welfare state. However, I argue that the case of Ireland reveals a new form of penality that requires conceptualisation. Following Foucault (1981) and Valverde (1998, 2017), Irish prison regimes were not welfare orientated, and were instead rooted in a pastoral political culture. Pastoral governing was a priestly form of power, ingrained in Christianity, though taken less literally it provides key ideas that more effectively illuminate Irish penal transformation, capturing the imprisonment regimes, political culture and historical-cultural context of 1970s Ireland that penal welfarism does not.

When pastoral power hybridises with penal aims it still uses the prison but openly acknowledges that prison always involves the inescapable infliction of pain, seeking to support the prisoners as they face the harms of confinement. As a result of this more benevolent and sympathetic approach to governing, the prison is to be made less oppressive rather than more effective – in fact, 'pastoral power is anti-quantification and anti-efficiency' (Valverde 2017:29). Pastoral penal power is instead 'highly personalised' and individuated, supporting people through the 'dark night of the soul' (Valverde 1998:47), caused in this case by imprisonment and familial separation; as such, it engages people's suffering without pathologising them. Specialists informed by a pastoral penal culture will therefore not be designated the task of diagnosing criminals and providing corrective treatment, such as in a penal welfare context; instead, their job will be to act as 'shepherds', providing 'advice and moral support' through lenience (Valverde 1998:47). Like others, the findings here show that in the 1970s Irish penal policymakers did not display any belief in the superiority of scientific knowledge professionals (O'Donnell 2008; Rogan 2011). Indeed, the Division described 'penology' as 'an area where folly abounds' (AOG/2014/23/1103). But this is not to uphold the ideational 'vacuum' often suggested. The lack of interest in experts, abstract scientific knowledge and efficiency was characteristic of pastoral penality. The Irish prison support services developed at this time – psychology, probation and education – differed in ideational orientation and practice to welfare approaches as they were not centrally linked to the aims of assessment, treatment and correction. They were intended to have a mainly caring and discursive quality, employing a 'pre-scientific knowledge of an individual's mind and soul' (Hannah-Moffat 1997:7). The aims of prison experts were focused on increasing a prisoner's ability to deal with imprisonment – the word 'coping' came up time and again in describing their work – in the hopes of reducing the corrosive impact of the prison upon a persons' social, personal and familial well-being.

The other primary motivation of a pastoral penal culture is communitarian, focusing on 'the flock' (Foucault 1981); the individual is seen as inseparable from the collective (Dean 2010). In this context the pastoral leader must return the fallen individual to 'the fold' of the community (Foucault 1981:229). The aims of pastoral power are conservative, to generate in citizens' hearts and minds a subjectivity bound to their place in the collective, and it does not share liberalism's desire to improve someone's sense of individual responsibility (Valverde 2017:29). We see this particularly in how an 'approach to living' was described as paramount among Irish prison policy aims: supporting a prisoner's relationships with family and friends and encouraging their community belonging, which was achieved in particular via Ireland's generous and informal parole arrangements.

The primacy of the flock was also highly significant in shaping the more dubious view of the prison. In total contrast to the welfare penal culture that was waning in the rest of the Anglophone world, in Ireland informal social controls of the community were not side-lined but actively embraced. Many in the Division were motivated by a conviction in the superior power of the 'collective efficacy' of the family and community (Sampson et al. 1997) because, in contrast to penal welfarism, there was a deep scepticism of the prison as a corrective site. In 1970s Ireland, techniques such as temporary release, skills training and open prisons were being expanded to help return the prisoner more regularly and more easily to the normalcy of community and family life.

Such techniques were possible because, unlike their welfarist counterparts in England and the USA, those working in the Prison Division in Dublin further differed in their penal approach because they were not so interested in reducing crime. In Ireland the view of the prisoner was as misfortunate, rather than the more patrician sentiments of the penal welfare habitus (Loader 2006) that viewed prisoners as a dysfunctional client to be treated (Feeley and Simon 1992). By looking after the collective, the pastoral leader also recognises the ascetic life and hardship of its flock and is fundamentally a 'lover of the poor' (Brown 1987, quoted in Dean 2010:96) who has a sense of solidarity with the less fortunate. Rather than treating their individual transgressions or recovering them from criminality, Irish penal policymakers recognised prisoners' poverty and suffering. The absences of diverse prisoner groupings, only categorically distinguishing 'subversives', also reflects the homogeneity and 'ordinariness' with which prisoners were understood. That was who prisoners were often believed to be by those in charge of Irish imprisonment: economically marginalised but unfaltering members of communities and collectives. That was how the ideal Irish nation was envisioned, and it was those ideas that were inscribed into the emerging progressive prison practices.

Lastly, pastoral penality requires a specific socio-political context to blossom. As outlined earlier, the ascendant political and cultural currents and social structures in Ireland were conservative, communitarian and traditional. Given that pastoral power is rooted in a traditional Christian culture, it also more precisely captures these social forms that helped support Ireland's 1970s penal transformation – buffering Ireland from the punitive trends that were occurring around it and ultimately giving it a distinct form of progressive penality.

We see, therefore, that similar penal tactics (e.g. release, incarceration, rehabilitation, prison education) should not be misunderstood as having sprung from identical social aims and political contexts. We must understand the nuances and differences between intentions and outcomes (Nelken 2005, 2009). Pastoral penality was founded upon conservative political and social forms. When pastoral penality provides the ideational basis for governing imprisonment, its aims are driven by compassion and community cohesion, not criminal correction; it is interested in reducing the pains of imprisonment rather than achieving individual rehabilitation. The prison was viewed sceptically, seen as inherently inhumane and inferior to the traditional institutions of family and community for returning an offender to normal life. In this context prison programmes favour discretion over effectiveness, employing open programmes and settings, job training, education and discursive support services that are directly aimed at supporting prisoners to cope with imprisonment and to develop as people. I argue that rather than being a late or superficial adopter of penal welfarism, it was pastoral penality that was reflected in Ireland's 1970s prison transformation and the intentions that informed it.

However, finally, to have a full critical and sociological understanding of pastoral penality we must situate this parsimonious form of penality within its contingent social control landscape. While the number of prisoners and prisons was expanding, in the 1970s the prison remained a peripheral social control mechanism. Ireland's traditional conservative political outlook had religion and morality as its bedrock, rather than legal concepts and order. Ireland's carceral archipelago of coercive confinement offers ample evidence of the primacy of other more explicitly morally attuned institutions charged with confinement. In addition to that religious welfare control, Ireland also relied on the 'emigration culture' as a 'safety valve' for its social problems (Fitzgerald and Lambkin 2008:51). In a country that was often excluding and oppressive in how it achieved social conformity, in contrast the prison operated as more benevolent, mild and tolerant. The pastoral-ism of the Irish imprisonment regimes existed not in spite of excessive and harsh Irish social control, but was partially a result of it: the Division could indulge and develop ameliorative imprisonment regimes because imprison-ment was peripheral, not the main coercive means of social control; and, in addition, crime was not a major social matter. This meant that the social goods of the family and the community could prevail within the Division's penal preferences.

By looking at penality in Ireland using the concepts of imprisonment regime and political culture, we may now see Ireland's 1970s penal culture anew. Those in the Prison Division were not secular liberal professionals with crim-inological expertise and a refined sense of civic citizenship; they were con-servative, culturally Catholic, civil servants. Their social interests and political intentions were shaped by communitarian ideals and obligations wherein the hegemonic image of the cohesive family was the central unit of Irish social order. The government's central job was to create a nation where citizens were indoctrinated as productive members of families and communities, and when it came to the prison, its techniques reflected these particular set of concerns. The aims of those in the Prison Division were tied not to modern-ism but to collective morality, giving rise to a pastoral penal culture, and as a result this meant that Irish prisons in the 1970s were coming to be 'ruled through leniency' (Melossi 1994).

While pastoral approaches are certainly appealing in their parsimony and humane thinking, there are limitations that must be acknowledged. While it was the dominant ideational framework during the 1970s, like penal wel-farism, pastoral penality was never wholly dominant in all prison practices (Goodman et al. 2017:72; Behan 2018). Pastoralism was also gendered (Hannah-Moffat 1997). Given that the prison system was almost entirely male, there were heteronormative limitations on the social imagination underpinning pastoral penality. This was benign inclusivity for men who could be recovered to the traditional and acceptable settings of the family, the workplace and the community. For convicted women, their double devi-ance often incurred a harsher patrician response, such as indefinite coercive confinement (Black 2018). There was also the risk of unbridled discretion being more punitive, where people deemed bad simply would never be con-sidered for release (Department of Justice 1984a), though this is an endur-ing problem of even the most regulated and bureaucratic parole systems and not limited to pastoral informality.

As a result of these social, political and cultural forces, this was undoubt-edly a period of progressive penal reform. The Division hoped that the sig-nificance of the 1970s as a decade of development could be continued. It was stated that the '1980s promises to be another important decade for the Prison System' (*Annual Report 1980*). However, negative transformations in the organisation of the Irish social field began to shape a much more difficult future for Irish imprisonment. It is to the unanticipated erosion of pastoral penality that we now turn.

Notes

i By the 1970s Ireland was exceptionally homogenous, with over 90% of people identifying as Catholic (Ferriter 2012:5).

ii Though Whyte (1980) writes that this only occurred on a few occasions. Inglis argues that the indirect influence of Church power was considerable, as displaying 'religious capital' was essential to advancing in Irish social and political life (Inglis 1998).

iii The Minister who had tried to implement the health scheme had to step down as a result. In his parliamentary resignation statement, he was clear about the Church's influence upon the policy: 'the Hierarchy has informed the Government that they must regard the mother and child scheme proposed by me as opposed to Catholic social teaching. This decision I, as a Catholic, immediately accepted without hesitation' (Dáil Éireann Debate, 12 April 1951 [available at http://www.oireachtas.ie/en/debates/find/?debateType=dail]).

iv The court found that the treatment was inhumane and degrading but not torture (Bonner 1978).

v The term 'big house' here is an entirely literal description and obviously means something significantly different to those big house prisons Simon identifies as closed prisons in the USA in the 19th and 20th centuries (2007:146–147).

vi Which, of course, were very much still part of the Irish prison system. But these changing perceptions inside the Division help us appreciate the changes occurring in how the Irish prison system was organised.

vii This draft ministerial address has no formal reference as it comes from a folder in the Department of Justice storage and was in a series of folders from the early to mid-1980s, but the copy I had was without a specific date.

viii These extensions of state power during the 1970s were not newly invented but rather a reactivation of once-retired acts and practices (Mulcahy 2002:284)

ix 'Subversive' became a category in Irish prisons during the 1970s; it had been used with less formality in the 1930s (Rogan 2011), though it has no formal meaning in law.

x In exchange for their assistance in going to Portlaoise, the members of the Working Party were given a greater percentage of remission.

xi Easter Sunday of 1916, the Easter Rising, is considered to be the uprising which set in motion the series of events which saw the end of British rule in Ireland by 1921.

xii The violence in the 1970s dulled what had been longstanding irredentist aspirations. After the formation of the Irish Free State in 1922 the nationalist project was focused on restoration of the island as a single nation and the inevitable annexation of Northern Ireland. This was formally written into the 1937 Constitution, which described the nation as 'the whole island of Ireland'. Moreover, survey data from 1972 to 1973 showed that 42% of Irish people disagreed that the North and the Republic were two distinct nations (Coakely 1998:49–50; Hardiman and Whelan 1998).

4 Pastoral penality losing ground

During the interviews, one former civil servant, Seamus, explained that in the 1980s 'the prisoner and the prison changed because the world outside changed. You see, the prison is a microcosm of society.' This astute statement ably demonstrates the challenges prison policymakers face in the everyday management and design of imprisonment regimes, reminding us that prisons always reflect who prisoners are perceived to be as well as the wider social context – though there is nothing inevitable about how broad social and political predicaments play out in the penal realm. The changing imprisonment regimes from early 1980 to the early 1990s, charted in this chapter, show that the emerging political panic was not exclusively about numbers (rising crime, rising committals). The dominant governmental perception of the prisoner, and view of crime patterns, so fundamental in giving precise expression to differing modes of incarceration, exhibited the shifting dynamics of Ireland's social and cultural landscape.

Because of a tendency in comparative penology to compare punishment using per capita imprisonment rates, there is sometimes a tacitly universalised image of the prisoner, overlooking changing crime rates, perceptions of the prisoner and patterns of criminality (e.g. Cavadino and Dignan 2006). The implicit assumption in these analyses is that the prisoner remains the same, views of crime are stable and it is only the political reaction to the prisoner that had transformed. This can be a decontextualised perspective, one that does not fully account for the changing social problems that a government is trying to resolve (Miller 2015, 2016), and consequently it undermines our ability to account for how and why the prison is mobilised to address those problems.

In this chapter I am interested in how those in the Prison Division made sense of, and responded to, the complicated changes that transpired in Ireland from the 1980s to the early 1990s. How were imprisonment regimes reorganised? What sorts of accommodations were made? And why? How did those sensibilities differ from the previous period? The discussion begins by showing the unfolding crises, economic recession, rising crime rates and an emerging opioid problem. The changing image of the prisoner became embroiled in these wider social anxieties and began to bring Ireland's pastoral political culture into disrepute. Panic and chaos consumed the working environment of the Prison Division, enabling the regressive changes that were later made to Irish imprisonment regimes.

Economic downturn and rising violence

The promise of the 1970s gave way to the harsh realities of the 1980s, as Ireland entered a period of serious economic decline. Unemployment rose to over 17%, mass emigration recommenced, the deficit increased and the currency was devalued (O'Connell 1999). After more than a decade of expansion of the Irish economy, the 'upward spiral of unemployment' was the biggest issue facing the nation (Department of the Taoiseach 1984:9), with one in three Irish people in receipt of social welfare (Inglis 2003:121–122).

Crime was now also on the political radar. There was a rise in violence during the 1980s. Crime peaked at an all-time high in 1983, and while this reduced through the rest of the 1980s (O'Donnell and O'Sullivan 2003), it rose again until the mid-1990s (Brewer et al. 1999). While understandings of the causes of crime were still largely tied to images of Ireland's poverty (Rogan 2011:165), it was also felt that 'the current mood in Ireland is one of serious concern about crime particularly its more violent manifestations: murder, rape, robbery with violence, attacks on elderly people, woundings and intimidation' (Committee of Inquiry into the Penal System 1985:29). Rather than being simply part of a national story of poverty, rising crime and violence was increasingly seen to be about a new but 'overwhelmingly urban problem' (ibid.) connected to Ireland's rapidly urbanising demography and the construction of new, large, suburban housing estates (Bowden 2014).

The politics of panic and retrograde regimes

With crime rising, the number of people being committed to prison continued to increase (see Figure 4.1) and there was an enormous daily struggle to manage the prisons. According to Seamus, the most pressing matters of this era were an absence of space and capital: 'The biggest thing was the overcrowding. You couldn't do anything without the resources.' In an internal note, the Division described the other consequences of their financial predicament as a dire impact on prison conditions and prison policymaking: '[We have] been managing the prisons on the cheap and at the expense of not only the review of prisons legislation but other crucial tasks too: for example, general inspections' (4 July 1984).

The Division now believed that they needed a 'near instant prison' to meet the demand for places (Treatment of Offenders Management Meeting, December 1983). Given the recession, any attempts to develop plans were hemmed in by extremely restrictive finances, and the Division was forcefully reminded of this by the Department of Finance: 'cost is a crucial issue… [new proposals would] be regarded as out of the question – unless they can be <u>clearly</u> shown to involve <u>no extra cost</u>' (JUS/2001/62/1; original emphasis).This created what seems to have been an utterly frantic working atmosphere. There was no more time for planning; 'everything was ad hoc', according to Jim. Seamus told a similar story, describing a feeling they were working in extraordinarily difficult times: 'Every day you wouldn't know what to expect…[events] set the agenda.' The terms 'chaos' and 'survival' were frequently used in recollections of this period:

> There was chaos, it was organised chaos…it was moving pieces all the time. Being run by a very small section in the Department…I remember going in in the mornings and you didn't know what was going to come at you that day, and that was the way it was every day. In terms of taking a longer-term perspective, a lot of the time it was about surviving.
>
> (John)

While the absence of resources is a major reason behind the decision not to build new prisons, the Minister for Justice publicly justified the decision by drawing on the familiar narratives that crime had complex social causes and imprisonment did not produce much social good: 'I would not like it to be thought that the problem faced by society in dealing with criminals can or should be solved solely by reference to the provision of more custodial places' (Dáil Debates, 27 November 1985). Lacking the finances and political will to build, the Division undertook a series of expedient expansions. A second wing was added to Cork Prison, while Loughan House, which had been a juvenile institution, became an open centre for between 50 and 100 men. At the same time, the Department opened the Separation Unit at Mountjoy to accommodate the remaining prisoners who were now being transferred from military detention in the Curragh back into the prison system. Wheatfield Prison, which had been thoughtfully developed to provide a modern prison for 150 juveniles and women prisoners (DFA/2009/120/200), and which the Division had noted they were fiercely committed to (TAOIS/2012/90/354), was hastily reconfigured.

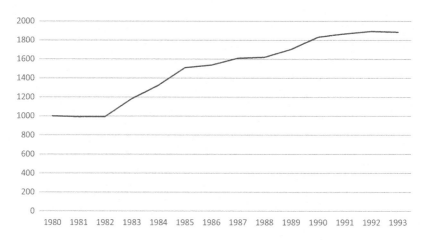

Figure 4.1 Daily average adult prison population 1980–1993.

Source: Annual reports on prisons, various years

When Wheatfield finally opened in 1989 it was a closed men's prison holding over 300 prisoners. Despite the promise of a new prison, Division officials predicted that Wheatfield would still not meet the demand for places (Treatment of Offenders Management Meeting, April 1984). More dramatic but financially feasible solutions were required if they were to accommodate the rising prison population.

We simply cannot understand the changes to the imprisonment regime from 1980 to the 1990s by seeing them as rational or instrumental responses to rising numbers and dwindling resources, or as the result of an absence of ideas. As Sewell argued, in studying history and transformation, one cannot ignore the emotive currents that guide decision-making and action: 'high-pitched emotional excitement is a constitutive ingredient of many transformative actions' (1996:865). Operating under duress compounds strain and this kind of tension gives a new permissibility to previously unthinkable and unacceptable imprisonment regimes (Bourdieu 1990:262). This was exactly what began to happen in the 1980s as the Department tried to curtail the chaos of the Irish prison system, making changes that only a few years earlier had seemed unthinkable, while also still trying to maintain the goals of their pastoral ethos.

Doubling-up

Until 1983, Irish imprisonment regimes were bound to provide each person in prison with their own cell, as per the 1947 Prison Rules. Removing this entitlement was considered a regression: 'Doubling up of offenders would be considered a retrograde step' (Treatment of Offenders Management Meeting, April 1980). Giving more prisoners early release was seen as 'preferable' to doubling-up (*Annual Report 1983*:8) and resistance to cell sharing was presented as an enduring and praiseworthy feature of the Irish prison practices (*Annual Report 1982*).

The continuing rise in prison committals, however, ruptured the boundaries between what had previously been expressly resisted, raising the threshold on earlier inhibitions. Doubling-up was now seen as a potential solution in a worst-case scenario: 'The "doubling up" of offenders offered a possible solution and must be seriously considered, despite the dangers inherent in this course of action' (Treatment of Offenders Management Meeting, October 1980).[i] There was a sense that something drastic, even unpalatable, had to be done: '[The] accommodation problem in the prison had reached almost crisis proportions. Harsh decisions would need to be taken if the situation deteriorated any further' (Treatment of Offenders Management Meeting, May 1982).

By 1983 doubling-up was a de facto practice in Cork Prison, and a prisoner there brought a legal challenge regarding the situation. The court found in favour of the government, but only due to a technicality. There was relief in the Division, but they felt they had now been forced to an impasse. The Department had to either eradicate de facto doubling-up or amend the

Prison Rules to permit it (TAOIS/2013/100/311). Given the aura of emergency around rising numbers and the threat of future legal cases, the Department formally authorised accommodating more than one person per cell 'for as long as the accommodation continues to be insufficient' (Memorandum for Government, May 1983). What had been a covert but largely resisted practice was now a strategic dimension of Irish imprisonment regimes and 'over-crowding received official sanction' (O'Donnell 2004:252).

This is a significant moment in understanding the changing governmental considerations that underpinned imprisonment regimes. This change legitimised practices that undoubtedly increased the onerousness of imprisonment. As Tom lamented: 'doubling-up was the biggest scourge…a disaster. No space, no light.' The punitive consequences of this doubling-up were illustrated by the Mountjoy Visiting Committee in their 1985 report:

> In May 1983 a statutory instrument was made allowing the prison Governor to permit 'two or more' offenders to occupy a cell when he judged that prison accommodation was insufficient to allow single cell occupancy. This represented a most serious setback to the possibility of maintaining and developing a humane regime within the prison…This imposes additional strain/punishment to the basic penalty imposed.
>
> (47–48)

Many in the Division agreed with these sentiments. But doubling-up was an expression of the prevailing atmosphere of panic, and as a regime change it became a pragmatic step to forestall further legal challenge.

Shedding – a rolling amnesty

But other, less confining adaptions were made to the imprisonment regime. In the 1980s temporary release was used to move an even greater number of people more speedily through the prison system. This came to be known as 'shedding' and was the most significant technique in managing the Irish prison population, seeking to reduce the daily average prison population. Shedding 'was adopted largely as a matter of necessity because of the pressure on accommodation…and it is, of course, one of the cheapest methods of keeping down the prison population' (Department of Justice 1984a:3).

The system had not been designed to deal with this level of mobility; there wasn't the administrative capacity or community infrastructure to release people in a sensible and supportive way. Previously, temporary release was achieved on a relatively orderly case-by-case basis. Shedding, by contrast, was chaotic and ad hoc, a crisis management approach reliant on systemic informality. Prisoners were not just released for family occasions, they were instead being liberated in order to free up beds for incoming prisoners. Respondents spoke of how the nuance had been stripped from their considerations about who to release; the most important issue now was to reduce the daily prison population:

A lot of the day was spent identifying who was going to be released this evening so that they can maintain control. The prisons were over-crowded so you had to everyday release ten or twenty people, maybe more....every day was a list of names with offences...and saying: yes, yes, yes. Out, out, out.

(Niall)

Those who received 'full' (and effectively permanent) temporary release were divided into those released under supervision and those who were not. In 1988, the Department stopped officially recording the distinction between supervised/unsupervised release when, of the 1,504 prisoners who received full temporary release, only 32 were placed under supervision. By 1993, of the 11,663 people who received temporary release, 7,335 of them were on full leave from prison (see Table 4.1).

Disorderly as this practice was, it was felt to be better to release people than allow extreme overcrowding. The Minister for Justice defended the 'extent of "shedding"...[because] The alternative has been the sort of crowding that has been resorted to in other countries'. The Irish prison system did not have 'enough space in our institutions to accommodate all committals in comfort' (Minister of Justice Speech to Prison Officers' Association, 25 May 1983).

While the Prison Division managed imprisonment regimes in a way that could radically alter a sentence length, the judiciary in turn still tended to respect the Division's discretion (O'Malley 2006). But shedding became publicly controversial, described as 'the most obvious and worrying symptom of the current chaotic state of the Irish prison system' (O'Mahony 1996:92).

Table 4.1 Use of temporary release 1976–1993

Year	Daily average prison population	Total number of temporary releases
1976	1049	1252
1977	1029	2720
1978	1179	3587
1979	1140	2842
1980	1215	3525
1981	1196	3292
1982	1236	4850
1983	1450	4375
1984	1594	7238
1985	1863	5746
1986	1869	5685
1987	1943	4883
1988	1962	6018
1989	2067	5830
1990	2108	8095
1991	2141	9038
1992	2184	8974
1993	2171	11663

Source: Annual reports, various years; O'Donnell et al. 2005

Between the pincers of low economic resources and high committals there remained a culture – albeit in a mutated form – in which prison accepted offenders, but continued to be more concerned with release than punishment. The 1983 Annual Prison Report declared that shedding remained justified within the existing humanitarian framework:

> Until additional accommodation can be provided, the present practice of releasing some prisoners in advance of their normal release dates to make way for committals will have to continue. It should be understood, however, that the practice of releasing some prisoners early has been followed for many years for resocialisation purposes.
>
> (p.7)

Shedding was the practical compromise that made the most sense – i.e. the prisons must accept everyone sent there, but to meet this basic demand the Division significantly increased the permeability of the imprisonment regime. The use of release was being justified as a means to maintain a semblance of humanity within the prison system under stringent economic times. The logic of pastoral penality had morphed and adapted to reflect the new financial realities.

This was not without negative side effects, however. Despite claiming that shedding worked within their desire to keep the system humane, it undermined their recent progress:

> The high level of early releases is a matter of grave concern...to the prison administration...On the one hand, unplanned releases disrupt resocialisation programmes for offenders and have the effect of negativing [sic] the significant advances that have been made over the last decade in the provision of education, work-training and other services for offenders who are now less motivated to make the best use of them.
>
> (*Annual Report 1981*:8)

Due to 'the level of transfers and early releases' (*Annual Report 1982*:21), fewer prisoners were completing courses in the Training Unit or engaging with education because they knew that they would likely be released without supervision in the near future if they stayed in an overcrowded prison (ibid.:24, 39).

The demands of shedding were such that it severely curtailed the Department's capacity to produce long-term prison strategies. Plans for consolidating prison legislation and updating the prison rules were side-lined. As they reported in 1984:

> the work which employs the largest number of (junior) staff is the daily chore of sifting through the prison population to find 'suitable' offenders for temporary release, 'shedding' etc [sic] in order to cope with the pressure on accommodation...In practice it has been found that day-to-day

pressure inhibit or preclude 'long-term' projects such as the review of the Prisons Acts and Rules.

(Department of Justice 1984b:12)

We might better conceive of shedding as a *rolling amnesty*, in the same way amnesties were also used in France and Germany to relieve prison over-crowding (Nelken 2011:110), though in Ireland they were organised on a day-to-day basis rather than en masse. These retrograde regime adaptions were a result of the Division having to 'muddle through' (Lindblom 1959), but, apt as it is, that concept does not capture the emotional intensity of these decisions, nor the stress that was endured. Reflecting on work in the Division by 1990, John was solemn, stating that 'the pressure on the prison system was unrelenting...[We were] on the treadmill running a system, just running'.

Authority under threat

By the mid-1980s, the scale of the Prison Division's challenges stretched beyond prison space and an absence of resources. The prison officer overtime bill had been ballooning and the government, needing to curtail expendi-ture, announced a civil-service-wide pay embargo in 1982. This was met with the greatest resistance from the Prison Officers Association (hereafter POA), who had grown significantly in power and size since the 1970s and gained Trade Union status in 1983, allowing them to go on strike – a facility that it used regularly and often with little forewarning. There were occasions when prison officers refused to unlock prisoners from their cells and banned visits, supervision of education, use of workshops and evening recreation. By the 1980s their protests had intensified in frequency (Committee of Inquiry into the Penal System 1985:307–310), and the POA had been identified as having 'a tendency to militancy' (Department of Justice 1984c:2). Liam, like others, described how the prisons now seemed to be unmanageable as the Department lost authority to the POA: 'I think the Department lived in fear of the POA. And ministers lived in fear of the POA.'

The POA demanded better working conditions, more staff, and increased pay and subsidies, and to get this they also demanded an inquiry into the prison system. In 1983, the government acquiesced and assembled the first independent penal review of its kind – what became known as the Whitaker Committee, which was accorded a comprehensive mandate to examine the prison system. In exchange, the POA suspended industrial action until the Committee's report was published.

The Whitaker Committee has a 'cultural afterlife' (Biber 2019), one that sees it celebrated as a seminal exposé that provided an unflinching critique of Irish imprisonment, lamented as one of the most significant lost oppor-tunities for progressive penal reform. It is still exhibited as the bar for Irish penal aspirations and continues to inspire activism (O'Donnell 2004; Behan 2018; The Katherine Howard Foundation, Irish Penal Reform Trust 2007).

The contemporaneous impact of the Whitaker Report instead tells a more divisive story. While its content presents an urgent and humane vision for penal reform, when situated in its own historical moment we see this aligned with much of the Department's existing political culture.

Within the Division they believed that a public body such as theirs, 'whose policy is not manifestly clear' (Department of Justice 1983:2), should probably be open to scrutiny. But they also hoped the Committee would provide them with legitimate and objective leverage against POA dissent (AGO 2014/23/1103), and they wanted the Committee to give support to their vision of imprisonment (Treatment of Offenders Division Management Meeting, February 1984). In an internal memo they wrote that the 'main purpose of the inquiry' should be tackling 'costs, increased committals and pressure on accommodation. It is obviously essential to the secondary purpose of winning public support for the prison system as such'.

The Division dutifully prepared numerous submissions for Whitaker (Department of Justice 1983, 1984a, 1984b, 1984c, 1984d, 1984e, 1984f, 1984g). These documents depict a Department with a sense of penological purpose and know-how. They suggested (Department of Justice 1984a:1–2) that the prison

> is extremely costly and for perhaps the vast bulk of offenders its positive achievements (training and education for example) can be substantially offset by its negative ones ('labelling', 'differential association' etc.). While the incapacitating effect of imprisonment for the duration of the term is obvious, any just alternative that is reasonably successful is better. Imprisonment ought to be kept to a minimum.

In these materials they proposed a number of ways to reduce committals and the overall prison population. They suggested that the Committee might investigate the usefulness of decriminalising homosexuality, drunkenness and the possession of cannabis, the possibility of weekend prison, increasing temporary release, and reducing sentence length. They also suggested taking comparative inspiration from the Dutch reliance on short sentences, West Germany's suggestion of decriminalising shoplifting, as well as the validity of international practices such as the Swedish day fine.

The Whitaker Committee released its report in 1985. It was rigorous and detailed and included research material provided by the Division. Its authors reflected much of what the Division advocated for and practiced, supporting the liberal use of release, the notion that prisoners were 'ordinary human beings' (Committee of Inquiry into the Penal System 1985:96), and that crime had social causes. The prison itself was affirmed as incapable of tackling crime, but it was likewise stated that prison should have the capacity to 'do something towards improving individual offenders' (ibid.). They also recommended a host of measures to reduce the use of imprisonment which, if implemented, promised to remove 500 people from the prison system (ibid.:112). The report also exposed a much more critical story. It included pictures cataloguing the dilapidated and grimy conditions inside the prisons, a very different visual story to what the annual reports had advertised in previous years. Both John and Gerard saw the pictures presented in the Report not as a story of Departmental incompetence; instead the 'pictures of dilapidated buildings…that was the scene which reflected years of underinvestment, no investment' (John).

The humanitarian demands made by the Committee were shared by many of those working inside the Division, to a greater or lesser degree – though this too seems to have offended the Department, who believed that many of the Division's ideas and aspirations had been erroneously and egregiously appropriated by the Whitaker Report:

> The reality is that in many regards the findings of the Committee endorse the policy already being pursued by the Government but without actually saying so. Indeed, the opinion is often created that the committee was breaking new ground.
>
> (marginalia, Memorandum for Government, 1987,
> Establishment of Prisons Board)

Inside the Department they were also startled that Whitaker diagnosed the Division as the source of problems for the prison system, and not the brinkmanship of the POA:

JOHN: The Department's reaction was that the Whitaker Committee was being simplistic in thinking the prisons board was going to fix this issue when the fundamental issue is about power.

LB: How do you mean power?

JOHN: The POA exercising power…and basically putting the gun to management's head to say if they don't get ten extra people on duty or get extra overtime they're going to, they're not going to allow management to manage.

The most intractable point of conflict that arose from Whitaker, therefore, was the suggestion of an independent prisons board. Prison matters had, the Committee wrote, 'drifted into the political sphere through the involvement of Departmental officials in such matters' as 'prison management and discipline' (Committee of Inquiry into the Penal System 1985:122). These were claims redolent of the POA's accusations (and those of other people who made submissions to Whitaker, such as the Governors and the Prisoner's Rights Organisation), and the Committee stated that it was 'satisfied' that this indeed was the case (ibid.:20). The prison system, they argued, rather than being sequestered inside the Department and shaped by their discretion, should instead have clear public leadership with stated objectives and greater responsibility delegated to staff inside the prison (ibid.:126). In sum, Whitaker recommended that the control of prisons should be removed from the Department of Justice, and hence the Prison Division, and instead devolved to an independent board.

The Department had no intention of creating a board. This was inconceivable in their conservative vision of government. For one, the existence of political prisoners was believed to be unquestionably a matter for government. Moreover, it was felt to be anti-democratic; the deprivation of liberty was 'an area so fundamental to the way a democratic society organises itself' that it would be an error to remove it from the political sphere (Department of Justice 1986:2). At a cabinet meeting, the Minister for Justice raised the idea of a prison board, stating that 'the diminution of control by the elected Government of the day should be approached with great caution' (Memorandum for Government, 1987, Establishment of Prisons Board).

Despite so many points of agreement, this aspect of Whitaker's recommendations was perceived to be against the Department, which ultimately undermined the credibility of the entire report in the eyes of the government and the administration. Rather than providing a way forward, in critiquing the lack of resources for prisons and the growing power of the POA, the Whitaker Report, according to Niall, 'further entrenched positions by this stage [the early 1990s]. And the spread of inertia.' The report's lasting effect was to create a stalemate between the POA and the Department, with tensions remaining high and unresolved, and progressive or large-scale policy change remaining as unlikely as before.

The 'new hardcore'

Another set of immediate problems presented themselves. From 1980 to 1993 the view of the ordinary prisoner as family man and community member began to negatively diversify. Increasingly conceived of as potentially dangerous, needy, recalcitrant and incorrigible, the ordinary prisoner was gradually less likely to be framed by tolerance, lenience and hope.

Drug addiction

When drugs first began to encroach upon the prisons at the beginning of the 1980s (*Annual Report 1982*) this was downgraded to a health rather than a penal issue:

> The abuse of alcohol and drugs is on the increase. In particular there is a marked increase in the use of the 'hard' drugs such as cocaine and heroin...The abuse of drugs and alcohol are victimless crimes and it was suggested that offenders in these areas might better be dealt with at a detoxification centre.
>
> (Treatment of Offenders Management
> Meeting, October 1980)

This attitude recalls the claim outlined in Chapter 3: that corrective rehabilitation was not an organising rationality for Irish imprisonment regimes.

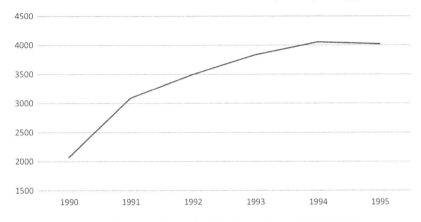

Figure 4.2 Number of persons charged with drug offences 1990–1995.
Source: Department of Justice 1997a:88

This confident complacency did not last, however. By the mid-1980s Ireland faced an 'opiate epidemic' (Dean et al. 1985), and the number of drug-related deaths began to rise (Kelleher et al. 2005, see Figure 4.2) – though this was generally seen as a Dublin – thus, urban – problem (Butler 2002). As Eamon suggested, there were fears now that 'the drugs were rampant around the inner city, but then it started moving around the rural towns and into the countryside. That was an eye opener to people and it got serious.'

The reality of drugs atrophied some of the ambition, permissiveness and empathy of the previous decade. Drug use in Mountjoy (other than cannabis) grew from 37% to 77% between 1986 and 1996, and in the same period serious dependency on hard drugs doubled from 31% to 63% (O'Mahony 1997). As prisoners with addictions and related health needs became a significant cohort in prison, the logic of what sorts of imprisonment regimes could be developed evolved correspondingly, becoming more pessimistic. For example, the Division feared that the Training Unit was now housing prisoners who were on drugs, meaning it was increasingly used for custody, eroding the Unit's 'unique spirit, esprit de corps' (Treatment of Offenders Management Meeting, April 1984). Overcrowding and the collapse of the previously growing industrial sector would have also undermined the open and permeable logic of the unit. It was suggested, though, that the practical changes in Irish imprisonment regimes were due to what they perceived as the reduced 'quality' of the prisoner:

> there was not the quality of offender to turn back a number of years. We had to use the Unit to hold short-termers unsuitable for open centres… Of course the choice of offender would never be as good as before.
>
> (ibid.)

The 1970s had established a pattern in which open prisons and lower security regimes were becoming an important feature in Irish imprisonment. In this same rationale, efforts had been made at the beginning of the 1980s to secure another open 'big house' (*Annual Report 1981*:5) as a response to rising committals. Acquiring large stately homes, such as Shelton Abbey, was lamented as less realistic by the mid-1980s. The Division believed they could no longer use prison in the same way because *who* was in prison had changed, meaning justifications for open regimes were felt to be less sensible. The outlook that had enabled pastoral penality in the 1970s now took on a less sympathetic, harsher tone: '[We] may be reaching the limits in our use of open centres – the hard core of the offender population is increasing all the time' (Treatment of Offenders Management Meeting, February 1984). There was a growing animus in the Irish public for the 'drug addict' (MacGreil 1996), and there was a consequent waning of empathy for the prisoner. A more diversified view of the ordinary prisoner emerged: one who was still vulnerable, sad, unfortunate and poverty stricken; but, by the beginning of the 1990s, the prisoner was also understood as addicted and more unpredictable, lacking strong community ties. The annual reports divulge this antipathy: 'The problem of drugs also continues to undermine the prison system. Many prisoners use prison to get off drugs. However, a small hard core do everything in their power to continue their abuse' (Annual Prison Report 1993:37). There were now prisoners who the Division believed did not wish to return to the fold of Irish community life.

Urban criminality

The paramilitary prisoners, while still a cohort within the prison system, were largely quietly contained within Portlaoise (Mulcahy 2002:291). The binary categorisation of ordinary/subversive began to fade through the 1980s, unable to capture the diversity of newly perceived prisoner identities and the complexity of Irish criminality. For a time in Ireland, joyriding became a huge news story (McVerry 1985). In response, the prison was employed as an expressive political tool for crime control. A former naval base on Spike Island, off the south coast of Ireland and only accessible by boat, was commandeered by the Department of Justice for use as a prison in March 1985. The Department installed a new prisoner population despite these buildings being in a state of disrepair (*Annual Report 1985*:15). Spike Island catered for males aged 16–25, an age category erasing the usual separation of juveniles and adults.

Recalling the vitriolic atmosphere at the time, Jim was exasperated at what he described as the divisive law-and-order atmosphere:

> In the 1980s there was a moral panic. As far as I remember it was the Evening Herald [newspaper] lambasting crime and a lot of joyriding. Sean McDermott St [in inner city Dublin] and handbag snatching was seen as a big thing. The Minister for Justice, Michael Noonan's response was to open Spike Island and put the 'young gurriers in there'.

This was a landmark moment in the transformation of how Irish imprisonment was governed. Spike Island was brought into use for the sole purpose
of exclusion and punishment; this was the first time the development of
prison regimes was explicitly linked to crime. John described his disapproval
at the decision to open this prison, which he saw as a political intervention:

> There was the joyriding problem and Spike Island was opened because
> the Department was told by the political system you have to find some-
> where to put these troublemakers who were driving up and down and
> getting out of hand and Spike Island was the solution. And that blew up.

Those final words refer to the riot that occurred in 1985, shortly after the
prison opened, wherein a fire destroyed much of the accommodation.

The Spike Island fiasco reveals a new political concern regarding *certain
kinds of crime* seen as distinct because they were associated with *certain kinds
of places* and *certain types of people*. These place-specific crime problems continued to percolate within the Department. The publication of *Urban Crime
and Disorder* (1992) documented emergent worries about new urban housing
estates and how they appeared to be producing a new 'hard core' population
(ibid.:23). As Eamon defined the problem at the beginning of the 1990s,
these new large estates were the 'bad areas' and seemed to create a culture
of crime, 'where from the time they were out of the cradle in those areas you
have to try and stop it [crime]'. Bowden asserts that the state responded to this
issue of place-specific crime problems by focusing on gaining 'sovereign power
over newly urbanized space' (Bowden 2014:51). Spike Island was historically
anomalous as a penal response to crime control; however, looking back, John
described this as one of the first signs of the erosion of Ireland's pastoral penality: 'it got lost around the Spike Island time, it got lost'.

Gangland crime

Entangled in the mire of urbanisation, poverty, unemployment and rising
drug consumption in Ireland was the emergence of organised criminal gangs
(O'Donnell 2005). These gangs 'introduced a climate of violence and intimidation new to the Irish crime scene' (O'Mahony 2000a:4), and the exe-
cution-style shootings between rival gangs became national news. Between
1972 and 1991 there had been two gangland-related murders (Dooley
1995:16); in 1996 there were eight (Dooley 2001:17). Even more troubling was the perceived impunity with which these gangs operated. Of the
15 gang-related murders between 1992 and 1996, only three resulted in a
conviction (ibid.:16–17), with the newspapers discussing gangland figures as
'untouchable' criminals beyond the reach of the law (Black 2016:403). The
opposition justice spokesperson in parliament, John O'Donoghue, described
1995 as 'the year of the criminal'.

Gangland crime resonated because it became a narrative about social order
disrupted. The new murder patterns were felt not just to be evidence of a

crime pattern, but also to be a signal of a changing Ireland. As O'Donoghue graphically illustrated, murder was once either domestic or rural, as such, linked to acceptable sources of community and family friction; now murders were the result of a vicious, urbanised Ireland:

> Until recently the State averaged approximately 20 murders per year and, while that was desperately tragic, criminologists considered it typical relative to the size of the population. The bulk of those crimes were rural crimes of passion or linked to feuds over land and families. In 1994 the number of murders was approximately 25 but so far this year the number of violent deaths had increased to 40.
>
> It is fair to say that 1995 — the year of the criminal — has been marked by the emergence of gangland murders…Tragically, it is now a fact of life — a fact of Dublin underworld life — that criminals are settling petty feuds by murdering people.
>
> (Dáil Debate, 28 November 1995)

Homicides were rising overall as well (see Table 4.2). The Division provided revealing value-laden descriptions of aggregate statistical crime rises: 'what is not brought out by examining the gross figures for violent offences is the fact that vicious crime is now more widespread' (Department of Justice 1994:27). The prison administration was not just addressing the prisoner numbers, capacity and overcrowding. Respondents who were witness to and involved in these events recalled this transition as justified, with Seamus stating that: '[Previously] the prisoners were more manageable…[then] the prisoner became much more dangerous. The gangs and then the drugs.' Diminution of the pastoral approach was due in part to changing perceptions of crime and the prisoner, which did not stretch to embrace Ireland's new social outsiders: the drug addict, the joyrider and the seemingly violent criminal. A distance emerged between Division officials and these more excluded prisoners, creating a new social 'boundary' (Lamont 1992) rendering some prisoner's history and background less relatable, less readily sympathetic, perceived to not share the same valued social mores. The changing perceptions of the prisoner were shared more widely, and had the consequence of recasting the Division's heavy reliance on shedding prisoners as an indefensible and reckless prison practice.

Table 4.2 Number of homicides 1961–2000

Year	Total	Average
1961–1970	131	13.1
1971–1980	259	25.9
1981–1990	294	29.4
1991–2000	439	43.9

Source: O'Donnell 2005

The revolving door

The shifting views of the prisoner as someone more dangerous and socially risky led to shedding being regarded with heightened hostility. Shedding came to be seen as *contributing* to public disorder and recidivism. There was a new popular and cynical portrayal of temporary release as a 'revolving door' – a metaphor intended to capture the cyclical pattern of releasing prisoners who reoffended, were re-sentenced, and perhaps shed again. The following quote from the Mountjoy Visiting Committee in 1988 highlights the newly connected ideas of liberal release and social risk:

> It is quite distressing for us to have seen prisoners released knowing with almost absolute certainty that they would in a very short time assault, rape or possibly kill some innocent person. For ourselves, the prison, and professional staff many of these crimes are predictable. Many could be prevented.
>
> (p.47)

The Garda Commissioner publicly levelled partial blame for rising crime rates at the use of mass release (O'Donnell and O'Sullivan 2001:46). By the beginning of the 1990s the government endured severe criticism for this penal practice from the opposition benches (Rogan 2011:13), and it 'attracted considerable public opprobrium' (Alyward 2002:575).

Arguments mounted that the problem was now more than a lack of prison space. The pastoral ideas and conservative agendas that had informed imprisonment regimes – which had favoured shedding to overcrowding and prison expansion – were now accused of bringing the principle of justice into disrepute (O'Mahony 2000b:13). New staff in the Division saw release as being 'grossly abused' (Gerard). Looking on from the political realm, Eamon recalled a 'strong belief that the laws were too lenient', as they 'were watching people walk out of the court system every week, people who were habitual offenders, robbing people's properties, robbing people's cars. You remember the saying "the revolving door", and they were walking in and walking out.' A former Prison Division psychologist denounced shedding as 'a travesty of justice…It is hard to imagine any policy better designed to subvert the intentions of sentencing and to undermine the authority of the judiciary' (O'Mahony 1996:92). Thus, this was not just a failure of the prison system, but a failure of the government.

Shedding, while controversial, still maintained credibility within senior quarters of the Department, for familiar reasons. The men being released were not fundamentally criminal, but compelled by poverty and hardship, rather than a criminal compulsion. Prison should prioritise space for 'real' criminals:

> You just had to get them out because there were no beds for people coming in. It's kind of a fundamental of prisons that you take in from the courts, you don't say 'house full'. So you had to do that every day,

and sometimes you'd be letting people out who maybe had come in that morning for things that, that's why you have to look at courts policy and the judges. Sometimes judges putting people into prison for very little, I mean, the television licences…there were people in prison who were not criminals at all. There were also another type of prisoner who unfortunately, a lot of those got out and that was people who were persistent offenders, they're a different category, they're a dreadful nuisance to communities and older people and so on. And some of them got out because their offences, they committed, were not so grave, knocking off handbags and that sort of thing. So, you always had to keep room for the bigger players…you know, people who did real offences.

(Niall)

Here the prisoners are 'not criminals at all', and repeat offenders were 'nuisances'. Moreover, the cultural motifs that explained crime were those related to monetary matters, the TV licence, the handbag thefts, what one might consider the petty crimes of poverty.

However, as the pressure to stem the flow of daily releases mounted, it was announced in 1992 that Castlerea, an asylum in the west of Ireland, would be converted into a prison. In the end, lack of funding meant that the project stalled after the prison wall was built (Rogan 2011:182). In the same period, apparently another set of plans for the new women's prison at Mountjoy were also cancelled. The Prison Division was faced with public ridicule, but was being denied access to the resources required to make major changes to the imprisonment regime. Evidently, despite the crime problem, building more prisons was still not a priority in Ireland.

WE see how Ireland 'edged' ever so slightly to a 'law-and-order mood' (Hall et al. [1978] 2013:272) by the beginning of the 1990s. We might also reasonably suggest that the imprisonment regimes simultaneously became more punitive as prisoner numbers rose, prisoners experienced doubling-up of cells, chaotic release undermined the support programmes and the Training Unit became less open. Apart from the opening of Spike Island, changes in how imprisonment regimes were organised were not intended to be punitive, nor were they a harsh expression of censure upon the prisoner. They were the consequence of practical compromises made in an atmosphere of panic, chaos and an absence of resources.

Pastoral penality continued to provide the ideas to solve many of the problems of the prison system, though those ideas morphed and mutated in the pragmatic process of solving those penal problems. Even in its hyperbolic form, the Division favoured using their power to establish a rolling amnesty to prevent even more overcrowding or having to expand the prison estate. Ironically, this undermined the practices of pastoral imprisonment, accused of now turning the prison into a source of social disorder. The benefit of a historical and sociological approach is that it allows us to observe new prison practices emerging, while also illuminating what practices fell out of favour and why ideas lost their relevance. However, more dramatic and concerted transformations in the imprisonment regimes and Irish political culture were to come, which were rooted in the destabilisation of this period.

Note

i They feared the consequences of overcrowding but also worried that cell sharing 'facilitates homosexuality' (TAOIS/2013/100/311).

5   The power to imprison

The previous two chapters have made a number of distinct claims which suggest that Irish imprisonment regimes were the outcome of political culture. Prison in Ireland had generally been moderate and maintained a humane streak; despite the tremendous difficulties of the 1980s, release remained a favoured form of imprisonment. This penal culture was embedded in the social context, political ideas and cultural fault lines of Irish life. Yet, if that is the case, then fundamental changes in the underlying social landscape can bring new political pressures and cultural conflicts, and unsettle even the most accepted penal sensibilities. By examining the social, cultural and political changes that occurred during the 1990s, this chapter argues that Irish social transformation ultimately expanded the responsibility of the government over crime and punishment, and radically altered the meanings of Irish imprisonment. The prison in Ireland was reorganised as a tool of crime control, no longer languishing at the periphery of social control machinery.

We start by charting Ireland's rapid and dramatic modernisation and the changes it wrought, both positive and negative, in the mid-1990s. Thereafter, using mostly interview material, we see the clashes and deep-seated disagreements within the Department regarding the fundamental purpose of both government and punishment. Some wanted to reaffirm pastoral penality. Others saw this as an egregious, naïvely optimistic and an anachronist policy prescription. The changes that followed in Irish imprisonment and penal politics were not inevitable, the immediate context and events also directed the course of action, providing the raw materials to make a punitive vision of imprisonment appear plausible and persuasive.

Ireland: A late moderniser

In the 1990s Ireland decisively shifted from being a traditional agrarian and rural society, entering a modern, global and capitalist phase of social order. The 1960s into the 1970s marked the first in a small rise in Irish economic fortunes, though the 1980s heralded a harsh reversal of these gains. In another dramatic swing, in the 1990s the Irish economy experienced exponential growth. This was the beginning of what is internationally known as the 'Celtic Tiger': a time of unprecedented economic prosperity. After being considered a 'semi-developed'

(Ruane 2007:xi) third world country as late as the 1980s, and certainly one that did not have a modern, developed capitalist system, during the 1990s the average GDP growth was a staggering 7% per annum (Coulter 2003:3). The country experienced a level of affluence not previously experienced in its history. The ceaseless flow of people emigrating came to an end, and in 1996 Ireland began to experience net immigration (Central Statistics Office 2003). This prosperity was also accompanied by peace. The IRA declared a ceasefire in 1994, which broke in 1996 but was restored in 1997 (McEvoy 1998), culminating with the momentous Good Friday Agreement in 1998. Suddenly, Ireland felt like a very different place. The literature and documents from the 1990s are riven with stories of Ireland's 'miraculous' (Sweeney 1999) social revolution, providing breathless accounts of rapid social change.

Among the most significant changes during these years was a rebalancing of social authority. In the second half of the twentieth century the Catholic Church had been losing its sovereign dominion over Irish life (Ganiel 2016). Inglis (1998:13), in a compelling analysis, describes how the Church's grip on Irish institutional, moral, political and economic order had 'helped maintain Ireland as a conservative, rural society and delayed its full modernisation until the second half of the twentieth century' (ibid.). As we saw in Chapter 3, governments had been gently pulling away from the symbiotic relationship with the Church since the 1960s, establishing government-sponsored state welfare and supporting the early stages of Irish industrialisation. The conservative image of the family, the bedrock of the Irish national narrative, became one that fewer people wished to perpetuate (Hardiman and Whelan 1998:69; Inglis 1998:238–239). The valorised and protected image of the Irish family was fraying and modernising as people were less likely to adhere to Catholic social dogma. The separation of Church and State was catalysed in the 1990s when the Church suffered irreparable damage to its own moral reputation. There was a series of sex scandals, public revelations regarding clerical sex abuse and stories about savage mistreatment in Ireland's Catholic carceral network, all of which confronted the nation with the harsh reality of the Church's heavy-handed control over citizens' moral conduct (Inglis 1998). The Catholic consensus that had coordinated Irish political and community life seemed to collapse. Divorce passed into legislation via a referendum in 1995 (only nine years earlier, in 1986, two-thirds of citizens had voted against divorce (see Dillon 1998)). Contraception was fully legalised in 1992 (Beatty 2013), and homosexuality was decriminalised in 1993. This was an evolution not in belief and religiosity but in social authority (Peillon 1998a:119),[i] wherein the Church lost its purchase as an important governing power bloc, as its dominance dwindled in directing Irish politics, education, welfare, health and family life (Inglis 1998). The abandonment of religious social control was abundantly evident in the demise of Ireland's carceral archipelago. By the 1990s the network of asylums, Magdalene Laundries, Mother and Baby Homes and industrial schools had declined in size and significance; the last Laundry closed in 1996, and the last Mother and Baby Home shut not long thereafter. The Church no longer monopolised the power to punish, their pre-eminent authority over social control and penal mechanisms had ceased, and the government continued to take its place as the central authoritative institution directing Irish social order (Inglis 1998).ⁱⁱ The 1990s was therefore a period when people were enabled to live a life that was less homogenously Catholic (Ganiel 2016). In 1996 the Minister for Finance declared that Ireland was now a 'post-Catholic, pluralist republic' (quoted in Inglis 1998:223). Not only was the content of the Minister's statement bold, but the very act of making a public declaration that opposed the authority of the Church was a stark example of a new secular political field (ibid.)

There was a sense of cultural and social renaissance. Ireland seemed to be emerging from a long and stagnant history as an aspiring agrarian Catholic island (Keogh 1994:29), quickly becoming a modern, urban, educated and diverse society. Rural Ireland dwindled, manufacturing and service industries proliferated and more people had access to education (Hardiman and Whelan 1998:68–69). This image of a prosperous society must be tempered, however, as the social changes of this period were also profoundly negative. Coulter et al. (2003) have berated what they saw as the undiluted optimism in analyses of Irish modernisation. While the 1990s was a time of greater affluence, the spoils of economic success were unevenly distributed across society. Ireland's advancing fortunes created a more professional class, who were better educated, better paid and had more disposable income. The buoyancy of Irish social change did not lift all boats equally, though, and those who lacked the skills and educational qualifications to access the new job market were excluded from the consumer lifestyle offered by the Celtic Tiger (Hardiman and Whelan 1998:69; O'Connell 1999:220). Both long and short-term unemployment figures were plummeting; however, those who remained trapped in unemployment were increasingly marginalised and socially excluded. While a newly empowered and financially endowed middle class may have been imbued with a greater sense of confidence, by the end of the 1990s Ireland's once largely homogenous and horizontal social structure had begun to polarise (Hardiman and Whelan 1998; Inglis 1998; O'Connell 1999).

In the 1990s, Ireland emerged as a 'late moderniser' (Tovey and Share 2003:42). The shifting dynamics of morality and social control meant that Ireland's social landscape was in the process of accelerated urbanisation, industrialisation and secularisation. The principle of subsidiarity, which had justified the Church's control over Irish social welfare services and moral authority, had diminished. But Irish society also became more divided as a greater social distance between class groups developed. It was within this social context that Ireland's imprisonment regime, and the political culture that informed it, underwent a correspondingly dramatic transformation.

Political and cultural conflict

By the early 1990s, management of the prison system remained chaotic. The reliance on temporary release – shedding and the revolving door – had brought the system into disrepute and it became the issue around which the function of the Division and imprisonment was debated. Mostly the Division had endured and rebuffed these incursions, remaining implicitly committed to their pastoral penal culture. But in the early 1990s dissent grew within the Prison Division, broadly reflecting the changing socio-economic and cultural norms in Irish life. When it came to prison policy there was 'an internal battle there about where to go with it' (Gerard). In quite discreet and restrained terms, Niall described what sounded like a burgeoning insubordination:

> [T]here were certain, certain attitudes within, in the situation within… there was a clique, a small senior clique of more senior people. Who, who I think were, they were a clique and had a slightly superior approach to other things and there was a bit of resistance there to some things [we were] trying to do.

Jim was more explicit, lamenting the growth of a new law-and-order attitude in the office – one that seemed to reveal a heightened emotional pleasure being taken in the idea of punishment: '[S]ome [senior civil servants] were very gung-ho, they loved this kinda stuff…[Other senior civil servants] would have had deep reservations about it all. There would be deep divisions.'Like Jim, John also felt this opposing view was rooted in the base penal sensibilities, suggesting that some people's views 'veered towards the primitive'. At that time, he recalled, 'people really had to work hard that the punitive reaction didn't take precedence over: we need to run a humane system here'. There was a much starker ideological and cultural division emerging in the office, and evidently the emotions and feelings being invoked by the prospect of imprisonment were also sharply diverging.

   Those opposing the prevailing penal parsimony within the Division questioned the processes, aims and motivations of their work; in particular, they were less compelled by the suspicion of prison as fundamentally harmful. People began to wonder why energy was being expended releasing prisoners rather than containing them? Gerard, who was part of this critical contingent, was vociferous on this issue:

> [Y]ou lived with the risk all the time you were letting an axe killer out… But it made a travesty of the system and a mockery of justice because people weren't serving anywhere remotely like the amount of time they can serve…It was a mess. It was a shambles.

Almost reliving the passions of the moment, he went on: 'the system is too small to cope, we must build more prisons, me must!'

   Gerard, like others, saw release as dangerous. The use of release and reducing imprisonment were now seen by some within the Division to be exhausted policies. As Eamon similarly recalled of the time, people began to advocate that 'the balance has to be on the side of the public, the side of public safety'. The previously sympathetic sensibilities towards the prisoner appeared to some as offensively misplaced. Why would the background of a prisoner justify Ireland's rolling amnesty? Prisoners were criminals, as Gerard, amongst others, saw it. In an account replete with agitation, he described how the efficacy of the community needed to be protected from offenders:

> [There were] people in communities who were being bullied and oppressed by criminals. Sometimes the narrative in the media about criminals is that they're the true victims, but I don't buy that. Absolutely, many of them have tragic histories but if you live in a high crime area, you're at the mercy of people, however sad their lives might have been; they are the oppressor. They're oppressing other people, and that gets forgotten. There's a lazy left-wing rhetoric that puts forward offenders as the real victims. But if you're living in a community where houses are being broken into all the time, old people mugged and there's, you know, all kinds of depravity around drug misuse in the neighbourhood that's a living torment to live in a community like that. And these people were truly their oppressors and we were releasing people like that onto the streets all the time and I found it appalling... even street-level drug dealers are a scourge, you know, they're a serious menace to society.

This graphic and viscerally disdainful account alludes to new understandings of justice, inclusion and exclusion, making it clear that the prisoner was being viewed by some not as a member of society, but as dangerously detached, a persecutor. The prisoner was no longer a trustworthy member of society, an inherent member of a community; trust and tolerance were being replaced by a certitude of dangerousness. To have such a person in the community rather than the prison was morally wrong and harmful to neighbourhoods – neighbourhoods the government should be protecting from the addict and the career criminal. Here we see a new exclusionary strain of conservatism, one which was still focused on community integrity, but the prison was now being invoked as a way to protect those conservative Irish touchstones – an inversion of the earlier view that the prison interfered with community and family. This was a far less inclusive, communitarian kind of penal conservatism. Government, it was felt, now needed to defend Ireland against the 'depravity' of modern Ireland.

The project of government and the purpose of imprisonment now aroused new feelings, generated debate and caused battlelines to be drawn. There was disagreement about who the prisoner was, how the prison should be organised and what sort of responsibility the government had in addressing crime – those fundamental features of political culture. John described this as a series of heated family fights: 'People on a personal basis didn't agree. And people were of the lock-them-up and throw-away-the-key [mentality]. It's like families, there was some serious disagreements about philosophies.' Others spoke about these new conflicts as 'clashes' in which people exhibited 'very different attitudes to prisons and to prisoners, and I think they had very different philosophies' (Jim).

Though a seemingly acrimonious atmosphere was becoming apparent, the penal sensibilities that buffered and motivated the system were diversifying and evolving rather than being dismantled outright, as shown in the previous chapter. As late as 1993, the annual prison reports continued to present a more humane image of the prisoner. They continued to be structured as an affective narrative, which remained largely distant from matters of crime control. These narrative sections could go on for pages, depending on who had visited the prison (charities, writers, community organisations, musicians, visiting speakers) and what sorts of activities the prisoners had been engaged in (community projects, work and training, newsletters, annual sports day). They spoke of how prisoners felt; success remained amorphous, more abstractly linked to prisoners' personal achievements and development and the life of prison community rather than strategic ends of rehabilitation, discipline or deterrence. The animus developing inside the Division remained contained as the prison continued to be publicly presented as a place where people lived, rather than were mainly disciplined.

Reaffirming pastoral penality

During the 1980s the Division had been lurching from one crisis to another and now risked being overtaken by internal demands for a hardline penal outlook. It was during this time that *The Management of Offenders – A Five Year Plan* (1994) was published. This was a seminal development, the first public prison policy document of its kind; it was a public presentation of a clear strategy for Irish prisons. *The Management of Offenders* was not ground-breaking in terms of ideas, however; rather, it was reaffirming. It reflected the political culture that had been dominant but was now strained and under threat.

The document was an occasion to publicly establish these penal sensibilities as formal policy. As Niall described it: 'A lot of what I felt about prisons at that time was in that [document]'. Jim explicitly linked *The Management of Offenders* with the particular set of pre-existing penal sensibilities, and saw it as an attempt to reignite and consolidate support for that ethos:

> people in prison [are] as much sinned against as sinning…[given] the deprivation most of them are coming from. There should be minimum use of custody and minimum use of security and normalisation of prison life…But you see some civil servants had that attitude and you can see it in the earlier document [*Statement of Objectives* (1981a)], and in *The Management of Offenders* in 1994.

After the years of protracted panic, industrial disturbances and overcrowding, the document was an attempt to reclaim as well as publicly assert the logic and conventions of Irish prison practice. The vision of the system's future success was contingent upon regaining the views and prison practices from the 1970s:

In recent times the temporary release system under the Criminal Justice Act, 1960 has been devalued by the perception that it is used *only* as a means to reduce offender numbers. It is not widely known that some (though not as many as would be desirable) of these releases are supervised and that in the 1970's [sic] a temporary release system with supervision provided a flexible system of parole which offered scope for the management of offenders in the community with little risk to the public and with very much enhanced prospects of leading offenders towards a more constructive lifestyle in the community.

(Department of Justice 1994:39; original emphasis)

In keeping with pastoral penality, the vision of prison propounded here was one in which release remained central. They desired a return to this imprisonment regime, in which 'those in prison remain valued members of society entitled on release to take a constructive place in society' (ibid.:22). Such was the reluctance to increase the use of prisons that *The Management of Offenders* advocated installing a formal cap on prison places, with a remit to build no more than 210 extra prisoner places. This suggestion was presented as credible because of the familiar idea that prison was inappropriate as a tool of social control, with rehabilitative capacities that were ambiguous at best:

There have, on the other hand, always been questions about the long-term value of imprisonment as a means of social control, about the success or otherwise of prisons in diverting offenders from a life of crime and about the possibility of developing more community-based sanctions.

(ibid.:29)

As crime was increasing during this period, the cap on prisoner places may seem radical, but viewed longitudinally this aligned with the pre-existing parsimonious penal cultural that had characterised Irish penal politics. In *The Management of Offenders* the prisoner was still a fellow citizen, but one who likely exhibited a particularly unfortunate history, a set of individual circumstances and, importantly, a potential future: 'The case of each offender usually presents a unique set of circumstances – up-bringing, family relationships, nature and circumstances of offence, willingness and capacity to make good' (ibid.:40). Hence, the 1970s still represented a practically and ideologically impressive era, when prison practices were perceived to operate more coherently, shaped by explicitly humane and communitarian objectives. They acknowledged that in the 1990s there were new challenges, such as a new disdain for the prisoner-as-criminal, and they accepted that the public and the victim were now participants and active spectators in policy decisions (ibid.:30). This policy document was trying to overcome that by attempting to create historical continuity in imprisonment regimes.

At a time when the administration of prisons was chaotic and in need of a guiding policy, *The Management of Offenders* established a set of formal strategies to provide a route out of their stresses. As Niall described the motivation behind the document, 'it was the first attempt at an overall strategy statement for prisons… to produce something that would oblige us to do something. It's in writing, now get that made policy, like a programme for government.' So why was this first strategy statement for prisons in Ireland 'shelved' (O'Donnell and O'Sullivan 2001:31)?

Researched 'from the inside' – from the experiences of those who were there at the time, and set against the historical backdrop – we see that the ideas formalised in *The Management of Offenders* now stoked contentious ideological divisions. Strengthening temporary release mechanisms and maintaining as low as possible prison population numbers no longer grasped the imaginations of the majority of key policymakers. As a strategy it failed to convince and persuade those who were demanding greater incapacitative penal power. One critic – and former Division psychologist – writing at the time excoriated the policies in *The Management of Offenders* precisely because of its restated commitment to the dominant logic of the 1970s. This was continuation, not innovation; to his mind it was no more than 'an unquestioning adherence to the status quo' (O'Mahony 1996:94).

As a set of ideas, *The Management of Offenders* now only represented one side in the internal conflict in Irish penal politics. It entrenched some positions, and others set themselves in opposition to the views espoused in that policy document. Tom despaired when recalling how some colleagues rallied against it: 'the number of fucking critics of that document, but the frustrating thing was not one of them wrote a line'. It was argued that pastoral penality as a way of thinking and organising imprisonment was no longer practical or realistic:

> [Pragmatism] means realism, being realistic. You have to respond to the world as you find it not the world as you wish it to be. A person who's in front of you might have had a tragic family up bringing but they've also offended grievously against society and probably represent a danger at the moment to society…It's like, you know, reality is at fault, [they] just couldn't live with the reality that you can't just turn a dial and tell the courts to stop sending people…it was a repetition of the same mistake and mantra…The mantra being cut the numbers and everything will sort ourselves out, we lock up too many people. Already in a country that was locking up less than practically anybody else…We actually weren't locking up enough people appropriately.
>
> (Gerard)

According to this divergent evaluation, Irish imprisonment regimes were too lax, the use of the government's power too concerned with *releasing people* rather than *containing criminals*. Individuals who were more steeped in humane and empathetic feelings and advocated a restrained approach came to feel like they were 'marginalised' (Jim) by the mid-1990s.

While *The Management of Offenders* was avowedly committed to reinforcing the existing penal logic, the forces from which this political outlook had drawn its strength and its common-sense appeal had waned. The communitarian class relations, the dominance of the family as a unit of social control, a marginalised but sympathetic prisoner, and the rationale of a state reluctant to directly intervene in the moral affairs of its citizens, had, by 1994, progressively diminished. Ireland was rapidly modernising, becoming socially polarised as those bonds of collective efficacy loosened (Peillon 1998a:117). However, many people in the Division remained committed to pastoral penality, and potentially it could have gone on to find its resurgence, but events conspired to fully marginalise it as a form of penal politics.

Signal crime

The reading of the prison problem in the Department had clearly become more fractious, and the debates concerning government intervention and the limits of imprisonment continued to undermine their ability to find a unified way forward. Externally, crime was still rising and public anxieties about drugs, violence and organised crime persisted. Then a crime occurred that was felt to be so significant that something akin to a state of emergency was declared (Kilcommins et al. 2004), in which crime, disorder, but also government weakness were seen as fatal causal factors.

Veronica Guerin, who was a renowned investigative journalist writing about organised crime in Dublin, was fatally shot while sitting in traffic in June 1996. This was an assassination organised by one of Ireland's notorious gangland leaders, about whom Guerin had been reporting. That such a flagrant and public act could be carried out was seen not as an anomalous tragedy but came to represent the terrible culmination of a changing Ireland. Guerin's murder happened shortly after the death of Jerry McCabe, a Garda who was killed during an armed robbery, leaving a residing sense that such acts could no longer be excused as one-off anomalies. At Guerin's funeral, the Archbishop of Dublin was reported to have told mourners that it was now 'time to reflect on the drift in the direction of our society and to ask how it may be halted' (quoted in O'Donnell 2005:106). In the Dáil, Guerin's murder was similarly understood as a crescendo of escalating criminality: 'This event is an indictment of how crime has been allowed to grow rampant in our society for many years' (Dáil Debate, 26 June 1996). Shortly thereafter, the government was recalled from summer recess to debate the urgent crime problem, the 'assassination' of Guerin and newly proposed crime control measures – including discussion of the use and capacity of the prison system. Eamon recalled the public impact:

> There had been a lot of talk of taking tough action and tough measures for years, but when Veronica Guerin was shot and people knew [who] had done it because of her writing, people said this has to be tackled in a different way...for the public, who were normally concerned with jobs, houses, education – the bread and butter – crime jumped up to the top of the list.

There was a sense that Guerin's death had an instant effect on justice, seeming to release the sorts of resources that had been frustratingly out of reach of the Prison Division:

> Veronica Guerin, the day she was murdered we got a phone call from an official in the Department of Finance. [They] rang up and said 'how many jails do you want?' Her murder led to a total change about resourcing from the Department.
>
> (Gerard)

This view is born out in financial records. In 1993 the expenditure on prisons was £96m, rising to £108m in 1995, but increasing exponentially to £189m by 1999 (O'Donnell and O'Sullivan 2003).

However, we must be careful not to think of this as being strategic action on the part of a penal populist government, shrewdly capitalising on Guerin's death. This was also a rupture in public sentiment, a pronounced sense of threat and emergency in regard to citizens' safety (Sparks 2006:40) and a feeling of panic, in which the moral cultural consensus was perceived to be unravelling (Hall et al. [1978] 2013). Guerin's murder was a 'signal crime', seen as a manifestation of Ireland's now permanent categories of 'risky people, places and events' (Innes 2004:336). Guerin's death provided a focal point for the absolutist and expressive feelings that had been mounting since the 1980s, tapping into a wider anxiety about new social problems such as drugs, urbanisation, and organised crime at a time when the nation was adjusting to a less authoritarian social order (Holland 1997; Peillon 1998b). Looking back, Eamon recalled that there was a sense that Ireland was 'moving into a barbaric state, and not just in Dublin'.

Politicisation of punishment

In the lead-up to the 1997 general election crime and punishment became charged political issues. The opposition party, Fianna Fáil, eagerly mobilised these fears as a means to gain political capital. They released an election manifesto (Fianna Fáil 1997a) and a policy paper, *Leading the Fight Against Crime* (Fianna Fáil 1997b), outlining their tougher stance on the 'cancer of crime'. Crime had not been an issue which had previously required assertive government intervention, but now, they wrote, 'Organised crime, once something we only knew through fiction and film, has suddenly emerged as a vicious reality in Irish society' (Fianna Fáil 1997a:9–10). It was time, according to Eamon, 'to fight fire with fire'.

Just like in other Anglophone countries in the mid-1990s (Jones and Newburn 2007), Ireland's political discourse became inflected with 'zero tolerance' rhetoric. Zero tolerance as a political strategy drew its power from Ireland's changing social conditions, grounded in the emergent worries and historical values. For example, the opposition's election campaign was couched in terms which reviled the changing Ireland, the erosion of national communitarian values and the rise of disorder:

> the task of the next government will be to use the human and physical resources in this country to confront the malaise of crime and to foster, in the Ireland of the twenty-first century, an environment in which the traditional values of community, compassion and caring can flourish. That task will not be easy...The social fabric of this country is being destroyed. The next government must wage war on the cause of that destruction. It must wage war on crime.
>
> (O'Donoghue, quoted in O'Donnell and O'Sullivan 2001:32)

Zero tolerance connected law and order and the prison with conservative values; it was about safeguarding the sanctity of the community – the 'fabric' of Irish life – from the influx of drugs and crime. In practice, zero tolerance may have 'had only a fleeting impact on procedures and practices' (Kilcommins et al. 2004:289). Zero tolerance, however, should be seen as an expressive political act which bespeaks a view of crime as 'an urgent political priority' (Garland and Sparks 2000:200). In Eamon's terms, zero tolerance was intended to highlight to the public that 'our criminal justice system was too weak'. It was symbolic of the changing relationship between government and crime control, and thus punishment, in Ireland in the mid-1990s. There was now a systemic targeting of crime that had not previously been apparent in Irish political history.

The politicisation of crime and punishment, along with the rupture of public sentiment, enabled unprecedented change in Irish penality. It was not that those proponents who had mobilised inside the Department and had been campaigning for more retributive penal responses in the late 1980s and early 1990s simply convinced others of their outlook. Rather, with the conjuncture of events, they found their punitive cultural schemas suddenly 'fit' with Ireland's changing governmental and socio-cultural environment (Wilde 2004:579). No one group or individual controlled the changes that occurred. This was a circumstance brought about as much by the happenstance of events, shifting social structures and changing penal sensibilities as by conscious effort.

Expansion of the sovereign state

Subsequent to these events the government began to rethink the uses of imprisonment, entering a self-confessed 'process of change' (Department of Justice 1997b:161). This was not driven by pragmatic and rational concerns regarding prison space (Rogan 2011). These reflections also reveal that more was felt to be at stake in the future planning of Irish imprisonment regimes than organised crime. They sought to fundamentally reorganise governing priorities and give a renewed 'clarification of their responsibilities' (O'Mahony 2000a:7). This was as much a political transformation as a penal one.

Under these conditions, any lingering commitment to pastoralism was finally marginalised, replaced by a new sovereign and punitive political culture. Crime had been rising since the 1970s, but in the 1990s the antipathy to the anti-social criminal and dangerous recidivist prisoner became dominant among policymakers' penal sensibilities, giving punitive purpose to their political culture. This political culture was also based on a new understanding of crime and criminality as governable objects. Hence, it was not merely the perception of crime that shaped and remade imprisonment regimes. How people are imprisoned equally reflects a changing view of government responsibilities and its place in Ireland's evolving social order – one that had once been shared with the Church.

The underserving prisoner

In 1997 a new criminal justice policy document was published. *Tackling Crime* (1997a) was the antithesis of *The Management of Offenders'* penal parsimony, the existence of which seemed to be erased by *Tackling Crime* being erroneously presented the 'first ever document of its kind' (p.5).

The document advocated new 'guiding considerations' that suggested the Irish penal system needed to revise the practical dynamics of inclusion, exclusion and justice:

> it is beyond dispute that society has the right to protect itself from the activities of criminals. The exercise of that right is a prerequisite for the maintenance of social order...the focus is on the position of the law-abiding majority whose rights are, without any justification, put in jeopardy day-in-day-out by a relatively small minority, some of whom will literally stop at nothing to achieve their criminal purposes.
>
> (1997a:13–14)

The idea of rights set out here shows a dichotomy between deserving and undeserving citizens – a forceful example of the emerging social divisions in Ireland in which offenders were no longer considered to share the same rights as fellow citizens. The greater disparity between villainous offenders and law-abiding public also recasts the conservative sensibilities and assumptions about the primacy of a prisoner's place among family and community – ideas that had previously motivated as well as tempered the use of prison. *Tackling Crime* was based on a frightening depiction of criminality: 'criminal elements are becoming more powerful, more callous, more vicious' (1997b:158). As Jim so solemnly recalled, this was a period in which something more fundamental than the machinery of imprisonment evolved. Rather, the pivotal conceptions of the prisoner shifted also, describing how in the 1990s there was 'a punitive turn in the way prisoners were seen'. The Division began to officially embrace an open hostility towards offenders.

There was a chastisement of pastoral penality, such orthodoxies were directly addressed and reassessed – making clear that there had been a reordering of penal priorities and the communitarian rationale within the Department:

> While it is necessary to take account of the fact (well supported by research) that circumstances of their upbringing can have a significant bearing on the way on which people behave in later life and that offenders may advance arguments of this kind to explain their wrongdoing, this does not mean – even if the substance of the argument advanced is accepted – that the wrongdoer must automatically go free. The public is not obliged to carry the risk of attack simply because the would-be attacker's tendency to misbehave has been exacerbated by negative personal experience or other personal failings.
>
> (ibid.:13)

This was an explicit reversal of the earlier ethos. An individual prisoner's background and circumstances could no longer justify prison's permeability. The social solidarity that underpinned temporary release was losing its authority and common-sense appeal.

While *The Management of Offenders* had reaffirmed the pre-existing penal restraint, *Tackling Crime* advocated a new assertive culture of penal practice: it was a declaration of intent. One must avoid mistaking talk for action. But this talk, the very fact of the document, its new assertions and sketched-out programmes were, to paraphrase Simon (2007:159), a reordering of prisons around the problem of crime and order. However, these changing sensibilities were not merely the outworking of crime anxieties or the disdain for the criminal; this was also about establishing a new, more authoritative state approach to governing crime.

A new governmental authority

It has been argued that the Irish transition from a penal system dominated by a carceral archipelago to one where the majority of confinement took place in prisons was the result of Ireland moving away from a rural economy (O'Donnell and O'Sullivan 2012). Under these conditions, the government took 'virtually exclusive control over the management and funding' of Ireland's system of confinement (ibid.:257). I suggest that this is only a partial explanation. The rational and instrumental economic argument does not fully illuminate the social and political changes that underpinned not only an increased use of imprisonment in Ireland at the end of the twentieth century, but also the changing forms and functions of incarceration (as we will see below). Second, it does not explain the transformation in Ireland's penal politics, which expanded, became more bureaucratised, gained new power and became more exclusionary in its penal ethos. These changes were founded upon the Church losing its dominance as a social authority. The Catholic Hierarchy no longer controlled Ireland's means of discipline and social welfare, a decline that changed the nature of the Irish government and political culture.

There was an aura of *mea culpa*: the government was now seen to be failing to live up to its responsibilities as a guardian of public order:

> We recognise that, as an organisation, we have various shortcomings – not least in explaining our work publicly. For one thing, we know that we are considered by some to be over-secretive and there is a view also that we are opponents of progress and change.
>
> (Department of Justice 1997b:160)

The government could no longer tolerate or lament changing crime patterns as an unavoidable matter, as had been vaguely apparent in *The Management of Offenders*, in which they had suggested that crime was best resolved in the community rather than punished in the prison. There was a new sense that the government must now act with assertive authority: 'there is an expectation that the institutions whose business it is to respond to that phenomena will perform effectively and coherently' (Department of Justice 1997b:158). The penal system could no longer be handled discreetly, political leadership must be shown, but this required a new kind of political authority to be established. The 1990s was a time of fervent activity around planning, strategising and reviewing in a way that was more publicly visible and authoritatively engaged. A week had passed since Guerin's murder and the government began to deploy what has become known as the '1996/97 anti-crime package' (Kilcommins et al. 2004:164), ushering in a raft of new legislation that would increase chances of convicting organised crime gangs. There was a slew of publications, such as reviews of homicide patterns (Dooley 1995, 2001), probation and welfare (Department of Justice 1999), a profile of prisoners (O'Mahony 1997), a review of the governing apparatus (Department of Justice 1997c), a strategy statement (Department of Justice 1998) and a report on communicative disease in prison (Department of Justice 1993). The government also commissioned a report that argued for the value of systematically measuring the impact of prison policy (Heylin 2001). This publication was necessitated by the 'developments in the Irish civil service' more generally. The document also sought to persuade those Justice officials who remained 'unconvinced of the merits of [policy] evaluation', as such, the new emphasis on bureaucratic techniques of prison management (ibid.:1).

They also explicitly *displayed* the new political style. The lengthy narrative of the previous thick annual reports (the last of which was in 1994) was replaced by a slick, thin and corporate-style A4 brief. The difference in prison experiences, programmes, initiatives and the general highs and lows in each prison was subsumed into a compressed and homogenous presentation, projecting Ireland's new political and penal culture. In this way the government intended to appear 'more transparent and penal decisions more easily subjected to the various demands for accountability' (Franko Aas 2004:384). As the first Director General of the Irish Prison Service (hereafter IPS) wrote at the time, a central goal of the new report style was 'to standardise the service we deliver...Justice and efficiency alike are impossible without consistency' (Alyward 2002:581).

These policy products were thus a signal that a different rationality of government had emerged – one concerned with establishing governmental sovereignty over crime, punishment and social order. There was a sense that social cohesion had ruptured: 'The last twenty years or so have seen drastic changes in the social fabric of Irish society' (Dooley 1995:5). These anxious expressions illustrate a Department now actively trying to catch up with their changing role in a modernising Ireland. The publication of a *Strategic Management Initiative* directly addressed its agenda towards what it saw as the 'changing world – an external challenge', in which it prescribed the problems thus:

> The pace of change, worldwide, in all fields – social, economic, cultural, communications – has accelerated enormously over the past ten to twenty years. Some of this change has been positive, enlightened and clearly for the benefit of mankind. There is also, however, the negative side – social exclusion, inequality, selfishness, alienation – side by side with a growing incidence and viciousness in crime...The task of the Department of Justice is to try to meet this challenge.
>
> (Department of Justice 1997b:166–167)

The Department's political culture, their habits of thought, their patterns of action, were adapted to Ireland's changing social circumstances and not just the Guerin murder and rising crime. This was reflected an overall shift in the understanding of government work, which was supported by the Public Service Management Act, 1997. This aimed to legislate for a new civil service mandate, 'to enhance the management, effectiveness and transparency of operations of Departments of state'.[iii] As such, it aimed to mature and expand the Irish governmental apparatus. When it came to the Department of Justice, the plethora of new public documents was intended to exhibit a new democratic, credible and assured political identity.

The government's expanding sense of authority, legitimacy, responsibility and accountability was grounded in Ireland's late-twentieth century secularisation. In England in the 1990s the government's penal responses were reshaped when confronted by the limits of their state power (Garland 1996). The Irish government, by contrast – and still a relatively new and now rapidly advancing nation – had a new sovereign mandate: it, rather than the Church, community or families, must be at the centre of Irish law and order, it must monopolise the power to punish. By the 1990s, neither the informality of the community nor the authority of the Church provided the kind of social control that had characterised Ireland in the first half of the twentieth century. The government was now understood as the entity responsible for providing discipline and control in the face of social disorder. The government was taking over the space vacated by the Church in Ireland's landscape of social control. This is evident in the organising rationale that framed the reports, emphasising that Ireland was rapidly changing and that social authority had come into crisis, creating new demands for government:

> Over the past decade, Irish society has experienced profound social, economic and cultural change. Much of this change has been positive. The rate of unemployment has decreased, enhanced employment opportunities exist for those with adequate credentials, and Irish society has become increasingly confident of its own capacity to determine its future. For some, this rate of change has been bewildering. *Established sources of authority in Irish society have been challenged,* and in many communities, traditional values have been eroded *which in turn places an extra burden on the State.*
>
> (Department of Justice 1999:5, emphasis added)

These forces of social change provided the raw materials for a very different political culture by the end of the 1990s in Ireland. The shifting hegemony in Ireland legitimated 'the recourse to the law, to constant and statutory power...it legitimated the duty of the state' (Hall et al. [1978] 2013:273). But it was not just that social change flowed through state agencies and actors – such forces are too broad and epiphenomenal to shape precise technologies of imprisonment regimes and specific actions of government. The Department were explicit about their new authoritative position, asserting that: 'The Department is at the hub of the law and order system...That is why it is now essential to decide what the core business of the Department actually is and to identify strategies best geared to secure effective discharge of that business' (1997b:164–165). As such, how these authorities perceived, interpreted and rationalised these broader problems, how they felt about crime, conceived of the prisoner, the objectives of government, and how officials' sense of the aims of imprisonment altered, all set the scene for a truly dramatic change in Irish prison strategy by the end of the 1990s.

The reinvention of the political apparatus

To further establish this new sovereign political culture, a new institutional apparatus was implemented, one that had been unthinkable only a few years earlier. After railing against it, a decision was taken in November 1996 – prior to the 1997 general election and shortly after Guerin's murder – to establish an independent prisons agency (Department of Justice 1997c; Alyward 2002). This administrative development conveys a remarkable change in vision and direction in how Irish penal power was organised – a moment that has not been singled out for analysis by other researchers. It was suggested that changes necessitated in the prison system would be better facilitated by the creation of an independent prison agency. In 1999, the IPS was established as a separate agency, physically outside of the Department though its independence was never formalised on a statutory basis. Thus, 'instead of being totally immersed in the day-to-day delivery of various services' (Department of Justice 1997a:17), the Department would become a 'policy driven organisation' (Department of Justice 1997b:179). Along these same lines, the Department of Justice became the Department of Justice, Equality and Law Reform in 1997, a declaration of their broader and loftier remit. The new organisational hierarchy and officious policy products formally institutionalised a new sovereign political culture in Ireland.

The promise of prisons

In this emergent political outlook the prison, it was now argued, should instead be seen as 'one of the essential bulwarks of civil society' (Alyward 2002:579); the prison could restore order, allay anxieties and display the new political authority. Incarceration was now explicitly named, without its former qualifications, as a 'law enforcement agency' (Department of Justice 1997a:17) and one of the 'primary instruments employed by society to secure protection' (ibid.:14). A prison system that had generally been concerned with maintaining the flow of prisoners now jarred with the new sovereign and punitive consensus of the political culture. The government thus sought to realise their new penal culture and address immediate social problems in the practical design of Irish imprisonment regimes.

Prisons – preventative detention and deterrence

Previously the use of prison was tempered by a fear that it could cause greater damage to citizens who were imprisoned. The new assessment provided in *Tackling Crime* presented an alternative outlook, wherein Ireland's imprisonment regime should be a tool of crime control. Thus, 'A major impediment to the effectiveness in the law enforcement system is the absence of an adequate number of prison places' (ibid.:107). Prison's failings were assessed to be a lack of space, but also – and this is a critical distinction – a lack of containment capacity. As Eamon put it, what they desired was to have more 'people in prison and in prison for longer'. It was not just that Irish prisons did not imprison enough people, they also failed to literally confine those who were sent there. If Irish political challenges and social problems were to be resolved, it was felt that the remit and size of the prison must be expanded.

A referendum was held in November 1996 which gave judges greater capacity to deny bail (O'Donnell and O'Sullivan 2001:33). Previously, due to a legal decision made in the 1960s (the O'Callaghan decision), bail could only be denied if a judge believed there was a risk that a defendant would either not be present for the trial or would interfere with a witness (O'Donnell 2005:101). This was an important restatement of the aims of imprisonment, now expanded to include preventative detention.

Among the new penal prescriptions was a belief that prison had untapped deterrent functions. The 1999 Criminal Justice Act provided for mandatory minimum sentences (Campbell 2010), establishing a new punitive dimension to Irish imprisonment. At this time, Ireland had few mandatory sentences, instead privileging the independence of the judiciary (Bacik 2002; Hamilton 2014). The new Act stipulated that those convicted of possession of drugs worth €13,000 or more faced a minimum ten-year prison sentence (Bacik 2002:351).

These 'mandatory sentences for drug offences were an attempt to reassure communities blighted by heroin abuse and infectious disease, and largely neglected by the state, that they had not been forgotten and that firm action was being taken on their behalf' (O'Donnell 2005:102). Together with the newly restrictive bail laws, these prison policies had an expressive capacity, demonstrating the new and expanding strength of penal authorities to wider society: not only can we confine our prisoners, but we can employ prison to exclude and punish the most egregious for longer, and now without exception.

Similar to preventative imprisonment, the mandatory minimum sentences for drugs swept more people into the system, a practice which would previously have been felt as unjustifiable. Balancing these consequences, Cormac reflected:

> [Y]ou may have locked up [more people] on long sentences, people who wouldn't normally, like drug mules, but you did take out some serious drug dealers who wouldn't have been before cause it was too lenient, so it wasn't all bad, it had some benefits.

This was a reversal of the older orthodoxy; the emphasis was now upon containment.

Prison works: techniques of intervention

A further marked departure in the imprisonment regime dynamic was the new suggestion that prison practices could be used to reduce recidivism (Department of Justice, 1997b:169). In the 2001–2003 Strategy Statement the aims of imprisonment now included supporting prisoners to 'address offending behaviour'. Eamon said in the 1990s they were aiming to have a 'humane' prison system 'that cured the evils' of criminality. The 'core issues affecting prisoners' were now believed to include their 'personal decision-making capacity', according to prison authorities (Alyward 2002:591). Thinking Skills courses were introduced in several of the prisons. These offered 'an offending behaviour programme...The aim of the course is to equip participants with a range of problem solving skills and social skills', and they homed in on 'anger management, evasion of personal responsibility and relapse prevention' (ibid.:587). The CONNECT Project was established in Mountjoy and the Training Unit. Rather than help people develop a better approach to living, CONNECT aimed to reduce recidivism from crime via vocational training (Lawlor and McDonald 2001:23; Alyward 2002:590). The irony is that the rehabilitation logic came to bear upon Irish imprisonment not as a progressive measure; instead, it formalised inside the prison an understanding of the prisoner as 'other', different from law-abiding citizens. Perfectly demonstrating that the ethos of humanity and scepticism was now subordinate to the new concern for punishing and reducing reoffending, Cormac described the aim of prison programmes at the end of the 1990s in these terms: 'you're here to help prevent crime by helping people, it's not just to help people'.

Punitive modernisation

There was now an 'accelerated prison building programme' (Rogan 2011:186), and so commenced a second wave of 'modernisation' in Irish penality. Unlike the prison modernisation of the 1970s, in developing these proposals key actors felt they were developing 'modern prisons' organised around 'tough laws and tough sentences' (Eamon). Between 1996 and 1999 Ireland significantly expanded the prison estate, increasing the number of prisons for adults from nine to 14. In 1996 the Irish government recommissioned Curragh Prison for the purpose of holding difficult prisoners, and four other prisons were also newly constructed: the Midlands Prison, Castlerea, Cloverhill and the Dóchas Centre for women.

From the lessons learned in Chapter 3, which charted the development of pastoral penality, we should know that prison expansion is not necessarily a wholly punitive endeavour. More space might have allowed increased room and capacity for support services, improved sanitary conditions, increased out-of-cell time, a chance to amend the 1983 doubling-up rule, a diversification of programmes and so on. However, the crime control rationale, the growing animus towards prisoners and the pronounced desire to punish more were formalised in the punitive dimensions that came to dominate imprisonment regimes. The most striking feature of these newly devised imprisonment regimes was the emphasis on confinement. All the new prisons were closed prisons. Even the new 'open prison' at Castlerea was built within a closed perimeter wall, mimicking earlier ideas of permeability but within the uncompromising context of tight security. Cloverhill Prison, also a closed prison, was the first designated remand institution. Irish imprisonment regimes could now live up to their preventative aspirations. The Training Unit was still part of the regime, but it was subject to a transformation: it was no longer for any kind of ordinary prisoner, becoming instead a 'step down unit' (Irish Prison Service 2006:15) for those prisoners at the end of their sentence. Those in power were also intent on ending the prison regime's permeability and ensuring that the Department could no longer treat the sentences handed down by the courts as discretionary (Department of Justice 1997a, 1997b). By the end of the twentieth century temporary release had been severely restrained. In 1999, the Minister for Justice announced that certain categories of prisoners would no longer be eligible for temporary release, such as those convicted for perpetrating violent acts against women and the elderly, serious public order offences and car theft (McCullagh 2002:599). In 1995, 21% of prisoners served their sentence on temporary release; by 2001 that had dropped to

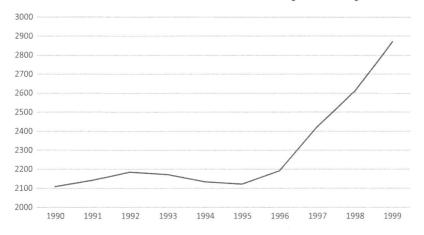

Figure 5.1 Daily average adult prison population 1990-1999.

Source: Annual reports on prisons, various years

only 6% (O'Mahony 2000b:550; O'Donnell 2004:261). Irish imprisonment regimes now placed a greater emphasis on the architectural capacities to confine prisoners away from society. Importantly, between 1994 and 1999 Ireland's growing prison population was not due to changing sentence patterns, these remained constant (O'Donnell 2005). Ireland increased its prison population by shifting the imprisonment regimes so that they held prisoners more permanently (see Figure 5.1).

The following quote from John encapsulates the nature of the change in the dominant governing sensibilities and ambitions in the mid-1990s in the Republic of Ireland. He described the control-orientated impulses which came to shape the very architecture of daily life for prisoners in this new era:

> The old school, one prisoner per cell and so on. That was an exciting time and there was a commitment in those times to developing education and develop work-training. But that came into conflict with the other school of thought, you know, our main business here is just to contain them...and Cloverhill was designed with I think the scope to accommodate two prisoners per cell.

This comparative reflection perfectly demonstrates that imprisonment regimes – how people were imprisoned – are always rooted in cultural tendencies, ideational leanings and governing rationalities. While the pastoral regime may have had limited funds, with them they developed the Training Unit, Shelton Abbey and Wheatfield (before it was redesignated) and increased the access to training, education, psychology and probation and welfare. Liam described how the new management styles and priorities of the late-1990s devalued these previous supportive techniques in favour of security: '[Senior

Management] wouldn't have seen therapeutic services as particularly relevant or positive, it was about secure containment.' Irish pastoral imprisonment regimes had been authoritatively and systematically dismissed and dismantled. Evidently, Ireland was not buffered from the 'punitive shift' during this period (Kilcommins et al. 2004:291). As the prison expanded exponentially, the promise of prison's potential to tackle crime had 'found its logic realized in physical structure' (Simon 2007:153). By 2000 Ireland's predominant form of incarceration was an explicitly punitive imprisonment regime.

The irony of the punitive turn

The changes in Irish political culture and imprisonment regimes at the end of the twentieth century were immense. This chapter has sought to provide a descriptive sociological analysis of the changes in Ireland's political culture, showing in close detail the evolution from pastoral penality to sovereign authority and highlighting how those ideas were expressed in the imprisonment regime.

Ireland's changing political culture was catalysed by the panic around the signal crime of Veronica Guerin's murder, but the seeds of social anxieties were sown in the preceding years. The punitive policies were intent on assuaging concerns about modernisation, such as rising crime, new social divisions and changing social authority. In addition, as the power of the Church and the perceived efficacy of the family dwindled, the Irish political system was burdened with a greater responsibility and unprecedented social pressures: to intervene, to protect communities from crime, to take control, to direct social relations. The changing political culture was therefore predicated on the government taking up the power to punish and to confine. Ireland's new penality was structured by the seismic shifts in Ireland's underlying social fault lines. However, these structural transformations did not reap material changes in imprisonment until they became embedded within Ireland's political culture, shaping practical choices and decisions.

The changes in Ireland's imprisonment regime were so clearly punitive; the prison lost something – its interpersonal nature, informality, predominant humanity and inherent scepticism had evaporated. More people were held in prison, not by accident but by design. The expansion of prison places was not a pragmatic calculus regarding size and space. It was a concerted effort at changing the imprisonment regimes so that their walls were less permeable, that people moved less freely from prison back into society, that their exclusion and punishment could be more certain and that the prison sanctions of the court could be better enforced. These changes reorganised the prison as a law enforcement tool, a crime control mechanism and an expression of intemperate social feelings. Given how drastic and stark these changes are in comparison to the pastoral penality that had preceded it, rather than being exceptional to the punitive turn (Kilcommins et al. 2004), Ireland may represent an exemplary case of a late-twentieth-century punitive transformation (Hamilton 2014) – though for reasons that were culturally, historically and politically distinct.

While political culture, and thus prisons, clearly became more punitive, what is an inescapable and fundamental part of this story is that during this period of the 1990s, Ireland had become a far less oppressive and censorious place, a less punitive nation in general (Inglis 1998). Irish citizens were gradually released from the extra-legal threat of being moved outwith society, forgotten and denied (O'Sullivan and O'Donnell 2007). As those other forms of confinement waned and new problems of social order arose, the prison – the government's own tool of punishment – was modified, adapted and expanded accordingly to reflect the government's own more centralised role in Irish social order. Changing access to opportunities of education, work and Celtic Tiger affluence created a pronounced social disparity, and a class-group whose social exclusion, subsequently, was deepened and reinforced by the workings of a newly extensive and punitive penal system.

Deciding, then, whether or not this was definitively a punitive or progressive social and penal change obscures the more subtle but critical point: the co-emergence of a liberalising nation and punitive imprisonment together tell the complicated story of social modernisation and political change; revealing how Ireland's transformation impacted unequally and differentially upon Ireland's communities and classes. By 1999 the Irish imprisonment regime promoted security, crime control and government authority at a time of rising crime and amplified anxieties about social dislocation The prison's increasing severity and expressive punitiveness were connected to changing meanings about justice and government, shifting sentiments about belonging and safety, as well as the progressive and social aspirations of modernisation and secularisation.

These cultural contradictions remade the prison. But the prison is not merely an 'echo' of social forces (Garland 1990a), modified after society itself has been reorganised. The prison is a beacon, a signal to society, particularly one undergoing a transformation, an example of what is and isn't permissible in terms of conduct, who is and isn't an insider, and who has social authority. New procedures for criminal accountability and new penal powers revise the relationship between government and subject, establishing a new social and moral order. Hence, Ireland's penal transformation also contributed in a small way to remaking modern Ireland by end of the twentieth century. Understood this way, we better illuminate the complexity of the prison as a political, cultural and social institution.

Notes

i One would not want to overstate this as a revolution in religiosity. Beatty writes that: '"Revolution" is one of the more abused terms in Irish historiography' (2013:116) because it overstates the 1990s social change as a total break from the past, particularly in relation to religious values. Irish people retained their faith and continued to hold onto Catholic values (Peillon 1998a). Modern Ireland remained a country committed to Catholicism (Hirschle 2010), although it should be noted that vocations did decline. Even in the 2011 census, 84.2% of people in Ireland identified as Catholic.

  ii For example, Inglis maintains that in the 1990s the social worker had taken over much of the power previously controlled by the priest in Ireland, like the right to knock on a home unannounced, gain entry and enquire about personal household matters (Inglis 1998:230–231).

  iii See: www.irishstatutebook.ie/eli/1997/act/27/enacted/en/html.

Section 2

Scottish imprisonment regimes and political culture, 1970–1995

6 The dismissive society

Discipline and exclusion in Scottish imprisonment

It has become commonplace to laud Scottish penality for avoiding the excessive and iniquitous penal developments that characterised England and Wales and the USA from 1970. In revisiting this period of Scottish penal history here, what is shown in this chapter will trouble this wider belief, and we will see that Scotland's imprisonment regime was monotonous, gruelling and often inhumane. Instead, Scottish imprisonment was reminiscent of a much more conventional rather than exceptional penal history. Explaining these carceral routines requires an exploration of the meanings of imprisonment held by those who managed the prison system. What did they perceive to be the causes of crime? How did they assess the aims of imprisonment? Who did they believe the prisoner be? How did they envision the ideal citizen? Where was the prison felt to fit in the wider social and moral architecture of Scotland? This chapter addresses these questions.

We begin, however, by sketching out the major cultural trends, social factors and political forces that were the central fault lines of 1970s Scottish society. The 1970s was an aspirational age, a justifiably glorified period, when Scottish welfare values were in the ascendency. It was also a time when poverty, concerns of unrefined masculinity, violence and moral turpitude provoked deep anxieties in the governing elites. Understanding the kind of place Scotland was during this time will enable us to fully illuminate the social meanings of imprisonment. By grasping the views of those managing the prison, and by then locating those sensibilities within their social world, we can establish why the prison in Scotland was understood and operated as a site of exclusion and confinement, why the prison was the place of last resort.

Scottish social landscape

When Scotland first became part of the UK in 1707 it retained its distinct legal and criminal justice system, which was organised and ruled by separate Scottish legislation and administration (Midwinter et al. 1991:11). In 1939 Scottish government departments relocated from London to Edinburgh, forming the Scottish Office – the equivalent to a Scottish Whitehall (Harvie 1977:51). Based at St Andrew's House, they were responsible for law, criminal justice, education, health, agriculture and fisheries. In the absence of a devolved government the Scottish Office became a powerful and largely independent administrative apparatus (McCrone 2001:117).

During the mid-twentieth century a progressive 'development philosophy' took hold in the Scottish Office, and civil servants were charged with urban and economic modernisation (Keating and Midwinter 1983; Gibson 1985:141–143). One of the most prominent events during this period occurred in 1965, when the seminal (and now historic) Kilbrandon Report was published. The Kilbrandon Committee had been tasked with investigating juvenile justice, and its report promoted the idea of providing whole families with 'social education' rather than criminal justice (McNeill 2005). Kilbrandon resulted in several transformative penal policies, the highpoint of which was the subsequent 1968 Social Work (Scotland) Act. In 1971 juvenile courts were replaced with a lay panel known as The Children's Hearings System. The Children's Hearings System had a wider remit, dealing with children who committed offences as well as those with an array of problematic, though not criminal, behaviour, such as school truancy. In this new reformist outlook, all cases were treated as welfare cases, focusing on children's needs, not their deeds, and identifying supportive interventions (Asquith and Docherty 1999:245). A second consequence of the 1968 Act was that social work was transformed into a generic rather than a specialised set of disciplines and, quite radically, probation was dissolved into newly general social work departments (Gibson 1985:148). The 1968 Act has been described as the single most significant piece of social legislation in Britain since the establishment of the National Health Service (Gibson 1985:149). In penological terms, both Garland (1996) and McAra (2005, 2008) have described the Kilbrandon Report as the quintessential penal welfare document.

Politically, what Kilbrandon achieved was seen as a 'breakthrough' for a new conception of Scottish law (Harvie 1977:197), a distinctly Scottish approach to social policy and criminal justice (Brodie et al. 2008). Kilbrandon was felt to be the first clear example of Scottish Office autonomy and policy distinction (McEwan 2002:72). Both the Report and the 1968 Act reflected a widely held belief about 'the necessity for, and efficacy of, governmental activity' (Brodie et al. 2008:701, referencing Stewart 2004) and a belief in the paternal state to create and support a more prosperous Scotland.

Simultaneously, urban planning was undergoing similar levels of intervention, though this had a longer history. Scotland had a predominately urban population, the majority of whom lived within the Edinburgh/Glasgow 'central belt' (Keating and Midwinter 1983), though there was a sharp class and culture divide between Scotland's two cities. By 1900 40% of Scotland's population lived in cities, with more than half that number living in Glasgow (Harvie 1977), where working-class people resided in some of the most acutely deprived and overcrowded housing in Britain (Johnstone 1992:76). So often, Glasgow was understood to be 'a filthy, slum-ridden, poverty-stricken, gang-infested city' (Damer 1990:5). As a means to redress these conditions, Glasgow was subject to 'slum clearances' during the first half of the twentieth century (Damer 1989; Keating and Midwinter 1983), a pattern that continued after the Second World War when local government again used relocation to significantly reduce Glasgow's urban population (Hutchison 1996:58).

Urban redesign and relocation – while explicitly concerned with improvement in living standards – were also motivated by a desire for urban re-moralisation. Glasgow was a place with a reputation, 'a deeply storied and mythologized city' (Fraser 2015:xxi), described as 'Scotland's Chicago' (Davies 1998, 2007a, 2007b; Fraser 2015). The stories and legends are often tied to the image of the 'hard man', and a 'cult of toughness characterised' Glasgow's working men (Johnston and McIvor 2004:138). A willingness to 'exchange fun for fists' was understood as Glaswegian cultural convention (Kirkwood 1935). The 'archetypical construction of masculinity in industrial Glasgow' (Young 2007:71) was a macho culture of heavy drinking, smoking, gangs and violence (Damer 1989:170; Bartie 2010: 385).

This cultural imagery contributed to Scotland's reputation as a violent country (McAra 2008:485), which was borne out in statistical reality. Scotland had some of the highest homicide rates in Europe and comparatively high rates of male victimisation, use of weapons, and more people dying from beating than in England and Wales (ibid.:486). Violent crime and offending had been increasing throughout the 1960s (House of Commons Debate, 26 March 1968) and murder rates increased fourfold between 1950 and the 1960s, compared with England and Wales where there was only a twofold increase (Smith and Young 1999).

Fears regarding crime and social disorder had a localised, place-specific character, therefore. While violence was a pervasive national stereotype, there was generally a distinct regional understanding that Glasgow was the epicentre of Scottish crime and violence (McAra 2008:486). These fears in turn stigmatised these communities. Moving people and razing areas were used as a means to address the 'social evils' that were long associated with Glasgow's inner city (Begg 1996:2).[i] Urban clearances sought to remake Glasgow's 'problem people' by ridding the city of its 'problem places' (Damer 1989; Pacione 1995). New 'overspill estates' and modern high-rise flats were built. Lacking the necessary amenities, such as schools, shops, pubs, recreational facilities and transport links, however, a number of these new housing schemes had higher rates of deprivation, male unemployment and infant mortality than the places they had replaced (Damer 1989:51). By the 1980s these 'peripheral schemes were themselves to pose some of the most severe social, economic and environmental problems faced by urban policy' (Keating 1988:24). Many of the 'overspill housing estates' came to be seen as 'delinquent areas' (Armstrong and Wilson 1973; Begg 1996; Bartie 2010). These estates were also perceived to instil drunkenness, anti-social traits, fecklessness and immorality in their residents (Damer 1989:52). To speak of life in many of Glasgow's overspill estates in the 1970s was to describe places besieged by deprivation, unemployment, vandalism and serious crime, as 'an atmosphere of decay and poverty' made these housing schemes 'notorious' (Begg 1996:154, 158).

As well as being an urban nation, Scotland, and particularly Glasgow, was also home to the heavy industries of steel work, coal mining, shipbuilding and rail works, and hence the percentage of people employed in heavy industries in Scotland was considerably higher than the British average (Perchard 2013). These were thus a major source of Scottish employment. At the beginning of the twentieth century, 10% of the Scottish work force was employed in a coalmine (ibid.:82). Tens of thousands of people worked in railway engineering, and at the beginning of the 1950s Scotland had 12% of the world's shipbuilding industry (Harvie 1977:174), giving Scotland a significantly less diversified economy than England. So, when the post-war years witnessed a period of massive technological innovation, shifting demand away from Scotland's industrial specialisations, there was mass unemployment: by 1971, 34.5% of men were unemployed (Carstairs and Morris 1989). Social inequality was further magnified, with one in five Scottish people living in poverty by the end of that period, with an even larger number of people existing on the margins of poverty (Norris 1983:29). This was a serious Scottish national crisis (Perchard 2013:86; Harvie 1977:174).

In the 1960s mortality rates had been broadly similar across the UK, but in the 1970s Scottish mortality patterns began to negatively diverge from their English and Welsh equivalents. This is seen as the result of the 'aftershock of deindustrialisation' (Walsh et al. 2010). Throughout the 1980s, mortality rates related to suicide, alcohol, drugs and violence increased in Scotland, most acutely in Glasgow and the surrounding west of Scotland (McCartney et al. 2012). From the 1970s Scotland contained 'some of the poorest parts of the UK...[and] some of the lowest life expectancies in Western Europe' (Campbell et al. 2013).[ii]

Thus, by the 1970s Scotland was experiencing a golden age of the social welfare ethos and, simultaneously, the problems of high unemployment, low income, poor health, urban inequality, violence and rising crime. The consequences of these forces contributed to new anxieties and the emergence of stigmatised groups and areas. It is within this context that we reconstruct the historical dynamics of the Scottish imprisonment regime and political culture from 1970 to the beginning of the 1980s.

Imprisonment in Scotland

In 1970, the Prison Division operated in a separate office beyond the hub of St Andrew's House in Edinburgh city centre.[iii] Managing Scotland's prisons had become increasingly demanding by the 1970s. The prison population had grown substantially in the previous decade. In 1964, Scotland had 3,250 prisoners; by 1971, the daily average number of prisoners had risen to 5,338 (*Annual Report 1971*; see Figure 6.1). The Division reported that it was 'alarming' that 'Two out of every 1,000 of the whole male population of Scotland are now in custody', which was a 'higher proportion than in most other Western countries' (*Annual Report 1971*:1).

In light of this, expanding the prison estate so that it could meet the needs of the courts was paramount among the priorities of the Prison

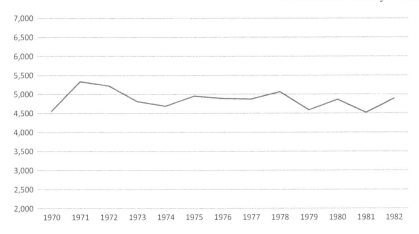

Figure 6.1 Daily average adult prison population 1970–1982.

Source: Annual reports on prisons, various years

Division. This was done by allowing multiple prisoners to occupy a cell and devising a prison construction programme aimed at keeping pace with the forecasted growth of the prisoner population. An extra 3,000 prisoner places were to be provided by 1978 (*Annual Report 1972*). This included three adult establishments, one of which (HMP Shotts) would hold up to 1,000 prisoners. The other two facilities would be built for a population of 500 each (HH57/322/52; HH57/322/60). In the meantime, two more prisons, Dungavel and Cornton Vale, opened in 1975. The latter was a female-only prison for 220 women and girls, and Dungavel was a medium-security prison for 150 adult men. Greenock, a young offenders' institution, was also being converted into a prison for 180 males. In 1970 the Prison Division was responsible for nine institutions for adult males, which expanded to 13 adult male prisons by 1983. The expansion meant that the cost of imprisonment was also expanding rapidly, from £6.55 million in 1971 to £15.76 million by 1975. While expansion remained the Division's central prerogative, it was severely curtailed when Britain entered a recession in 1973, due in part to the decline in heavy industries and the oil crisis. As a result, the planned 1000-person prison, HMP Shotts, had to be built on a phased basis. In 1978 phase one opened: a drastically smaller, 60-place unit. Despite these fiscal restraints, by the end of the 1970s Scotland had Europe's highest incarceration rate (Moore 1978).

All prisoners were categorised into discrete security classifications which distinguished them in terms of danger and risk of escape:

Category A: Those who if they escaped would be highly dangerous to the public, the police or the security of the state;

Category B: Those prisoners for whom the very highest conditions of security are not necessary, but for whom escape must be made very difficult;

Category C: Prisoners who cannot be trusted in open conditions but who do not have the ability or the resources to make a determined escape attempt;

Category D: Prisoners who can be trusted in open conditions (MacDonald and Sim 1978:8).

Prisoners were also subdivided within these groups into short- and long-term prisoners, with the latter group being divided again based on their perceived level of risk. This range of prisoner categories resulted in Scotland's diversified imprisonment regime, divided into mainstream prisons (Aberdeen, Barlinnie, Edinburgh, Low Moss, Greenock, Shotts and Perth), a remand prison at Dumfries, as well as open or semi-open prisons (such as Dungavel and Penninghame) and segregation regimes (Inverness, Peterhead and the Barlinnie Special Unit).

Mainstream imprisonment

Addressing prisoners' 'health and hygiene' was a central concern of Scotland's mainstream imprisonment regime. Annual reports monitored the aggregate number of people with diseases of the bowels, teeth, skin, and respiratory system, eye and ear problems, as well as 'infestations'. Prisoners were taught about the 'hazards of venereal disease' and personal cleanliness (*Annual Report 1970*:16–18). Over-indulgence in alcohol and alcoholism were seen as a major reason for imprisonment (*Annual Report 1975*). Abstention from alcohol, drugs and cigarettes was promoted to prisoners, and in 1971 a small alcohol treatment unit was opened at Low Moss prison (*Annual Report 1971*:13). Prisoners (most often short-term), were thus not seen as being subject to punishment but, as it was referred to, a regime of 'penal medicine' (*Annual Report 1982*:20).

The imprisonment regime relied further on this 'medical-somatic' approach (Johnstone 1996) using consultant psychiatrists to address the prevalence of 'mental disorders' among the prisoner population. Each year thousands of prisoners were diagnosed with these pathologies. These were described as prisoners who exhibited nervous disorders and neuroses, or who were emotionally disturbed or mentally unstable (*Annual Report 1981*:19). Within the broader remit of psychological disorders, there was a notable preoccupation with prisoners who exhibited 'personality disorders'.

The other most important dynamic propelling the daily regimes of Scottish mainstream imprisonment was work. Prison industries were not aimed at 'capacity building' (Garland 2013:501), and there was comparatively less education available within Scottish prisons (Wozniak 1987). Almost all prisoners worked within the prison (*Annual Report 1978*:14), involved in making and repairing mailbags, mat making, net making and mattress making, as well as domestic duties such as cleaning, orderly work and working in the library. A small number of around 100 prisoners were involved in trades such as carpentry, plumbing, painting, plastering and labouring. These were a cheap and effective means to keep prisoners usefully occupied (*Annual Report 1972*:14), to 'counter boredom' (*Annual Report 1970*:12), stimulate industriousness and prevent prisoners from succumbing to 'idleness' (*HMCIP Annual Report 1981*:12).

Prison industry was also lauded because it provided a systematic and simple template for prisoner control and prison order, contributing to 'the efficient management and control of prisoners and prisons by providing a stable and regular routine' (*Annual Report 1985*:5). Therefore, full employment for all prisoners was a key aim of the mainstream imprisonment regime (*Annual Report 1985*:5). The Division acknowledged that, to increase the rehabilitative capacities of prison industry, industrial labour would have to be better aligned with outside job opportunities, but within the prison system low-level factory work was over-emphasised (*Annual Report 1972*:17). Such unskilled work activities were prioritised so as to maximise the output of 'inmate labour' rather than welfare (*Parole Board for Scotland Report 1972*:15).

The idea of utility was so deeply ingrained that an increase in the prisoner population was also viewed positively, resulting in increased productivity because, as they described it, the prison now had 'a larger workforce' (*Annual Report 1972*:16). When there was a small reduction in prison numbers in 1981, it was reported that 'it caused short manning on lines of production' (*Annual Report 1981*:14). The Division monitored the 'value of work done', calculated via output of products and the financial value of goods produced by prison industry (*Annual Report 1970*:12). Using these figures, the Division tracked, compared and reported the annual sales turnover per inmate. Any signs of the rehabilitative ideal were subordinate to the economic rationality:

> modern industrial work under enlightened conditions gives no worse a result in terms of positive rehabilitative benefit than other more expensive forms of institutional treatment. Well organised and well managed prison industry can be carried out for up to 8 hours a day at virtually no cost whatsoever to the Exchequer and, in some cases, at a significant profit. The cost/benefit to society as a whole therefore of expanding and modernising prison industries is an important factor which deserves special consideration in the overall planning of treatment programmes.
>
> (*Annual Report 1974*:13)

Long-term imprisonment

Adult prisoners were also categorised as either short-term (sentences of less than 18 months) or long-term (sentences of 18 months and above, including indeterminate sentences). The majority of the average daily prison population in Scotland was made up of adults, about one-third of whom were long-term prisoners. Despite their being in the minority, the Scottish prison system of the 1970s was preoccupied with the long-term prisoner and the risks they posed, and had several special systems set up specifically for them within the regime.

Upon entering the prison system, long-term and life-sentence prisoners were assessed by the National Classification Board (made up of governors, chief officers, social workers, industrial managers and specialist officers) who tested these prisoners on areas such as cutting joints, arithmetic, IQ, etc. (McNeill 1988; Adler and Longhurst 1994). This process was used to iden-tify and distinguish 'trainable' prisoners: those prisoners who were likely to be compliant and docile and thus could enter prison industries at main-stream institutions, such as Perth or Edinburgh. But if the Classification Board deemed the newly incarcerated person as recalcitrant, or if the pris-oner refused to be assessed, they were labelled as disruptive and subjected to a much more austere regime, such as Peterhead (Scraton et al. 1988; Coyle 1991). In that way, Scottish long-term imprisonment was organised hierarchically.

Release

For prisoners to begin to move out of the prison prior to their official release or remission date, they required parole. For Scotland parole was a relatively new innovation, a product of the 1967 Criminal Justice Act which stipulated that only those serving more than 18 months were eligible for early release (McManus 1999:231). A prisoner was considered for parole after complet-ing one-third of their sentence or serving one year, whichever period was the greatest in length.

The entire process was a staged series of 'screenings' (*Parole Board for Scotland Report 1979*:14). Each prisoner considered by the Parole Board would have an individual dossier compiled by prison staff and social workers. This contained a plotted history of their criminal and social background, a review of their conduct on any previous supervision in the community, details of the current offence, comments or observations made by the Judge, and insights into their domestic life and how they had responded to the imprisonment regime. But the most vital concern was public safety, and the risk of future offending was paramount among their concerns (*Parole Board for Scotland Report 1972*:9). This data would then be examined by a local review committee, who would determine whether or not to recommend the applicant to the Parole Board, which then ultimately decided whether a prisoner would be recommended to the Secretary of State for early release.

In 1979 it was reported that the Parole Board recommended that 72.8% of applicants receive parole, a total of 236 people (*Parole Board for Scotland Report 1979*) – a high rate of parole success. But if we look at this figure measured against the entire number of parole-eligible prisoners, what we see is that in fact 29.5% of prisoners eligible for parole were successful in their applications.[iv] For those who did receive a release date, the Parole Board would recommend a series of preparatory steps, which would expose a prisoner's 'weaknesses and strengths' (*Parole Board for Scotland Report 1972*:9). Having progressed to this stage, any evidence of misconduct or doubts about 'their suitability for release' would mean that a prisoner's parole date could be withdrawn, and they would descend back into closed conditions (ibid.). Parole was not something that one just received, it was 'a privilege to be earned' (ibid.:12) as long-termers journeyed 'on the road to liberation' (*HMCIP Report on Penninghame 1982*:3).

Progression: training for freedom

Underpinning the hierarchy of Scottish imprisonment, and shaping a prisoner's passage to parole, was a distinct pattern of movement known as progression: long-term male prisoners were circulated around the prisons in a process intended to work as a rational system of rewards and punishments. One could ascend upwards through the prison hierarchy, towards open prisons like Penninghame, which had room for 74 inmates, or to a Training for Freedom Hostel; there were 8 Training for Freedom Hostel places in Aberdeen, 16 in Edinburgh and 11 in Perth. Before that prisoners would likely serve time in Dungavel prison, a designated midpoint between an open and closed prison (though physically a closed prison). Prisoners who reached Dungavel, Penninghame or a Training for Freedom Hostel could potentially attend evening classes in the community or work for an outside employer, and the majority would receive five days leave for Christmas. Nonetheless, a tightly regulated system prevailed. For example, if a prisoner had progressed to Category C in Shotts and had served four months under that category, they were then permitted an afternoon home visit every three months (*HMCIP Annual Report 1985*:6). That leave was still largely escorted, even from the open prison at Penninghame and Dungavel (*HMCIP Annual Report 1985*:6; *HMCIP Report on Dungavel 1985*). The prison kept its grip on a person as they were cautiously being released back into society. This 'support' helped prisoners 'contribute positively to local life and, equally important, the community itself may be better protected because the ex-offender under supervision appears less likely to offend again' (*Parole Board Annual Report 1980*:11).

'Responsible citizenship' was the central motif of progression (*Annual Report 1971*:22; *HMCIP Report on Penninghame 1982*:3). Progression was an attempt to 'train' prisoners to be responsible by moving them – literally (through progression) and metaphorically (through the process of socialisation) – towards a better prison with more privileges and, as part of that, 'becoming reasonably responsible citizens' (*Parole Board Annual Report 1972*:12). For example, the Dungavel regime was 'designed to encourage individual acceptance of responsibility appropriate to life in the community' (*HMCIP Report on Dungavel 1981*:12).

Such training meant that when they moved up the next wrung to Penninghame open prison, it needed to rely less on 'physical restraints'. Instead,

'Formal controls are replaced by a high degree of personal discipline and if it becomes apparent that an individual is incapable of exercising an acceptable level of control, he is transferred to another establishment' (*HMCIP Report on Penninghame 1982*:15).Progression constituted a game of 'snakes and ladders' (McNeill 1988), rarely allowing a linear journey to freedom. It was considered that 'The greatest controlling factor in an open institution is the sanction of being returned to closed conditions' (*HMCIP Report on Penninghame 1982*:14). Discipline, training and control in Scottish imprisonment regimes were thus connected to prisoner mobility, and prisoners knew that there was the risk of being segregated outside the mainstream system.

Segregation: the deep end

The Scottish imprisonment regime had a 'deep end': those institutions that existed at the bottom, and even outwith, the mainstream prison hierarchy. These were what Sparks has called '*termini*': the lowest points 'on an ostensibly rational system of incentives and sanctions' (Sparks 2002:559, original emphasis). Those of 'Peterhead classification' (Coyle 1987:145; Scraton et al. 1988:255) were the most recalcitrant, too disruptive for the mainstream. Peterhead was Scotland's maximum-security prison and was officially designated as the 'end of the road' (*HMCIP Report on Peterhead 1981*:4), a 'place of internal exile' (Sparks 2002:576). Thus, it became a notorious prison for notorious prisoners. The Chief Inspector described the incendiary atmosphere at Peterhead: '[it] experiences an uneasy calm which can erupt into violence without warning' (*HMCIP Report on Peterhead 1981*:3–4). Throughout the 1970s Peterhead endured intense bouts of prisoner resistance, such as rioting, roof-top demonstrations, escape attempts and hunger strikes.

Internally, Peterhead relied upon its own exclusionary techniques to maintain order, adding greater depth to this already extreme form of imprisonment. Working inside the prisons at the time, Alistair outlined the predicament. Inevitably, some prisoners would never accept the authority of the prison and the legitimacy of their sentence. The prison authorities therefore required measures to both punish and deter prisoner disorder:

> [Peterhead] was the end of the line, and once you were there, there was nowhere else to go, and once you take hope away – you know the usual argument....if you create the end of the line, you need an end of the line at the end of the line.

More restrictive segregation existed in the form of 'the Digger' at Peterhead (Sparks 2002). Andrew Coyle (1994), a former Governor of Peterhead, described the Digger as austere, barren, devoid of light and entirely intent upon total incapacitation. The Digger was Scotland's oldest segregation unit, but by the 1980s it was but one node along an axis of exile. 'The Cages' at Inverness (Boyle 1977; Wozniak 1989) opened in 1966 for prisoners deemed to need 'complete physical separation from the normal prison routine' (SHHD 1971:13). These were cages in the literal sense, set up inside prison cells (Steele 1992). Ostensibly they claimed to provide the necessary short, sharp shock of extreme deprivation (HH57/1794), holding prisoners in a regime of mostly solitary confinement. Its 'basic philosophy' was 'that any prisoner who showed that he was violent or subversive could be sent to the unit at Inverness until such time as he demonstrated his fitness to return to his normal prison classification' (SHHD 1971:4).[v] In reality, segregation operated a system of extreme deprivation and mortification:

> [N]aked before prison officers in a 'cage' 9 feet by 6 feet the prisoner underwent a full body search three times each day. The solitary confinement and personal humiliation of the cages represented the ultimate loss of dignity for any individual receiving punishment.
>
> (Gateway Exchange 1987:29)

This degradation, violence and inhumanity of the system became part of Scottish prison folklore (Boyle 1977), with one former prisoner writing that it 'was rumoured that blood was coated on the walls from the beatings handed out there' (Steele 1992:211–212).

In 1972, there was a particularly violent incident at the cages. A prison officer lost an eye, other officers were stabbed and two inmates were seriously injured (HH57/1742), which led to the temporary closure of the unit. Scotland had only abolished the death penalty shortly before these incidents in 1965. Without the threat of execution, the Division had been adjusting the imprisonment regime to meet the perceived potential dangers of the long-term prison population (Cooke 1989a). Confronted first with these troubling incidents, as well as Scotland's rising murder rate, it was feared that in abolishing the death penalty the Scottish penal system had lost its most serious deterrent (HC Deb, 26 March 1968).

In this context of deep desperation, there was a small but profound innovation in Scottish segregation regimes in the early 1970s, as the 'crisis of violence' opened a window of opportunity for more radical solutions (Nellis 2010). St Andrew's House intervened, establishing a working group on 'The Treatment of Certain Male Long Term Prisoners and Potentially Violent Prisoners'. Their job was to explore the possibility of another alternative regime for the endemic problem of unrelentingly disruptive prisoners. The working party argued that the abolition of the death penalty had indeed exacerbated the dangers of the prison (Scottish Home and Health Department [hereafter SHHD] 1971:3). However, the threat of the cages had not brought a reduction in prisoner misconduct. Inspired by prisons such as Grendon in England, they suggested an experiment: a radically alternative segregation unit, one based on a therapeutic model (HH48/100/34; SHHD 1971:2; Circular No 73/1973; Stephen 1988). As a result, the Barlinnie Special Unit (hereafter BSU) opened in 1973.

Operating in the small, disued women's unit at HMP Barlinnie, the BSU held up to eight prisoners, some of whom were renowned as Scotland's most dangerous men. The BSU was part of Scotland's segregation network, yet its internal regime was far from segregative. It was less regimented; unconcerned with industrial training, they favoured the arts (Nellis 2010). The BSU returned autonomy to prisoners, allowing them and the staff to evolve into a single 'community' rather than maintaining the distinctions between officers and prisoners. Everyone engaged in a democratic kind of governing arrangement which centred around weekly meetings. At these meetings, any member of the community (prisoner/officer) could be requested to take a place in the 'hotseat', where he could be subject to questioning from the rest of the group (Boyle 1977). Together, they decided to relax censorship outwith stipulated prison regulations; they allowed the free use of workshop equipment and telephones; and, in a highly symbolic act, the group decided to remove the door from the punishment cell. This was also undoubtedly a more permeable prison. Prisoners moved in and out of the prison with greater freedom, and also enjoyed liberal visiting regimes, including visits in their cells (HC Deb, 13 February 1978). This demonstrated that those perceived to be among the Scotland's most dangerous criminals were not beyond redemption, as one politician characterised penal practice at the BSU: 'The Barlinnie experiment was, and is, based on the premise that lifers and other hard nut offenders will respond positively to being treated like human beings' (HC Deb, 12 February 1980).

The Unit also gained a wide audience of admirers (Sparks 2002). In many ways, its acclaim reaffirmed Scottish distinction to a Scottish elite that saw itself as dealing with 'needs not deeds' of those who came into contact with its criminal justice system. Some of its prisoners – particularly Jimmy Boyle, who produced a biography and sculpture while at the unit, as well as Larry Winters, who wrote poetry – gained celebrity status as they and the unit entered the Scottish cultural imagination. Yet it remained an exception to the normal prison regime; it was pioneering, and it was anomalous. It was 'developed "apart from" rather than "part of" of the prison system' (Working Party on Alternative Regimes 1985:11).

The BSU was also not the only separation unit opened in this period. The Inverness Cages reopened in 1978, and a new Individual Unit (1976) and Ten Cell Unit (1982) were constructed within Peterhead. According to the Under Secretary of State for Scotland, these units would provide 'facilities to deal with prisoners who require, for whatever reasons, to be removed from normal circulation' (Working Party on Alternative Regimes 1985:14). So, while the BSU presents a remarkable and distinctive moment in Scottish penal history, it should be seen as part of this network of segregation. All prisoners held in the Ten Cell Unit, the BSU, the Cages and the Digger were beyond the mainstream prison system. As Derek described it, a prisoner in the BSU was considered 'out of the system'. Segregated prisoners could not progress until they returned to the regular routine of the mainstream prison system (Sparks 2002; Bottomley et al. 1994). The ideal dynamic of Scottish imprisonment regimes was to encourage long-term prisoners to circulate, to travel upwards through the prison hierarchy, embracing personal responsibility. While the BSU was far more progressive than other types of deep segregation (and maybe even mainstream imprisonment), it was not progression.

Political culture

How come the character of imprisonment in Scotland from 1970 into the 1980s displayed such paradoxes? The imprisonment regime was defined by hyper-vigilant security, fuelled by an unquestioned belief in the necessity of expanding the prison estate, and concerned with disciplinary circulation of prisoners. Why was mundane industrial work and health and hygiene so central to mainstream prison life? The motivations driving Scotland's prison practices emerge when we examine the assumptions, meanings and political values that informed the power to imprison. Scotland's distinctive imprisonment regime was based on the preoccupations, sensibilities and objectives of the Scottish political culture of *paternal liberalism*; a distinct political outlook that combined otherwise contradictory components of political thinking and cultural meaning.

Liberal aspirations

The imprisonment regime's aspiration for prisoners to achieve good citizenship and develop personal control were rooted in the 'key requirements' of liberalism, emphasising freedom, individual responsibility, rationality and independence (O'Malley and Valverdre 2004:27). These liberal ideas provided the accepted penal logic, particularly in the use of progression and open units. Progression was a disciplinary technique, and the ideal outcome was not just reduced crime and better prison behaviour; prisoners also needed to demonstrate that they understood 'the idea of good citizenship' (*Parole Board Report 1974*:7) and could exercise responsible 'self-determination' (*HMCIP Report on Penninghame 1982*:3). The prisoner had before him the opportunity to graduate up through the prison hierarchy and, ideally, in the process learn to master the self-control of 'personal discipline' (*HMCIP Report on Penninghame 1982*:15). If getting prisoners to develop liberal individual responsibility was the goal, then it was 'not enough to simply conform to prison rules and regulations' (*Parole Board for Scotland Report 1972*:12); such docility is not a celebrated liberal trait. The prison rules were external constraints, but to progress the prisoner was expected to demonstrate that they had internalised the 'instinctive habits' of the liberal citizen (O'Malley 1999). As the Parole Board reflected in their 1974 report:

> A man's behaviour in prison...[is] usually to a considerable extent in his own hands. He can see prison as a challenge and decide to make use of such opportunities as it provides, or he can simply conform and pass his time quietly.
>
> (*Parole Board for Scotland Report 1974*:6)

As Derek described it, progression was a way to reveal the prisoners who had the appropriate type of internal disposition, which enabled them to adapt to the responsibilities and expectations of freedom:

> Sometimes they were happy to be sent back [from an open prison] because they couldn't cope...I think most prisoners would have adjusted, human nature makes the best of a bad job...But some couldn't cope with the freedom.

This reflects the belief that freedom placed a tremendous demand on prisoners. The 'new found freedom' in the higher tiers of the prison regime, 'far from being a soft option[,] imposes responsibilities requiring personal decisions' (*HMCIP Report on Penninghame 1982*:3).

This widely shared liberal outlook also explains why the BSU was kept 'apart from' the rest of the prison system. There was a sense that the BSU undermined attempts to train prisoners to be rational, that it perverted the established progression and circulatory logic of Scottish imprisonment. The Special Unit was seen as a potential 'incentive for bad behaviour' and was lambasted because, it was argued, there should be 'no carrots if good must be emphasised' (HH57/1622; original emphasis). The BSU was felt to undermine the liberal system of incentives and punishment that organised the Scottish imprisonment regime and sought to train prisoners to develop rational calculation.

It rarely appeared that training for freedom was engaging prisoners pre-existing liberal dispositions. Instead, the regime used progression to 'encourage the internalisation of liberal democratic values, the creation of individuals who would learn how to rule their selves' (Dumm 1987:6, quoted in Melossi 2004:86). As the Chief Inspector for Prisons wrote, when a prisoner was 'exercising a personal choice on most occasions', it was likely 'a relatively new experience' for the prisoner (*HMCIP Report on Penninghame 1982*:10). This alerts us to the underlying understanding of prisoners as people who had not been inculcated in the ways of socially acceptable behaviour.

The majority of prisoners were not viewed as capable of this kind of inherent liberal rationality, reflected in the fact that self-control was an ideal but marginal expectation in Scottish imprisonment. The most effective form of prisoner rehabilitation, it was suggested at the time, would need to 'liberate the prisoner from the effects of the social, educational and emotional conditioning which have rendered him unable to function effectively and acceptably in our society' (*Annual Report 1971*:20–21). We cannot fully understand prison practices by looking at political ideas alone; we must also examine how liberal ideas fused with Scottish cultural sensibilities and anxieties.

Dangerous places, dangerous prisoners

It is clear from the description above that forms of imprisonment were deeply concerned with the prospect of violence and danger. The possibility of prisoners being dangerous, as well as disordered or hapless, were connected through a web of social narratives and cultural imagery from which Scottish imprisonment drew its degrees of legitimate force and common sense justification.

Serious crime and violence loomed large in the imaginations of those charged with managing Scotland's prison system. It was felt that the worst and most endemic crime and disorder tended to belong to the 'central slum parts of the city with a long-established reputation for containing a disproportionate number of habitual criminals, prostitutes, drug addicts and the like' (SHHD 1975:10). These places were described with florid and often unsympathetic detail: 'gardens strewn with refuse and broken glass, vacant houses boarded up, gang slogans on the walls of properties, neglected pets etc...These are the characteristics of areas which contribute disproportionately to crime' (SHHD 1975:11). The descriptions of these areas verged on the dystopian, as communities of drunkards, people living in self-made wastelands, who had high mortality rates and even higher unemployment: 'the cultural setting, in which the overwhelming majority of violent offences occur, is itself characterised by the acceptance not only of heavy drinking but also of violent behaviour' (SHHD 1975:17). During the 1970s, Henry said people's concerns were focused on 'the problems of violence in Glasgow'. Robert similarly recalled that one could *see* the differences between Glasgow and Edinburgh criminality:

> [In] Glasgow the jury trials all seem to be more serious. And we have two heavy duty guys from the west of Scotland and I thought we [in Edinburgh] rarely get guys like that. And they had suits on and they looked like ancient boxers. I rarely see people like that. So there is a significant difference in that. I think the other thing I did see that shocked me...this tribalism and all this display of bigotry. I was just horrified.

For Peter, the shock of Glasgow became the inspiration to work in public policy:

> I decided I wanted to work in public administration really, partly because of what I saw in Glasgow there seemed like a lot, you know, a lot that needed to be done...Glasgow was in a bad way then. All the shipyards were being closed down, unemployment, poor housing. You know being brought up in Edinburgh, you know, you can see what it's like, and being in Glasgow you saw something quite different.

These places inspired anxiety precisely because they were seen as communities with a persistent vicious streak, a cultural proclivity for violence, and a tolerance for crime and cruelty in general:

> there was a degree, a threshold, I still think there's a different threshold between Edinburgh and Glasgow. Edinburgh are more fussy and

> more likely to call the police...in Glasgow where there is probably a lot more inherent violence, and something happens in your garden and your house and they get slashed in the face, but I'll not bother calling the police.
>
> (Robert)

This quote explicitly illustrates that it was not merely crime, but also the quick resort to brutality that was perceived to be part of the routine domestic life of Glasgow and Scotland's impoverished enclaves. Violence could erupt in 'your garden' or 'your house'; an 'inherent' aggressive impulsivity simmered below the surface of normal social relations in those kinds of places. Edinburgh, on the other hand, was more likely to work with the law. Euan felt people were anxious about Glasgow, afraid of what it represented. He described an information-gathering trip to one of west Scotland's poorer and more marginalised areas where some colleagues did not want to venture too far as they were afraid of 'the natives'.

Glasgow rested in the political cultural imagination as a 'territory of disorder' (Bowden 2014), presenting the problems of crime not as structural inequality but as bound to 'the alleged pathology of its tenants' (Damer 1989:12), thereby stoking uneasiness and appealing to the administration's interconnected fears of untameable incivility, social disorder and violence. The 'territorial stigmatisation' (Gray and Mooney 2011) that had long troubled Glasgow came to shape the view of imprisonment. As Philip stated, 'that was what Scotland was like, you've got a tough job with a tough population'. In telling the story of prisons, Douglas and Alistair spoke of 'notorious gangsters' and known hard men from Glasgow. Robert described the 'problems in the West of Scotland: hard drinking, buckfast and Valium mentality'. In this way, the political culture governing Scottish prisons was inflected with wider social anxieties regarding Scotland's 'urban predicament' (Begg 1996) and pockets of 'dysfunctional cultural milieu' (O'Malley and Valverdre 2004:35).

Reflecting upon the low use of parole for long-termers, Peter noted that it was 'not punitive', though it might appear as such. Rather, he argued, it was a reflection of their being 'cautious', given the kind of people they were releasing and the nature of the communities to which they were returning. As the Parole Report in 1972 recorded: 'In the nature of things many offenders come from areas of high crime and delinquency...where the downward drag [of their community] may well prove almost irresistible' (*Parole Board for Scotland Annual Report 1972*:11). They went on to suggest that the most productive intervention to reduce recidivism that could occur would be for the prisoner to leave prison and discover that the area they were from had 'been pulled down and redeveloped' (*Parole Board for Scotland Annual Report 1972*:11). It was believed that many prisoners were drawn from places lacking in 'community spirit and social controls' (SHHD 1975:25). These place-specific narratives delineated a sharp line between respectable and disreputable classes. This group were repeatedly depicted as Scotland's savage underclass, presented via tropes such as hard men, heavy drinkers, career housebreakers, brawlers, petty thieves and gangsters. For government actors, prisoners were not one of them; they did not share values, views or manners. Prisoners were perceived to be from a different place, one that was morally and socially worlds apart.

Prisoners' perceived irascible incivility necessitated and legitimised the greater use of coercive and sometimes brutal control. While liberalism advocates restraint, it also has a despotic side which allows for a rationally justified authoritarian mentality (Valverde 1998). This is seen as a seemingly logical response to subjects who are unlikely to succeed at self-improvement and whom, as a consequence, must be permanently excluded, controlled, dominated and subject to penal exile. The function of segregation was to keep 'the mentally or inadequately aggressive out of ordinary circulation' (HH57/194). William lamented segregation, but, he reflected, volatile prisoner responses to the segregation units (especially frequent dirty protests) only reinforced the belief in the need for segregation: '[That] was all you had to show those in Operations convinced for the need for militaristic management.' The perceived erraticism, self-debasement and violence of the prisoners (often in response to the harshness and inflexibility of the prison system; see Gateway Exchange 1987) justified the extremity and regularity of the segregation control to which they were subject. Adam remarked that the benefits to the system were understood as a means to control:

> It was a response to the loss of control. In the end if you [the prisoner] don't consent you can't rule these people, if they were willing to take all the risks they take then you can't control these people.

Prisoners 'perceived dangerousness reinforces their isolation' (Simon 1993:253). The violence of the system – in this case, segregation – was 'rational, purposive, and controlled through values, norms, and procedures external to violence itself' (Sarat 1995:1134). The dehumanising physical control of segregation and penal exile was intended to oppose and dominate its penal subjects, a 'civilizing violence' of authoritarian order against social disorder (ibid.). Gaining control of this population was felt to be the Prison Division's burden.

The feckless and disordered prisoner

But much of mainstream prison life was mundane and dull, where prisoners were meted out medical care and worked a daily routine in low-skilled industries, reflecting what was a dismal and hopeless view of most mainstream prisoners. There was a sense that prisoners were, by and large, Scotland's most sad and disorderly citizens. When oral history respondents described the prisoner, they provided straightforward and timeless descriptions – lacking in either heightened emotional sympathy or open disdain, offered as flat facts. While they were recalling the past, they spoke in the present tense about their belief that the prisoner was, and is generally, incompetent – to them a universal trait:

> The majority of the prison population are...the poor, the feckless etc., the illiterate. (Douglas)

> The majority [of prisoners] are feckless, they don't know how to organise their life, they've never known any better. (William)

In one correspondence, prisoners were described as people who were not 'fully aware of, and responsible for, their actions' and likely had a 'below average IQ' (HH57/1794).

The perceived identity of the prisoner as feckless and incompetent was implicit in the specific metrics presented on prisoners' health and hygiene. The emphasis was on venereal diseases, self-inflicted injuries, alcoholism, diseases of the teeth, and lice or infestation. These were plotted, typified and materialised through the Annual Report statistics. This array of diseases and disorders presented a vivid and stigmatising statistical outline (Goffman 1963). The implied narrative was that the causes of prisoners' disorders were somehow internal. The most common type of carceral subject with whom Scotland contended was contagious, infectious and morally weak. If the ideal Scottish citizen was a master of a liberal sensibility, then prisoners were those suffering from 'diseases of will' (Valverde 1998). When it came to health, hygiene and mental health, prisoners were believed to lack the 'the principles they would need to observe if they were to lead more successful lives after liberation' (*Annual Report 1970*:18).

Many of the mainstream prisoners were also understood to have dysfunctional emotional and cognitive capacities, which rendered them beyond the spectrum of normalcy and unlike the average Scottish citizen. Matters of health became more endemic and problematic when it came to prisoners who suffered from 'disorders affecting the mind', such as neuroses or personality disorders (*Annual Report 1972*:21; *Annual Report 1978*:17). A personality disorder, however, was explicitly defined as a non-medical issue (HH57/1794) and it was rarely required that these prisoners be transferred into medical settings. In 1978, 2,872 people in prison had problems of the nervous system, though only 10 were diagnosed with medically recognised psychoses that required a transfer to a hospital. Prisoners' mental disturbances were often 'not treatable in a mental hospital' (*Annual Report 1983*:3). In 1983 the Division wrote that prisoners with 'treatable mental illnesses are not kept in penal establishments' (HH57/1794); thus, the prison was dealing with those who fell on the other side of the 'dividing line between treatable and untreatable' (ibid.).

From 1970 to the beginning of the 1980s, the manner in which the prison regime diagnosed, plotted and categorised prisoners as diseased, alcoholic or disordered was a reflection of Scotland's liberal and paternal political culture – which itself was orientated towards the practical problems of a deindustrialising economy and a society in decline. These were moral judgements as much as they were medical diagnoses. These categories, evident in the interviews, publications and reports, did not generate or inspire sympathy, but evoked unworthiness. Prisoners were thus constituted as individuals who had scarified their autonomy by living a life marked by poor choices and incompetence. They were socially, mentally and physiologically constituted as 'other', thus justifying – even demanding – extra-state intervention.

Prison: the terminal position

Contrary to mainstream deceptions of Scottish penal history, then, we see here an authoritarian paternalism and a commitment to liberal individualism giving the prison system its central meanings and logic, and not collective and social welfare sentiments. The Special Unit was undoubtedly innovative, participatory and progressive; it was a moment when the welfare ideas and segregation concerns of the Scottish prison intermingled and coalesced. But it was aberrant, a minuscule aspect of a much larger imprisonment regime. What purportedly widespread supportive practices there were – the snakes and ladders of progression, the routine of industry for 'trainable' prisoners – are better understood as tactics of discipline (Foucault 1977).

Yet, we know that Scotland's welfare state and progressive ideas of inclusiveness were at their high point during this period (Brodie et al. 2008). Why, then, does the use of the prison stand in such stark and bleak contrast to these developments? Imprisonment regimes were evidently designed, expanded and maintained in a manner that reflected wider social insecurities and liberal ideals. In order to fully illuminate the underpinning conditions that gave Scotland its distinctive penal culture, however, we must understand that the prison system was a product of the exclusionary dynamics of Scottish welfarism.

After Kilbrandon, social work was reorganised to better support children in need and vulnerable citizens. But in practice, local authorities faced growing social disorganisation, poverty and community need. Social work with offenders and ex-prisoners appeared to receive little funding when compared with groups considered more worthy of welfare interventions, such as the elderly, the sick and the young. The discretion accorded to local government to allocate funding to generic social work was subsequently criticised for creating an 'opportunity for the operation of the doctrine of less eligibility' (Moore 1978:39). As Adam described it: 'offenders were smelly, children were needy. So, criminal justice became the poor relation.'

These people were imprisoned partially because they had failed at the art of self-control and could not be helped by social welfare interventions. This reasoning was made evident when Peter spoke about the problematically high rates of Scottish imprisonment and the use of prison sentences for petty crime. He was especially progressive in his general views of punishment, yet even he concluded, with some exasperation, that the fault was not with the criminal justice system, but in the failure of individuals to grasp alternatives:

> [Sheriffs] will say, because I've had many conversations, tell me what I should do when a man, to whom I have given community service because you encouraged me to do that, comes back for the tenth time

having the same thing, or having failed, or alternative or community service and hasn't turned up to do it, what am I meant to do? And their only answer is, and there aren't alternative answers, but their answer almost eventually has to be to put him in prison, you see. And, that's, that is their answer, it is quite a difficult one to counter really if somebody is completely failing then the only answer to carry on putting them on probation, but it can lower the public belief in probation if a person is out, as it were, on approval and they're carrying on shoplifting ... I think the Sheriffs, they're always being put upon, and they are sending too many people to prison but I can see their point of view they have to come up with, and we having been trying this for a long time, to try and come up with other ways to stop people reoffending...and prison for certain people who have to send them to prison, I mean murderers and very violent people need to be in prison, but minor dishonesty, but then what do you do with the people that carry on?

High prison populations were assumed to be the result of many prisoners' prior unwillingness or inability to desist. To give such people probation would undermine the public's positive perception of the welfare system. Prisoners were those whose crime, either by severity or persistence, rendered them beyond the welfare system; prison was for the intractable and incapable, those not reclaimable. Prisoners' 'disruptive behaviour', their 'severe emotional problems and very disturbed personalities' were attributed to their being 'high grade defectives' (HH57/1794; *Parole Board for Scotland Report 1972*:10; *Annual Report 1982*:19). Prisoners' choices, the culture of their communities and their lack of personal discipline were understood as endemic, pathologically engrained and hence beyond help. As Carlen (1983) wrote with such force and clarity of Scotland during this period, these dysfunctional citizens ended up in prison not because they were morally unworthy of social welfare support, but because they were believed to lack the 'moral *capacity* to respond to welfare intervention or medical treatment' (ibid.:183 original emphasis). Prisoners were presented and reproduced as 'disordered' and 'untreatable' (ibid.:194).

Prison was thus the end of the line. It was for Scotland's deviants who had nowhere else to go and other avenues were seen as either exhausted or futile. Imprisonment regimes functioned for those deemed 'as being beyond the remit of the treatment agencies, without hope and beyond recognition' (ibid.:194). Alistair best summed up this view when he said the prison was designated and designed for those 'for whom there were no other options'. These prisoners may seem unworthy of imprisonment, they explained at the time, but 'in many cases [there is] no alternative to confinement' (HH57/1794). This governmental paternal inclination towards incarceration was best summed up by Henry: '[we] were trying to save people from themselves'.

Such a dismal view of the prison and its relation to the welfare system helps us to understand how little effort was given to rehabilitative or supportive regimes. It was considered to not be 'necessary, or indeed possible, to think in terms of positive treatment towards rehabilitation in custody for all inmates'. For those short-term inmates and 'others serving longer sentences…The prison service's role…is primarily therefore one of containment and physical care' (*Annual Report 1971*:2).[vi] Care may sound nurturing, but what it meant was a dismal commitment to provide prisoners with basic medical treatment, habits of regularity and periods of exclusion from society. Among the meanings constituted in Scottish imprisonment regimes was the need to incapacitate, exclude and control a population of 'lifetime clients' who, while not necessarily dangerous, were social failures, and therefore must be 'maintained securely at the lowest possible cost' (Simon 1993:259). In this way, containing intractable social dysfunction was the prison's practical social function.

If Kilbrandon had led to a welfare system interested in social education, the prison system was for those who simply could not learn. Operating as the coercive arm of social welfare framed the understanding of imprisonment regimes: 'The prison Service [sic] will continue to have an important social role to play in the care of this vulnerable group of offenders' (*Annual Report 1975*:20); thus, for many the prison was 'a social as well as a medical service' (*Annual Report 1982*:20). Despite these interventions, it was felt that 'in so many cases' prisoners would 'rapidly lapse from grace on release and return again and again to the care of the Prison Medical Service' (ibid.). Imprisonment was understood to be the result of irresponsibility, those wayward citizens resistant to community-based support. Scottish prisoners were 'perceived as failing to use available opportunity for advancement in the various approved runways of society…they represent failures in the motivational schemes of society' (Goffman 1963:171), thus necessitating government intervention and legitimating repeated or extended imprisonment. As Philip described the people given prison rather than social work supervision, these 'Adult offenders were quite different. A different ball game altogether. The usual categories of permanent offenders… someone who is not suitable for probation'. The welfare system worked with responsible and cooperative liberal citizens; the prison worked upon their opposite: those people viewed as 'ineligible for non-custodial supervision' (Carlen 1983:154). The prison reflects Scotland's

> *dismissive* society, a society where penal policy is retributive rather than rehabilitative and where, ironically, either despite or because of the ideology of generic social work, a rigid distinction is still made between criminal justice in particular and social justice in general.
>
> (ibid.; original emphasis)

Thus, we see the expansion of the Scottish prison system at the exact same time as the progressive reinvention and extension of Scotland's welfare state (for a discussion of this welfare/penal dynamic, see Barker 2017).

While the social work innovations sought to help people flourish in the community through social support, the prison worked to maintain order, welfare integrity and public safety through social exclusion.[vii] The aims of imprisonment were articulated as being a social service of last resort for those perceived as adult degenerates beyond hope. In the minds of prison policy-makers, Scottish imprisonment regimes began where welfare interventions ceased; prison was contrived as a 'terminal position' (Garland 1985:28). In this way, despite its large and growing prisoner population, the prison in Scotland was already understood to be operating as a measure of last resort.

There were consequences of this system, however. Given that prisoners tend to be drawn from a small number of often impoverished geographical locations (Houchin 2005; Goffman 2015), the heavy reliance on imprisonment would likely have also eroded community cohesion and entrenched social exclusion, class stigma and its consequent disorder. As such, it would have further degraded the informal social controls that were understood to buffer against criminality. The high use of imprisonment would have de-stabilised family units (Comfort 2008; Jardine 2020) who found themselves in a 'web of shame' as the stigma of the prison extended out into their lives (Condry 2007). Ironically, Scotland's division of social control labour, between patrician welfare intervention and authoritarian paternal exclusion, would likely have only further deepened the need for an extensive prison system as a coercive measure of last resort. In so doing, Scotland's field of social control – underpinned by the dynamic of prison and welfare – reinforced and perpetuated the characteristic classed divisions between worthy/unworthy, treatable/untreatable and social insider/social outsider. However, given that the Scottish adult prison system operated and functioned partially as the welfare system's safety net, its 'failure never mattered' (Muncie 1990).

FROM 1970 until the early 1980s, Scotland developed a disciplinary and exclusionary imprisonment regime. Through the administrative choices to build certain prisons – to routinise particular kinds of discipline, to organise the prisons hierarchically, to expand segregation and keep industry a mainly low-skilled endeavour – Scottish political culture influenced the material form and functions of the prison system. Visions of blameworthy diseased, alcoholic, disordered and dangerous prisoners provided prison with its intentions, and inspired its methods of redress, such as its characteristic progression, its extensiveness and its lack of capacity-building programmes. Such regimes were rationalised within a liberal and paternal political mentality, which shaped the bounds of what was thought of as possible.

Reassembling Scotland's politics of punishment in this period offers new insight into and explanation for Scotland's austere and punitive forms of imprisonment. Scotland may have produced Britain's quintessential penal welfare document, but the imprisonment regime did not operate on these principles because this credo did not inform the prison's governing political culture. Ideas of welfare ineligibility legitimated such dismal, disciplinary and exclusionary imprisonment, because the prison and the prisoner evoked such a strong sense of dismay and disdain. Prisons held those people considered too violent, too intractable or too inadequate to be in the care of welfare.

Scotland's social problems of the 1970s continued. By the 1980s unrest, protest and rebellion began to spread across the prison system, no longer confined just to Peterhead. Exclusionary and disciplinary forms imprisonment were well established, but how and why these forms of imprisonment were magnified and intensified in the 1980s are historical tasks of description and analysis, to which we now turn.

Notes

i Begg argues that housing in rural areas of Scotland was equally as poor as the urban slums.

ii In recent years this has become known as the 'Glasgow Effect', where morality rates are still considerably higher in Glasgow than in other equally deprived post-industrial British cities, such as Liverpool and Manchester (e.g. Reid 2009; Walsh et al. 2016)

iii The Prison Division was also sometimes known as the Prisons Group, referring to it as a collection of administrative units. Throughout, and for the purposes of consistency, I will refer to it as the Division.

iv I calculate this by using the figures from the 1979 Annual Report. This calculation commences at the very beginning of the parole process, including the 764 eligible prisoners plus a further 36 people considered by the parole board (so, 800 people) and the final figure of 236 who received parole.

v These were relatively small numbers in comparison to the size of the rest of the system, but, nonetheless, a regular feature which was relied upon.

Year	Number of Prisoners	Avg Length of stay
1968	32	2 months 3 weeks
1969	17	4 months 2 weeks
1970	11	3 months 3 weeks
1971	14	2 months 1 weeks
1972	17	2 months 3 weeks

Source: HC Deb, 24 November 1978.

vi This predates the 'Nothing Works' development, showing Scotland was practising pessimistic containment before the crisis of rehabilitation.

vii There is a risk here of presenting too optimistic a picture of social welfare. Social work (including work with offenders) was likely less dedicated to enhancing peoples' opportunities in practice than its policy discourses might suggest. However, that such a utopian view of social welfare existed in the minds of policymakers is the critical distinction here, shaping prison policy.

7 Crisis management

If we are to grasp why penal cultures differ or cohere across nations, then we must also understand the trajectories of penal transformation, discerning the styles of reasoning and motivations that shape and remake uses of imprisonment. We know now that Scotland's political culture of paternal liberalism made it vulnerable to antipathy, punitiveness and apathy as well as authoritarian uses of penal power. Political cultures provide the basic ingredients for decision-making, and therefore they must adapt to the world as it appears and is understood. This helps us comprehend how punitive adaptions and changes were made to the Scottish imprisonment regime from the middle to the end of the 1980s, while the political culture remained largely consistent.

This chapter shows that during this period Scottish prisons became engulfed in internal turmoil and, responding rapidly and reactively, in this time of crisis, there was a proliferation of Scotland's geography of segregation. We begin, though, with an outline of the extreme pressure on the Scottish prison system in the mid-1980s, spurred by a series of unprecedented crises.

New prison problems

In 1983, the British Home Secretary, Leon Brittan, announced new parole restrictions on prisoners serving five years or more, who from then on would only qualify for parole under exceptional circumstances. With the threat that those changes may come to bear in Scotland, the Secretary of State for Scotland, George Younger, initially restated the fact that Scotland had a distinct and separate legal system. However, in 1984 he reversed his commitment to divergent parole policies and the more restrictive changes were implemented in Scotland (McManus 1999:239). Writing of the negative impact this change in parole practice had on long-term prisoners in Scotland, the Chief Inspector stated: 'what light there had been at the end of the tunnel had been extinguished' (*HMCIP Report on Peterhead 1987*:64). An ominous atmosphere prevailed as it was feared that prisons now risked turning 'the man of violence' into a 'no-hoper', who then may 'become a serious danger to prison officers and other prisoners' (*HMCIP Annual Report 1986*:15). The second urgent problem faced by the Division during the 1980s was overcrowding (see Figure 7.1). Prisoner numbers, already high, rose to 5,588 in 1986, and the

Figure 7.1 Daily average adult prison population 1982-1988.

Source: Annual reports on prisons, various years

numbers 'peaked at an all-time high of 5,797 on 4 March 1986'. Overcrowding, the Division noted, had now become a 'crisis' (HH57/2070).

But a third and even more serious set of issues were to culminate within the prisons. In the mid-1980s, a sustained pattern of disorder and rioting erupted across the Scottish prison system, which was described as 'unprecedented in its intensity [and] duration' (SPS 1988a para 1.6). What came to be considered the first major riot in a long series of disturbances occurred in January 1984 at Peterhead, where prisoners took over a hall for 18 hours. The following year, in March 1985 at Peterhead, nine members of staff were taken hostage in the course of an abortive escape attempt (*Annual Report 1985*:15). Not long thereafter, in November, and again at Peterhead, seven members of staff were held at gunpoint during another escape attempt (though afterwards the gun was revealed to have been a replica; ibid.).The Governor of Peterhead wrote an internal report in 1984, reaffirming Peterhead's inherent danger: 'The history of Peterhead Prison is littered with incidents of one degree of ferocity or another, and this latest was simply another chapter in that history' (HH57/1622). These incidents were initially defined down, seen as the customary outbursts of Peterhead's extreme setting.

Some degree of prison unrest was not seen as out of the ordinary, with protest and demonstration seemingly routine, but from 1985 the scale of these incidents expanded exponentially. Dissent began to spread. Alistair recalled a new and extreme level of prison disorder:

> Basically, up until then, incidents in prison had always been things like hostages, individual prisoner took an individual officer or another prisoner hostage. How do you deal with these incidents? Then in 85/86 we

had the first incidents where prisoners took over a landing or a hall, and we never had that before.

Within a small window of time these disturbances evolved into a discernible and perturbing pattern, no longer isolated to Peterhead nor merely sporadic, but rather a recurring feature of Scottish prison life. There were several fire-raising incidents, dirty protests at a number of prisons and numerous occasions when prisoners refused food. In 1985 there was another riot, this time at Dumfries Prison (which had only recently been converted into an adult prison from a young offenders' institution), during which four prisoners held another prisoner hostage for more than 10 hours. Shortly thereafter two roof-top protests took place at Barlinnie Prison.

Prisoners at Longriggend Remand Centre destroyed furniture and set fire to their cells in 1986. Then there were two serious fires at Peterhead, which meant that 150 prisoners had to be transferred due to loss of facilities (*Annual Report 1986*:15). There were further roof-top demonstrations at Barlinnie and Edinburgh prisons, more dirty protests and two more fires at Peterhead. In another escalation, in October 1986 at Edinburgh, an officer was held hostage for four days by prisoners (Scraton et al. 1988). At the time, this was the most serious incident in Scottish prison history – but it was almost immediately superseded in November 1986 when a prison officer was held hostage for five days at Peterhead by 32 prisoners.

The Division was now facing a frightening challenge. The Chief Inspector was commissioned to investigate the causes of the disturbances, though he focused only on Peterhead. His report, published in 1987 (Scottish Home and Health Department 1987), argued that Peterhead had a small group of prisoners who were 'pernicious by nature and often volatile in temperament' (chapter 12). From that, dissent emanated. The Inspector concluded that control could be regained through increased segregation and that four segregation units, each with 15 places, should be built at the mainstream adult prisons (Perth, Shotts, Glenochil and Edinburgh).

Despite this effort to identify the problem and solutions to prison disorder, the pattern of traumatic incidents escalated in 1987, and across the country Scotland's prisons erupted into violence. In January, a number of prison officers were held hostage for six days at Barlinnie. For two days in April, two prisoners held a group of fellow prisoners hostage at Perth. Then in September, a prison officer was held hostage at Shotts prison. Just as the incident at Shotts drew to a conclusion, the following day, on the 28th of September, two prison officers were taken hostage at Peterhead in what became known as the 'Peterhead siege'. One prison officer was reported to have been 'held hostage, subject to assaults, humiliation and threats' (Scottish Prison Service 1988a: appendix 2). This incident was also an unparalleled spectacle, as 'television viewers around the world witnessed an officer being dragged across the roof of Peterhead Prison with a chain around his neck' (Coyle 1992:8). The siege was not resolved until a dramatic decision to send in the British

Special Air Service (SAS), who stormed the besieged hall at 5.15am on the 3rd October (Scottish Prison Service 1988a: appendix 2).

Despite this extreme emergency response, this was not the end of Scotland's prison turmoil. The following day (4th October 1987) a prison officer and a group of prisoners were taken hostage at Perth prison for 33 hours. After the quick succession of hostage-takings and the havoc of these distressing sieges, the Division took what was felt to be decisive and firm action to immediately stamp out the danger across the prison system (Scottish Prison Service 1988a: para.8.4). All adult male prisoners were denied association. A further 60 prisoners, believed to pose the greatest threat to the mainstream, were removed to Peterhead (Coyle 1991:143).

These were authoritarian responses, but they are not understandable without also appreciating the distressed emotional state within the Division and the incendiary atmosphere of Scottish imprisonment. The prison administration described themselves as 'under intense strain' (*Annual Report 1986*:15) and noted that this had been a 'traumatic period' (*HMCIP Annual Report 1986*:14). For many interviewees, speaking about this time evoked distressing, visceral memories. Ken reflected the feeling that a small carceral civil war had erupted:

> for a while, about two, three years, we were in a warzone… a lot of staff were held hostage, injured, a lot were traumatised, a lot of staff felt they couldn't really cope. It wasn't why they were in the prison service. A lot of staff retired and left. I suppose it damaged people. It was a very difficult time.

A sense of conflict had engulfed the prison system. Prisoners stood on one side, pulling against and clashing with the physical environment – the building, the landings, the cells –and those agents of power, the prison officers, who every day sought to manage and control them. A cycle of hostility and retaliation began to shape life in Scottish prisons: dirty protests, riot gear, landings blockaded, negotiations failed, homemade missiles launched, rooftop protests and hostages taken. Expanding the segregation facilities in the Scottish prison estate was thus a pragmatic if reactive response, undertaken in a turbulent and fearful climate, that aligned with and amplified their underlying political culture.

Though these troubles were severe, they came to be understood not as exceptional, but as an extreme form of the inherent difficulties routinely faced by Scottish imprisonment. These disturbances were defined as a 'microcosm of the problem in general' (HH57/1622). They were believed to reflect pre-existing problems of Scottish prisoners, who were cast as disordered and dangerous. The broader assessment of the situation depicted these incidents as, according to the Governor of Peterhead, 'inevitable' and as having 'everything to do with the character of the participants', which he went on to characterise as being 'consumed with hatred' (ibid.). It was believed that at Peterhead there was a 'Premier League' group of violent and disruptive prisoners (ibid.). The Chief Inspector gave this view official confirmation in his 1987 report, in which dangerous long-term prisoners, as well as identifying new group of 'very long term prisoners' (VLTPs), were singled out as the central causal factor driving the prison riots (*HMCIP Annual Report 1987*).

The Scottish prison population as a whole had been expanding, but the number of adults serving three years or more had increased at a quicker rate. By the end of the 1980s, 45% of convicted prisoners were 'VLTPs' (*Annual Report Prisons 1986*:1; Scottish Prison Service 1988a), with whom there was a growing preoccupation. The background characteristics of this group were painted with familiar imagery: truanting from school, broken family, raised in the slums of inner-city housing, lacking morals and having had long criminal careers wherein violence 'predominates' (*HMCIP Annual Report 1986*:15). Now this group were larger and imprisoned without the promise of parole to incentivise them, apparently making them particularly 'bitter' and 'uncooperative'. They were thus 'liable to be disruptive, anti-authority and may inflict physical injury on prison officers or other prisoners' (ibid.). The fundamental functions of the imprisonment regime were seen as sound: prisoners were individuals who generally could not be coerced into rehabilitation, but the rational 'carrot and stick' system of progression and downgrading to incentivise good behaviour was, and should, remain paramount within the imprisonment regime (ibid.:16). The tactics of using a civilising violence against prisoners needed to be reinforced if control was to be reinstated.

Rather than seeing these incidents as a blunt statement of the failing of segregation arrangements to deter prison disorder, instead they were understood only as exposing their lack of capacity. Segregation needed to be intensified and expanded. Within the Prison Division it was believed the incidents 'served to highlight the need to tackle the question of facilities for difficult prisoners' (HH57/2070). This marked a period of extreme security consciousness, an obsession with the dangerous prisoner and reactive prison policy. In 1986 the Chief Inspector of Prisons (*Annual Report 1986*:17) suggested that governors in Scotland required a greater array of options 'for the removal of disruptive prisoners at short notice', which would allow them to concentrate on maintaining the stability of the mainstream prison system. Following the first major incident at Peterhead in 1984, the 18 cells in B Hall at Peterhead were sealed-off, these cells were fortified and the whole section transformed into a segregation lockdown facility (Scottish Prison Service 1988a: appendix 6; *HMCIP Peterhead Report 1985*). The Prison Division continued to tighten perimeter security at a number of Scottish prisons (*HMCIP Annual Report 1986*:14), while new 'punishment blocks' and security systems were provided at Greenock, Barlinnie, Aberdeen and Shotts (*Annual Report 1985*:14). There were already 78 special handling places for disruptive prisoners at Aberdeen, BSU, Inverness and Peterhead.[i] Shotts E Hall was added to this inventory in 1987, but its function was slightly different to the existing units. The Shotts Unit was a new progression point where prisoners leaving conditions of limited association at Peterhead could be assessed before being returned to the mainstream. It was also a 'time-out' site for those prisoners who may not necessitate complete segregation but who required downgrading out of the mainstream (Scottish Prison Service 1988a: para.9.13). Another six-cell national unit opened at Perth prison, designed to segregate prisoners from any of the long-term prisons. A further alternative unit that could hold 12 disruptive prisoners and an 18-cell segregation lockdown facility were opened (*HMCIP Peterhead Report* 1985:5; *HMCIP 1988*:iii; Scottish Prison Service 1988a, 1990b; Adler and Longhurst 1994).

A new military style of control was developed in response to prison disturbances. In trying to be proactive and plan for the future security of the prison system, the Division developed two mobile military teams: Alpha and Beta. These were run by senior governors and would be, according to Alistair, 'dispatched around the country' in response to major incidents. Ken described this response as an extreme but necessary firewall: 'We were very much trained in the dark arts of handling major incidents. The three major incidents led us to set up incident command teams...So that was our insurance policy solution.'New practices of observation were also implemented. The Division reviewed how they assessed long-termers, and a revised system of increased monitoring was introduced for prisoners serving five years or more. These very long-term prisoners were now subject to an individual annual report until they were eligible for release or parole (*HMCIP Annual Report 1986*:iii)

Finally, with matters of security and control being addressed, the need for space now required renewed efforts. To expand the adult imprisonment regime, a number of young offender institutions and detention centres were converted into adult male prisons in 1986 and 1987. These included Greenock (for adult males serving three years or more), where capacity had been increased from 180 to 231 with the use of doubling-up; Glenochil came on-line as a long-termers' prison; and Friarton (just under 100 prisoners) was for adults serving 9 months or less.

The period 1985–1988 was one of significant expansion and modification of the imprisonment regime's most severe practices, and reflected the belief that Scottish prison violence was now an 'epidemic' (Cooke 1989b). Senior management within the Division then decided to make a 'high risk' systemic alteration to adult imprisonment regimes. The entire prison estate was to be reorganised under an operation called Grand Design. This was their 'game plan' to reclassify five prisons which would, they hoped, 'meet the accommodation need of the Scottish Prison Service for at least the next three years and perhaps even into the early 1990s' (HH57/2070). Dumfries and Greenock, the latter of which had only just been reclassified as an adult prison, were converted into young offender institutions (*Annual Report 1988*), and an open prison, Noranside, was established in 1987 (HH57/2070). During this time the delayed Phase II of Shotts prison was finally completed after a long gestation. This increased Shotts's capacity from 60 to 528 prisoners.

These organisational actions were both reactionary and tactical. The Division was trying to ameliorate the problems faced by the prison system, and they were trying to safeguard the future from further chaos within the Scottish imprisonment.

Refining care and control

What people described from this time was a profound sense of fragility. They felt that the whole order of their work and the system had become severely weakened. As Alistair said with such frankness: 'We really thought we were going to lose the prison service.' The Division needed to find a new means to reassert its control and authority. At the end of the 1980s a more proactive approach to prison administration emerged. In 1988, two policy documents gave formal footing to the bifurcated view of prison's role as somewhere of last resort for the most vulnerable and a place of exclusion and control for Scotland's most dangerous criminals: *Assessment and Control – The Management of Violent and Disruptive Prisoners* (1988a) and *Custody and Care – Policy and Plans for the Scottish Prison Service* (1988b). The Division had rarely published detailed policy reports. Now these documents exhibited signs of a new governmental leadership for Scottish prisons.

Assessment and Control addressed itself towards 'the specific issue of inmates who present violent and disruptive behaviour' (para.1.5). In doing so, it reaffirmed the traditional view of the inevitable subculture of dangerous, incorrigible and wilfully subversive prisoners. The diagnosis of the problem at this time remained coherent within the established political culture. It was asserted that, in 'the experience of the Prison Department', the nature of the violent, gang-related, disordered, anti-authority long-termer led to these incidents (1988a para 2.13). In this view, the problem remained the behavioural patterns of individual prisoners and that:

> rather than looking to changes in the way in which the Prison Service as a whole goes about its task, a more productive approach may be to concentrate attention on the individual personality and 'repertoire' of particular disruptive and violent inmates.
>
> (1988a para 2.11)

The logic which followed stated that with greater numbers of long-term and very long-term prisoners there was naturally a greater volume of violent incidents. Moreover, the capacity of segregation units was now insufficient to address the problems posed by Scottish prisoners. It was assessed that previous practices of security and control were no longer adequate (1988b para 1.2). Emboldened by the expansion of segregation, the Prison Division said they needed to think bigger and more ambitiously, planning a 'new generation' of maximum-security units for the end of the 1980s. This would include a 60-person unit to be built 'as quickly as possible', given the 'Department's anxiety to make progress' (1988a para. 8.3–8.8).

But *Assessment and Control* also posed the possibility of softer control techniques, such as assessment tools for 'control profiling' risky prisoners (1988a para.3.5). As seen in Chapter 6, the Division had favoured a more physical rather than psychological form of security intervention (in the form of segregation and medical treatment): their 'policy of minimum intervention in the lives of prisoners' (para.4.8). Rather than merely continuing to react to incidents, now the Division suggested prevention must also be a policy objective (para.4.9.2). The document outlined that prisoners should be seen as 'responsible' and thus 'accountable' for their actions (para.4.9.1), and the system should develop means of ongoing interventions, such as 'control risk profiles'.

Custody and Care took a wider view of the mainstream regime, providing an outline of the central objectives of the Prison Service: (1) 'security', defined as containment and the prevention of escapes; (2) 'control', achieved through disciplinary measures and (3) and maintaining 'quality of life'. Like *Assessment and Control*, *Custody and Care* largely reasserted existing principles and practices rather than establishing new ones. For example, the more positive dimension of quality of life meant access to 'basic services', such as medical attention, along with 'opportunities for work and other activities' (1988b para.2.9), which, as shown in Chapter 6, were basic tenets of the existing Scottish prison practices. *Custody and Care* did, however, extend the idea of care, and pressed for more institutional responsibility towards prisoners. Ideas of intervention were proposed in this document: 'routines and discipline' should seek to 'stimulate a positive contribution and response from inmates' (para.2.9). Staff, it was argued, should provide more support to prisoners to help them build better prison-based relationships, and prison regimes should encourage prisoners to turn away from crime (ibid. para.2.11).

The plans forwarded in *Custody and Care* aimed at improving the progression process, and a new mechanism of surveillance and control was suggested: 'sentence planning'. This was described as a more 'dynamic process of assessment, [and] review' for long-termers. A file would be kept in which a prisoner's response to prison, the rules and his sentence would be consistently recorded. These files would serve as early warning systems for prisoners 'who cannot or will not come to terms with their sentences', alerting staff to those who would require 'intensive assessment' outside the mainstream (Scottish Prison Service 1988b para.9.7–9.9). The reports would become like a surveillance diary, a subtle new technique which aimed to reinforce control and prevent future disorder.

These policy documents, released within the same short period, exhibited a marked comparative contrast in their substantive focus, revealing the distinct operational logic and penal sensibilities underpinning Scottish imprisonment regimes. *Custody and Care* explicitly did not address Peterhead (para.7.14) or the segregation units, but did cover the rest of the system, namely progression and the provision of care. It was interested in the routine patterns for the mainstream, but also the 'carrot' of persuasion through progression. *Assessment and Control*, however, addressed the 'stick' element of coercive imprisonment tactics. These documents were a material demonstration of the cultural delineation between *the mainstream* (the willing and coopera-tive prisoners) and the *outgroup* (the non-compliant prisoners), a dichotomy which the Division sought to reinforce in the face of their prison crises.

The problems confronted by the prison system from 1985 were substantial, yet the common sense thinking and affective criteria that inflected decisions regarding the uses of imprisonment had not altered, but were magnified. The riots and protests were felt to be the result of bad prisoners – the hard core, the Premier League prisoners, antisocial and filled with hatred. Those prison-ers must be removed from circulation or potentially subject to preventative policy such as personal assessment, profiling and observation as a means to reduce the risk of future prison disturbances. And in the worst-case scenario, the Division could also employ their own military response. In 1987, the Secretary of State for Scotland, Malcolm Rifkind, issued a statement which reinforced the balance of sympathies which ordered the prison system:

> Prison regimes by their very nature will never be ideal for those who have grievously offended against society. It is my view that we have had, in recent times, too great a concentration of attention upon the criminal element. The lawbreaker does not have the sympathy of the population at large. Their support lies with the forces of law and order, and while the Scottish prison system is passing through a particularly trying period our support for them is not in doubt and never will be.
>
> (quoted in Kinsey 1988:116)

There was now a strong signal being communicated to the public and the prisons alike. The prisons had been stabilised.

Legitimacy crisis

For years, the Division had been seeking a return to an equilibrium within prison through a reactionary phase and now a demonstration of proactive thinking via the new policy documents. Despite these best efforts, and even with the Secretary of State's support, the legitimacy which had underpinned those actions had been seriously and irreparably eroded as the prisoners had become ever more irreconcilable to their imprisonment. An atmosphere of hostility and anxiety lingered. The Division's attempts to subdue and con-trol the prison system had not quelled the frustrated internal administrative struggles that had developed at this time. There were demands for greater introspection, reflection and fundamental change. Across the period of dis-ruptions, key actors within the prison service had begun to critically probe the logic of the imprisonment regimes, suggest new ways to engage with prisoners, advocate for a distinctly Scottish approach to imprisonment or aver against certain regulations (such as the recently formed Association of Scottish Prison Governors; see, e.g., Bruce 1982; Spencer 1983; Withers 1984–1985; Walker 1987). They began to be perturbed by the use of excessive force which underpinned, but failed to control, the Scottish prison system. There was a growing concern about the adverse impact of the rigid security classifications, the crude use of 'downgrading', the lack of policy initiative from the Division and the idea of disciplinary training (HH57/1622; HH57/1794). The Chief Inspector now criticised the arbitrary use of progression and the systems for long-termers as 'inadequate' (*HMCIP Annual Report 1986*:5). The Chief Inspector also noted what he described as a clear 'degenerating trend' among a number of prisoners subjected to segregation and exclusion. He stated that it had become 'less clear how to discourage irresponsibility and past experience is not encouraging. The usual way of dealing with anti-authority behaviour is to impose tighter control', and while 'Some prisoners respond, other [sic] merely become more bitter, anti-authority and dangerous' (ibid.:16). Despite the expanded use of prison's civilising violence, Scottish prisoners had continued to breach the rules and disrupt the order of the prison with intensifying frequency. Perhaps the problem was not just with the prisoners, but with the imprisonment regime itself.

For the most part, Scottish prisons had not been exposed to intense public or political intervention or criticism from the period after 1970. Rather, the Special Unit had initially drawn public intrigue and was praised in the media. Given the highly publicised events of the mid-1980s, however, the Division began to draw public opprobrium for their reactive responses to prison disorder. The Scottish Prison Officers Association, along with the Scottish Council for Civil Liberties, wrote to the Scotsman newspaper to critique the ineptitudes of Prison Division in the face of the current crises of violence and overcrowding. An independent review published a report criticising the abuses at Peterhead and the official responses to the disorder (Gateway Exchange 1987). Critical aspects of an internal and unpublished report were leaked to the press. These blamed the current prison problems on a lack of accountability from the Division and highlighted an unfair system which provided little reward for a prisoners' personal obedience and efforts (Kinsey 1988:108).

In addition to these admonishments, there was a new strain of uncertainty within the administration, as they felt they could no longer secure the basic objectives of control and containment. Interviewees told moving stories of senior managers 'breaking down' in tears in public or on television broadcasts, or not returning to work after taking leave. William described it as a resounding sense of fragility: 'The prison service breaks down, it can no longer manage...[The Division] lost the plot.' The trauma, the sense of crisis and chaos was felt to have taken an understandable toll upon those in charge. Derek referred to the departures of senior Division civil servants as 'casualties': 'At the time of the troubles...[there were] casualties among governors and managers, who were suddenly away.' These were visceral tales of a government department which had 'exhausted' its well of authority and unsettled the consensus about how best to control prisons and prisoners, and now found itself in a new form of internal crisis. Senior officials in charge of prison left their posts, leaving Scottish prisons in a transient state.

The Division was challenged on two fronts, within the prisons and within the Division itself, by a 'crisis of *delegitmation*', which Sparks defines as the 'withdrawal of consent' (SPS 1996:15, original emphasis). There were suggestions of unfairness against prisoners, and ongoing incidents and public identification of the Division's weakening authority. Each of these waves of rebuke served to undermine the dominance of paternalistic liberalism and the appropriateness of disciplinary and exclusionary imprisonment. Some absence of legitimacy inside the prison had always been accepted, evident in the existence of the downgrading and segregation so characteristic of Scottish imprisonment regimes. As crisis and prisoner dissensus was no longer an exclusively (and mainly private) Peterhead problem, but a Scottish prison problem, the intractability of the prisoners now became seen by some as a consequence of Scottish penal authority.

As a result of this crisis within prisons, by the end of the 1980s the hegemony of Scottish political culture, which had characterised the approach to prison management in the 1970s and 1980s, unravelled – and a 'crisis of authority' emerged (Hall et al. [1978] 2013). The riots and disturbances had become prolonged and distressing; public and internal critique continued. Consequently, the bounds of Scottish political culture, such as what uses of prison and penal power were deemed possible and legitimate, began to be fundamentally rethought.

A climate of fear gave rise to an exceptionally draconian period in Scottish penal history, wherein brutality, rebellion and violence were recurrent. In response to the perceived size and intractability of the problems faced, the penal state adopted a reactive strategy of increased segregation and prison expansion. The cumulative effect of this strategy was to render Scottish prisons more punitive in the 1980s. In chronicling this history, I have sought to empirically identify how the actions and decisions of actors within the Division gave rise to these punitive adaptions within the imprisonment regime. The meanings which actors attached to those decisions were consistent with established penal sensibilities, social narratives and political rationalities, reflecting the sentiments and outlook of the pre-existing paternalistic liberalism. Scotland's imprisonment regimes remained deeply embedded in the logic of the dismissive society.

Note

i This official figure only includes the specific segregation and exclusion spaces within Peterhead; it does not include the almost 130 people at Peterhead deemed too dangerous and thus sent to Peterhead because they were being excluded from the mainstream.

8   Civilising Scottish imprisonment

Given the avid commitment to punitive prison techniques displayed in response to the riots, it makes Scotland's subsequent, and swift, progressive penal transformation from 1990 all the more startling. This chapter traces this dramatic and impressive metamorphosis from the inside. What fresh ambitions motivated these changes? What new visions of the prison enlightened this novel penal outlook? These changes will then be situated within the wider social and political context as a means to explain this striking penal transformation, showing the influence of the otherwise opposing movements of Scottish nationalism and Conservative neoliberalism.

By avoiding the reductive and limited binary depictions of punitive/progressive and lenient/severe penal transformation, this chapter probes the deeper meanings and intentions motivating these changes. The chapter provides a critical analysis, outlining the difference between *civilising* and *humanitarian* penal transformation. Humane prison practices are radical, seeking to reduce the use of the prison and penal control given the inevitable personal and social problems they cause. Alternatively, the civilised prison is one that appears progressive but is far less radical in its aims. Civilised penal practices use evidence-based expertise to refine the aesthetic of penal control, protecting the prison from the prisoners' dissent and instilling prison administration with greater power and resilience such that, when imprisoned people experience tragedy, it is seen as a blip that has occurred *in spite* of the prison, rather than *because of* the prison. The civilised prison revises the pains of imprisonment, such that they become deniable, and therefore successfully inures itself from blunt-force critiques levelled at overtly punitive institutions that are overcrowded, with poor physical conditions and degrading treatment.

Progressive penal transformation

Reassessment

The Division was now embroiled in a period of introspection, still reeling from the tumult of the last several years. At times of crisis, as Hay has written, 'disparities between previously unquestioned cognitive frameworks and the 'realities' they purport to represent are starkly revealed' (Hay 2002:214). As such, it is at moments like these that transformation can take place.

During 1988–1989 the Director of the Prison Division stood down and 'a group of young Turks took over' (Derek). The new Director stated that 'New approaches and new ideas are needed to avoid further disruption' (McKinlay 1989:4). Now, in a volte-face, the failings of the regime were described as the overt violence of Scottish imprisonment – evaluations which had previously been reserved for the prisoner. The Prison Division became embarrassed about the physical excesses of incarceration. As Ken mournfully reminisced:

> Our response was a very hierarchical, forceful, coercive response. We were out there knocking the hell out of prisoners … It was a very violent time. The response was violence by the authorities back, and we locked down and we locked up. And we damaged a lot of people, a lot of prisoners.

William described prisons as 'pretty nasty places…we were treating them as animals'; Douglas recalled that it appeared to him that 'Prisons used to systematically brutalise people'.

It was further suggested that Scotland's prison administration was responsible for the disorder. It was argued that management's punitive and uncultivated ideas about imprisonment had proliferated the disturbances. Reflecting this, William described Scotland's prison policy of security and segregation as illogical and needing to be repudiated:

> It came from the common sense: we have 50 bad apples, or 200 bad apples in the barrel, let's take them out, but let's do something for the rest but let's get these guys out…[It] was about 'let's get a cage somewhere and let's forget about them'…[new senior management were] able to say [this] was shite.

Douglas also wanted to invalidate the Prison Division, describing it as a 'semi-performing' Department that hadn't been able to function when the riots persisted. Similarly, Adam described how the prison administration suffered from a powerlessness that he defined as 'learned helplessness'.

The problems with imprisonment were now firmly identified as problems with (1) management; and (2) the dehumanising penal philosophy that shaped the treatment of prisoners. New management was intent on transforming the Division and, in so doing, more effectively taming the disorder in Scottish prisons. Having made these diagnoses, the new management, acting with all the zeal of reformers, felt they could radically alter the foundation principles of imprisonment: 'ideas on the organisation of prisons are under challenge from the new perspectives' (HH57/2071), and, they wrote, the 'fundamental philosophical concerns' of incarceration were now subject to a 'programme of change' (Wozniak and McAllister 1992:10).

The Scottish prison service

Scottish prison administration underwent a transformation, becoming SPS (Scottish Prison Service) at the beginning of the 1990s. The creation of SPS marks the beginning of a fervent period of bureaucratic expansion, policy production and reinvention. The deliberate reconfiguration of the 'culture' of Scottish prison governance was to be made literally and physically evident (Frizzell 1993). For example, the reception at SPS headquarters was to be redesigned on the instructions that it 'portray a positive image of a forward-thinking service' (HH57/1897). In becoming SPS they acquired a logo (a unified symbol that the previous prison administration never had) that adorned their documents, their letterhead, their staff IDs, etc., demonstrating and consolidating their new managerial unity. SPS for the first time set out a mission statement in which the concerns of custody, order, care and opportunities were precisely stated. These developments allowed SPS to produce new referents by 'which to define itself and advance its claims' (Geertz 1983:143) as a professional and cohesive organisation, no longer a mere administrative set of offices.

Scholars have identified a trend in England and Wales whereby imprisonment was inflected with a new austerity in the 1990s. Stripped of their reformative aims, prison policies were no longer the preserve of insulated researchers and civil servants. These experts were displaced from the policy-making process, which was increasingly beholden to popular sentiment and punitive politics (Cavadino and Dignan 2006:230; Loader 2006). Contrastingly, in Scotland, a space for evidence-based policy was created, and at the beginning of the 1990s a new SPS research unit was established (*Annual Report 1991-1992*), where they hired and also commissioned work from criminologists to establish 'what works'. These experts were highly regarded, and their new conceptual frameworks led the way in Scotland's penal transformation. There was now an avalanche of academic publications from SPS: a series of extensive research reports, bulletins, policy documents, business plans and strategic reviews. SPS was motivated by a desire to evaluate effective interventions, refine prison policy and improve prisoner intervention,[i] an approach that seemed totally unknown to the previously reactive administration. Policy documents provided SPS for the first time with evidence to make decisions, helping it establish a strikingly reformist penal identity. As William described it:

> We transformed the quality of what was brought to the board, just transformed. Two pages became 22 pages. Things had references to academic work, footnotes – that was never ever part of that agenda before.

As William indicates, these publications also *looked* different: adorned with the new SPS logo, they were sleek and glossy A4 documents. They began to include pictures of smiling visiting families, new facilities and prisoners involved in uplifting activities. These allowed SPS to raise the standard of the previous archetypical prison administration, the way it looked, the form it took and the outlook it communicated. This in turn allowed '[new] ideas to get supremacy' (William). As such, these documents were a tool of penal transformation; setting the foundations of a new professional and authoritative prison management, these documents sent visible signals that SPS was an 'enlightened' (Douglas) and 'thinking organisation' (Alistair).

Scottish penal transformation was in direct response to the destabilisation caused by the continuous disturbances, but the character of these changes was partially the result of wider political shifts occurring in British politics. In tandem with changes in Scottish penal values, the whole rationality of government had been evolving. Throughout the 1980s, Margaret Thatcher's Conservative government, armed with a newly dominant doctrine of free market economics, launched an assault on the social democratic developments of Britain's post-war settlement. Under Thatcher, the ideology of Westminster politics shifted to the right. These changes entailed alterations to the normative vision of the citizen. Social structures were dismissed as a determinative force. Instead, citizens were to be understood as autonomous agents fully responsible for their own well-being and circumstances. In its policies and discourse the UK government began to advocate and encourage citizens to be entrepreneurs of their own fortune (O'Malley 1992; Garland 1997; Rose and Miller 2010). In wanting to foster this kind of neoliberal citizenship, ministers sought to minimise citizens' dependency on government by reducing social provision in education and health, and curtailing the abuse (as they saw it) of welfare benefits (Gamble 1994). Government itself was to be shaped by a 'business-type managerialism' (Rhodes 1994:144). The civil service should follow the corporate doctrines of performance measurement, efficiency, greater accountability and consumer responsiveness. In addition, government agencies should be decentralised, becoming independent in order to reduce costs (Hood 1991:4–5). The ascendance of this outlook was to have a major impact on SPS's specific aims and managerial organisation as they confronted the problems of Scottish prison disorder.

What came to distinguish SPS's organisational DNA from that of the Division was that it adopted exactly this kind of corporate identity (SPS 1990c). In 1990 the annual report changed so that it corresponded with the financial year instead of the calendar year. In this period SPS published a *Business Plan* (1989) – an extensive organisational review conducted by a private consultancy firm. They then produced *Organising for Excellence* (1990a), which illustrated how to improve accountability and establish a strategic management style. SPS pursued the opportunity to become an independent agency (ibid.), which they achieved in 1993 (SPS 1993). As Douglas – who was directly involved in this bureaucratic conversion – defined it, becoming an agency 'empowered headquarters... it gave [SPS] the freedom and trust that we needed'. However, during the 1970s and '80s the Division had been largely free of the downward pressure from central government at Westminster and the leadership of St Andrew's House. Freedom and trust can be more accurately interpreted as increased penal power. Adam described the reinvention as one which moved prisons away from administrative bureau-cracy and towards a more powerful corporate system: SPS became 'a man-aged place rather than an administered place, you can't do any of these things [reforms] without a grip on the business'. As a corporate-style organisation SPS had more power and was able to create a 'coherent line management structure with clear accountability for the overall direction and control of prison operations' (SPS 1990a:i). As Douglas defined it, they were no longer merely administering prisons. Becoming an agency 'empowered headquar-ters…That was when we made the most of our progress.' The SPS structure was now warranted to 'endorse the new philosophies' envisioned for Scottish imprisonment (*Annual Report 1991–1992*:ix).

The reformed Scottish prison and the responsible prisoner

SPS was in a process of producing and reifying their organisational moti-vations in their managerial paraphernalia, but it also recalibrated the penal philosophy underpinning imprisonment, reflecting the entrepreneurial nor-mative vision of citizenship that was now in the ascendance in UK politics. During this period SPS produced their most seminal document, *Opportunity and Responsibility* (1990b). While the practical focus of the document was trained upon the long-term prisoner, *Opportunity and Responsibility* reads as a manifesto, re-articulating the aims of imprisonment.

Central to *Opportunity and Responsibility* was a new view of a prisoner's rational subjectivity, one that became the bedrock of Scottish prison pol-icy. It asserted that Scottish imprisonment had 'concentrated excessively on individual pathology'. This was now seen as defunct. To align the prisons with its campaign for a new organisational culture and penal philosophy, SPS set about transforming imprisonment regimes into a single efficient and business-like system. While disciplinary and exclusionary penal culture had shaped a system that relied heavily upon the logic of segregation and exile, SPS inverted that thinking. Their new general objective for Scottish imprisonment regimes was 'mainstreaming'. No longer would attention be directed towards the expansion and oversight of segregation; instead, it was retrained upon the mainstream system, supported by new techniques of pris-oner intervention, responsibilisation and pacification.

As described by the Chief Executive of the SPS, the prisoner was neither 'sick' nor 'an inferior kind of person who is unable to exercise decision mak-ing' (Frizzell 1993:206). The new ethos accepted that prisoners possessed at least a degree of rationality and credited them with the potential for self-con-trol and responsibility: 'we believe that the prisoner is a person who is respon-sible for his actions and who should be encouraged to act responsibly, then it follows that we must believe that he is a responsible person' (HH57/2112). However, 'It is not sufficient to say: "Be responsible", responsibility must be learned in a context' (SPS 1995a:14). They could no longer just do things to prisoners. They envisioned a system of 'mutual responsibilities' between the regime and the person confined (ibid.:18). But this would place new demands on the prisoner. As the new Director of Prisons stated, 'prisoners claimed their rights. Many [in senior management] feel they did so without living up to their responsibilities' (ibid.). Control would be better achieved through 'facilitative change', by giving prisoners 'opportunities' to develop and display their responsible character, rather than using a 'coerced cure' that had relied on intrusive punishments, such as segregation (1990b:17). Now, 'the whole thrust of SPS policy was to encourage prisoners themselves to adopt a more responsible approach' (Minutes of the Scottish Prison Service Extraordinary Board Meeting, 21 June, 1995). Training prisoners to be responsible had been a marginal practice in the 1970s and into the 1980s. By 1990 it was the dominant concern of Scottish imprisonment.

The twinned ideas of opportunity and responsibility permitted a much more internal and psychological form of prisoner control. SPS implemented interventions such as cognitive behaviour groupwork and disruptive prisoner programmes, seeking to make prisoners compliant through a personal evaluation of their criminality and acts of prison disorder (SPS 1998:10; *Annual Report 1994–1995*). The imprisonment regimes evolved to include new techniques of intensive micro-management, as Personal Development Files and Sentence Management were introduced for long-term prisoners in 1992. These dossiers would enable prisoners 'to address personal development issues and problems' (SPS 1998:9). All prisoners sentenced to two years or more could also take part in the Sentence Planning and Personal Officer Scheme (*Annual Report 1991–1992*), whereby prisoners were appointed a personal prison officer with whom they would agree the best way for them to make the most of their time in prison (Coyle 1992). Existing prison programmes, such as education and work, were rhetorically repackaged; these too would 'give prisoners the opportunity to address their offending behaviour and to assist and encourage them to make constructive use of the available facilities' (SPS 1998:10). These techniques promised the Scottish prisoner that he could now be 'master of his own destiny', according to a former governor (Coyle 1992:6). It was not simply that the Scottish prisoner became responsible because people expressed that belief, but rather that these new rationalities materialised in the altered shape of the imprisonment regimes which sought to 'encourage' prisoners into the kind of 'responsible citizens' they desired (SPS 1994:26). In Scotland during the early 1990s, the responsible prisoner was both 'imagined and moulded' (O'Malley 2010:14).

SPS also attempted an additional rhetorical repositioning of the prisoner: labelling them as 'customers'. SPS was spreading this new mantra through workshops at which staff were 'learning a business approach to forward planning, focusing on quality of life service and customer needs' (HH57/2071). At senior management meetings they began to refer to prisoners as 'customers', 'SPS customers' and 'prisoner customers' (ibid.; HH57/1897). With this in mind SPS developed the Prisoner Survey, described as 'a major market research study' of prisoners' views (Wozniak and McAllister 1992:10). The survey was extensive and directed SPS's efforts towards the process of *mainstreaming* – namely, improving the mainstream prison system to reduce disturbances and the need for segregation. In response to the findings of the survey, SPS set about improving the quality of life for prisoners in the mainstream prisons. Visiting facilities were upgraded; information booklets for prisoners and prison visitors were produced; food was improved (*HMCIP Report 1993–1994*); and a new grievance procedure was introduced in 1994 when an Independent Complaints Adjudicator was appointed.

Mainstreaming was intended to minimise the need for special handling units. SPS also shifted the use of classification terminology for long-term prisoners. First, at a stroke, SPS reduced the number of long-term prisoners by increasing the threshold for long-term imprisonment from 18 months to two years, and then to four years. SPS had decreased the problem prisoner category by making it more difficult to qualify for that classification. In 1993, the Standing Committee on Difficult Prisoners was replaced with a lay membership and given the banal and unprovocative new title of Advisory Committee on Prisoner Management (*Annual Report 1993–1994*:42). Similarly, while the existing segregation units remained, they were rebranded with the more civilised terminology of 'small units' (SPS 1990b, chapters 8–9) which would provide opportunities for facilitated change by addressing prisoners' anger issues, 'criminal attitudes, values and beliefs' (SPS 1994:42). Rather than relying solely on spatial and temporal control, small units would also help normalise the prisoner – not for society at large, but for the mainstream prison system. Segregation was now a site for more proactive intervention with the dangerous and disordered prisoner. Within this same normalisation endeavour, a National Induction Centre for newly convicted long-term prisoners was opened. This was an independent unit for up to 52 prisoners at Shotts, where prisoners serving a sentence of ten years or more were sent after sentencing (excluding sex offenders). There, prisoners underwent a 2–3 week induction programme. This provided 'a supportive regime for prisoners' at the beginning of their sentence to help them adjust to the mainstream prison system, and decisions were made regarding a prisoner's security category (SPS 1998:10). It was hoped that this would reduce long-termers' hostility towards the system; according to Douglas, 'The induction unit at Shotts [aim was] to get more long-term prisoner inducted into the system in a way that would hopefully make them less likely to be disruptive.'

Finally, to reinforce a coherent mainstream prison system, SPS set about transforming imprisonment regimes into a single efficient and business-like system. The annual reports no longer provided summaries of health, personality disorders, hygiene, discipline, activities, etc., but set an agenda for each prison which was assessed one prison at a time. The annual reports now had the character of a report card, organised around performance measures, targets and strategic objectives for facilities, conditions and security as each prison was to be aligned with the Service's business outlook.

Bolstering the mainstream like this, however, put the Barlinnie Special Unit in a precarious position. The BSU had always been outside the mainstream system, and had been lambasted for perverting the progression system as it was often perceived as a reward for bad behaviour. Now it was criticised for undermining the mainstream system and harbouring prisoners who were opposed to SPS's positive interventions (SPS 1994:40–41). As Douglas put it, '[the BSU] was also sending strange messages to the system, we were giving confused messages in those days, it was rewarding violence'. The Unit became emblematic of a prison system that had fallen into disarray because of incongruity between regimes (ibid.:41); it was now an anathema to the governing ideas of systemic consistency and mainstream efficiency. In the era of mainstreaming, the BSU was seen as a relic, as having become 'mummified' – an historical oddity in the new modern organisational field of imprisonment. William, recalling this time, characterised the BSU as being 'completely beyond its sell by date'. Alistair felt similarly, saying that 'the Barlinnie Unit had outlived its time'. By the 1990s the BSU, once considered Scotland's great prison experiment (Sparks 2002), was a prison out of time, in both senses of the term.

More than the ostensible logical opposition to the Unit, it inspired feelings of contempt. These hostilities resonated with the undercurrent of rancour that had persisted since the Unit was established, which were now openly embraced by those who appeared to be on the side of positive penal change. Douglas reflected the distaste for the Unit when he described it as 'rotten to the core'. Interviewees, who would otherwise be considered among the leading reformers of this era, were openly disdainful when describing the prisoners at the Unit, who they saw as a ragtag bunch of misfits. They were repulsed by the in-cell visitations, which, as went the widely held secret, had permitted conjugal visits at the Unit. Hinting at this, Douglas said they 'discovered things that were going on that were making it insupportable. To be honest, it was outrageous.' William was explicit about this: '[The BSU was] completely rotten to the core…Hookers come in and shagging…they bought quiet, they bought the lack of violence, conjugal visits. The cells had couches!' SPS's progressive programme of mainstreaming made BSU's position as a penal outlier untenable, as encapsulated by Douglas's account: 'we felt we were improving the whole system. The arguments for it [the BSU] were becoming less and less.'

SPS commissioned a report on small units (Bottomley et al. 1994) from people they believed they could 'trust' (William). However, that report was largely positive about the character and routine of the Special Unit. This was absolutely not what the Division wanted to hear, according to William, and the report was left unpublished for some time (Sparks 2002). Within SPS, marginalia notes on a copy of the external review were vitriolic. Admiration for the Unit was chastised. As far as they were concerned, such positives actually reduced morale for mainstream prisoners As it concluded, '[w]hat about the system?' Their desire for a coherent, orderly modern prison with compliant and consenting prisoners not only made SPS immune to the Unit's positive claims, it also predisposed them to reject a future imprisonment regime that had a Special Unit of this nature in it. The report was alighted upon as the evidence that could garner support for closing the Unit. Prisoners' largely self-directed life was offensive to senior managers' modernising sensibilities, who described this as 'Evidence for need to remove'. The external review was open about the fact that in-cell visits allowed for privacy, which could include sex (Sparks 2002). The small section that confirmed this known secret of life within the BSU was leaked to the press, sensationalising what had been the vaunted public image of the Unit (ibid.). While certainly not what the authors of the external review would have intended, for SPS the report still managed to serve the function of garnering political support to close the Special Unit.

Shortly thereafter, another working group on small units, this one internal, was established. Its criticisms were decisive and unambiguous (SPS 1994). Prisoners at the Unit did not want their regime to be brought into line with the new mainstream. It was felt that '[t]he prevalence of such attitudes makes it impossible to reinvigorate the BSU's regime' (1994:41). It would seem that the routine of autonomy and responsibility that had characterised the BSU would be consistent with SPS's new rational regime of opportunity and responsibility. However, the Special Unit came to be seen as a potential threat to the authority and practices of the newly homogenised mainstream system. Prisoners were to be offered autonomy, but no prison could be autonomous from the mainstream. The BSU was not improved, reclaimed or realigned. It was, as Sparks has written, 'a standing admonition of the very system that the reformers believed they had superseded' (2002:576). In 1994 Scotland's acclaimed and humane carceral experiment was disbanded and the prisoners distributed across the mainstream system.

During this time SPS did not build new prisons; instead, they modernised and ameliorated some of the harsher and objectifying aspects of Scottish prison life. SPS sought to increase the legitimacy of the system among prisoners and de-dramatise prison policy. Yet many of the developments in Scottish prison policy and prison administration were not so different to those occurring in England and Wales (though England did not close its own therapeutic special units), where responsibilisation and managerialism were also being ushered in. However, in England a punitive political rhetoric emerged to envelope public discussions of prison policies (Sparks et al. 1996; Garland 2001; Liebling assisted by Arnold 2004). In Scotland, these same policy changes were perceived to display the Scottish commitment to an enlightened and egalitarian approach to penality (McAra 1999). How come, in contrast to England and Wales, Scottish prison policy and administration were seen as abandoning overt punitiveness and embracing progressiveness? What cultural forces and social occurrences were transpiring in Scotland that were not present in the rest of Britain? That similar prison and administrative practices signalled very different penal identities in Britain at this time means that Scottish penal transformation is not best categorised as either a neatly choreographed case of neoliberalism or progressive penality the same as any other – such sharp distinctions prevent us from seeing the complex forces that gave Scottish penal culture its character. It is only by developing a fully contextualised history that we can understand the different meanings actors gave their actions when devising and justifying their prison policies.

Nationalism and fear in Scottish prison administration

Managerialist ideas were not thoughtlessly replicated by SPS nor imposed by Westminster; rather, they were actively and eagerly deployed by SPS managers. What makes SPS's fulsome embrace and pursuit of managerialism all the more intriguing is that the Thatcherite brand of liberalism was highly contentious in Scotland. During the Conservative government's reign from 1979 until 1997, the majority of Scots voted for Labour MPs. This did not necessarily represent a democratic deficit in the UK, as under their political system the party with the greatest number of seats across the UK wins the mandate to govern. However, within Scotland it was felt that they were being ruled without democratic consent. Constitutional difficulties and cultural divisions emerged in the 1980s as the Conservatives pursued neoliberal policies that were felt to be particularly harsh on Scotland, such as the poll tax; curtailing social provision; introducing privatisation into healthcare, electricity and transport; and re-ordering education and local government funding. Scotland's higher reliance on public provision, extensive social housing, higher unemployment rates and having some of Britain's most deprived areas meant that Scotland 'had much to lose' from Thatcher's economic policies (Stewart 2009:120). Accusations followed from leading Tories that England was subsidising a dependent Scotland, which now needed to develop a culture of enterprise (Mitchell and Bennie 1995:94).

Scotland gained a devolved parliament in 1998, the popular momentum for which developed from the middle of the 1980s as Scottish public dissent against Thatcher and the Tories grew. By the 1970s Scotland bore 'cultural scars' (Perchard 2013) from the loss of industry. As a result, during that period a 'resurgent' and 'powerful national narrative' emerged (ibid.:78). Scotland's local government, civil society and media engaged in a protracted resistance against the commodification of public services, the responsibilisation of citizens and the destruction of the Scottish welfare state (Holliday 1992; Stewart 2009). Consequently, the policies pursued by Westminster alienated Scottish voters, provoking the proliferation of Scottish 'civic nationalism' (Perchard 2013:n14),[ii] and fuelling demands for Home Rule (Stewart 2009:139). Scotland, rather than Britain, was 'construed as the unit of political and economic management' (McCrone 2006). The view that Scotland should free itself from 'internal colonialism' (Perchard 2013:86) became influential. By the end of the 1980s, Scotland had become a 'restless nation' (Munro 1999; see also Midwinter 1990), taking on a distinct new identity and increasingly depicted as 'different' (McEwan 2002:79): culturally distinct, collectivist, left-wing, sitting in stark contrast to the neoliberal ideology of individual responsibility in British politics (Perchard 2013). As a response, the Scottish administration found ways to embed an image of national distinction in departments and policies; this period, more than any other, was the 'tartanisation' of the Scottish government administration (McEwan 2002:72).

A vital source of change that helps explain the particularly positive glow around managerialist penal change (McAra 1999) was rooted in how the prison became imbricated with devolution sensibilities. The image of punitive penality in England and Wales served as a nationalistic foil: transforming the prison reflected the desire to implant a distinctly Scottish identity in the penal system. Undoubtedly there was something amoral (O'Malley 1992) in how SPS now conducted itself and treated prisoners. But when interviewees recalled this time, their stories were also charged with the nationalism that had been mobilised in response to the Tory policies of the 1980s. Interviewees were appalled by Thatcher. Philip stated that the difference lay at the level of values: 'She made some terrible decisions, and her value system was just wrong.' Showing the overlap between these anti-Thatcher sentiments and the positive Scottish managerialist motivations, Douglas commended Westminster managerialist policies but described Thatcher's influence as totally 'toxic', dividing Scotland from England: 'the Thatcher years [...] were toxic because she was a south-east England posh lady and anybody with that type of accent doesn't go down well here'. These statements conform to what Mitchell and Bennie described as a source of Scottish nationalism: a deep personal dislike of Thatcher, who was felt to personify 'anti-Scottish' Westminster politics (1995:96). The penal reforms enacted gave a new discursive life to the distinctly *Scottish prison* – a shift that was a reflection of the contemporary 'neo-nationalist sentiment' that McLennan described as forming an image of 'New Scotland' in the collective consciousness, representing a 'distinctive national civic culture of progressive pluralism' (2006:592). Douglas best summed up the nationalist charge within Scottish penal cultural:

> During the 1990s we had the Tory government and we had people like Michael Howard in England preaching about prison works and all that stuff and a very right-wing agenda, and of course we weren't quite following that here. We were trying to be a bit more evidence-based rather than politics-based...Scotland didn't like the Tory government. Scotland hates the Tories.

Prisons in Scotland would not follow the politics south of the border. Alistair similarly described the Scottish penal changes of the 1990s in contrast to England: 'It worked quite well, and quite different from England and Wales.'

While SPS embraced managerialism, they opposed what was felt to be the imposition of any English prison policies or practices. As a result, the Secretary of State averred that SPS policy 'betrayed "wetness"' for lacking the tougher character of imprisonment in England. SPS managers saw this as evidence that this English minister did not understand that Scottish prison policy was now fundamentally different (Minutes of the Scottish Prison Service Extraordinary Board Meeting, 24 July 1995). Scottish divergence from penal culture in England and Wales was now clearly evident. SPS's actions, its name and the way in which it declared its organisational rationale and penal intentions all affirmed it was now 'other-to-England' (McAra 2008:493). There was a distinct way of doing things north of the border that was less right wing. Progressive changes in Scottish prison policy and organisational culture allowed anti-Thatcher views and growing nationalist sentiment to find some practical expression.

There was another inescapable force driving Scotland's prison system and penal state transformation – something much more visceral. After the prison disturbances, the public outcry and the crisis inside the Prison Division, the pre-existing certitude about how to address prison disorder unravelled. The enthusiastic embrace of managerial ideas in Scottish penal culture reflects the desperation and anxiety which had overtaken the Division. There was no protest and angst around the implementation of these signature Conservative policies in Scottish prisons as there had been when they were grafted onto other areas of Scottish social provision. SPS was high-spirited and jubilant about the managerial transformation in Scottish imprisonment regimes and its supporting governmental processes; as William described it: 'The atmosphere was great. It was mental, it was a party.' This is because it appealed to, and could assuage, the fears summoned by the prisoner riots. From 1989 until the mid-1990s, the senior prison administrators were seeking a return to order by dramatically reorganising the most provocative and inciting aspects of their rule; managerialism provided the tools for that project. Actively pursuing the new public management agenda bestowed SPS with the power and a complete set of ideational resources to take firmer control of prisons and purge prison management of its emotional intensity.

The motifs of managerialism were concerned with the distribution of a stabilising effect across prison life, which had been marked by chronic chaos. The language of the customer, objective pro forma of performance measures, the new business ethos and the orderly outlook also safeguarded the organisation against future vulnerability. These changes reflected 'a logic of resiliency', which, according to Lentzos and Rose (2009:243 in quoted in O'Malley 2010) improves the ability to cope, 'to anticipate and tolerate disturbances in complex worlds without collapse, to withstand shocks, and to rebuild as necessary'. By being more proactive and managerial, SPS were seeking out forms of safety and protection as much as managerial efficiency: 'Prisons will always be potentially volatile but I believe that the more professional we become at managing the Service, the less violence will occur' (*Annual Prison Report 1990–1991*:3). The new managerial systems and evidence-based penal stratagems, and the responsibilisation of prisoners, provided SPS with a means to prevent 'potentially traumatic futures' (O'Malley 2010:488). Scottish prison managerialism deviated from the neoliberal ideas that forged them because they were employed progressively, to make prisons calmer, safer and ultimately more manageable. They provided SPS with new controls to prevent future disorder and disarray. Managerialism gave people a renewed sense of confidence.

These contrasting influences – changes in the nature of British liberalism, an insurgent Scottish cultural outlook and the emotional demands of fear and fragility – provided new ideational resources to assertively address the Scottish problems of imprisonment.

Civilising imprisonment

The changes that took place at this time were intended to reposition Scotland as a penal exception, a country that was leading the way in progressive prison reform. Speaking in 1991, a senior governor reflected that through their reforming efforts SPS had 'overtaken and passed traditional penal reform groups, such as the Howard League' in the development of new practical theories of incarceration (Coyle 1992:6). These striking transformations are all the more astounding given the violence and disorder that preceded them. The Prison Division was replaced by SPS. Prison conditions were being modernised, the general quality of prison life was improved and physical segregation was softened. Yet, I aver caution against too positive a reading of this period of change. That is because the nature of the penal reform that took place in Scotland was a *civilising transformation*, rather than a *humanitarian* one (Garland 2010).

A humanitarian shift in penal sensibilities would have curtailed the very act of inflicting imprisonment (Halttunen 1995), making the imposition of harsh or invasive punishment unacceptable (Garland 2010:148). There were few traces of humanitarian sensibilities, such as an increased empathy or social identification with the plight of the prisoner – their life trajectories, poverty or background. By contrast, I identify Scotland's penal transformation as civilising rather than welfarist and progressive. Civilising imprisonment has three key features: (1) it is calculated to protect the prison from the instability and emotional turbulence that tends to be experienced by more overtly punitive prison systems; (2) it does so by intensifying prison control; (3) it simultaneously submerges the brutal and disturbing aspects of imprisonment beneath progressive penal tropes.

Central to civilising imprisonment was a broader process of refinement (Elias 1978). As shown above, in confronting the prison problems, an embarrassment crept in among the SPS professional managers, who expressed open discomfort at the physicality and brutality of Scottish imprisonment. Euan recalled prison now as something despicable and inexcusable. Looking back, he felt what he described as a

> horrible kind of, this impression of grey, they [prisoners] ate off tin plates... And they had sex offenders sewing mail bags. It was grim, absolutely grim...I know that sounds bad, and when I look back no one was interested in these and what was going on in these places.

They had seen it, but had not always acknowledged that the prison was dismal and routinely inhumane. By 1989, and in the face of continued violence, 'forms of cruelty that had once gone unquestioned' were increasingly hard to justify (Halttunen 1995:303). SPS's new squeamishness in response to prison severity helped secure a 'diminution in the gratuitous suffering' imposed upon prisoners (Morris 1966:628). These realisations had clear benefits for prisoners: improved food and visiting facilities, better clothing and access to a complaints commissioner.

However, what happened in Scotland was not a reduction in the use of the prison, but a concealment of its penal pains. These changes expressed an unease and embarrassment about the prison's excessive force, but not about its aims, social function, levels of exclusion or stigmatisation. Both Adam and Douglas outlined the spirit of the change as humane, but their pairing it with the terms 'efficient' and 'evidence-based' reveals a concern for preventing penal impropriety rather than preventing penal pain:

Adam: [We] made policy a bit more humane, a bit more efficient.

Douglas: I would say sensible, I would say humane, I would say evidence-based and legal.

SPS's civilising desires were more ambivalent about the infliction of pain: not doubting its necessity, but appalled by its brutality and vivid existence. Managerialism and evidence-based policy were part of this civilising process, making the administration of prisons dispassionate. Crucially, this 'offered a variety of narrative strategies designed to distance' SPS 'from any imputation' of barbarism as well as Home Office punitiveness (Halttunen 1995:328), and thus was 'an aesthetic of refinement', reducing 'the sight of pain' but not 'its infliction' (Garland 2010:150).

The BSU had been a humane prison. It reduced the use of penal pain, acknowledged prisoners as people and was managed with greater discretion. The Unit, however, offended the sensibilities of many senior SPS officials; it transgressed a civilised system – thus evoking irrational emotive responses, evident in how William and Douglas contemptuously described people there, the way they looked and how they conducted themselves, as 'outrageous'. How could a prison system that strived for a more rationalised form maintain this peculiar, even deviant, experimental outlier – and one which appeared to have abandoned civilised order? The closing of the BSU epitomises how the civilising agenda was privileged at the expense of humane penal reforms.

This resulted in new penal tactics and tropes. Prisoners in Scotland were not to be viewed as alien and subhuman. The Scottish prisoner was no longer passive, but an active consumer, 'an entrepreneur in his own personal development' (Garland 1997:191) who was being taught how to manage their own risks and potential. Prisons employed control techniques that relied directly on the 'pains of self-government' (Crewe 2011b). These included highly intrusive psychological and cognitive programmes that promised 'pseudo-autonomy' (Crewe 2011a), encouraged self-regulation and promoted rational decision-making, all while providing an 'implicit inducement' for non-compliant prisoners to conform to the mainstream as well as 'subtle ways of undermining' the resistance and protest of prisoners (McEvoy 2001:252). The civilising reforms implemented ideas of rationality and opportunity that made prisoners more visible and accountable for their progress. If prisoners failed inside the mainstream, the blame must rest with them and not SPS, who, rhetorically at least, could say they offered prisoners a programme of positive engagements. These seemingly progressive changes exerted a 'broader and tighter grip on behaviour and cognition' (Crewe 2011a:460).

This civilising reinvention and concealment were also a strategic transformation and expansion in Scottish penal power – which, as shown above, was felt to be much needed. These reforms helped win back management's ruling prestige, reducing the quotient of violence, while returning the prison to some form of predictability. Similarly, improving the mainstream facilities further demonstrated SPS's more magnanimous approach to achieving their ends of containment and control. Reflecting this, Adam recalled that giving prisoners more rational prison interventions gave SPS improved control over prisoner behaviour:

> In the events at that time we formed a Mission Statement of the prison service, and there had to be order, that's the first. Order, 100%, that's your job. You can't do anything unless it's orderly. You do have to take care of them, you have to feed them...[that's] why we get sentence planning and all that do-goody stuff. And we have control.

Civilising imprisonment, using 'do-goody stuff', steadied the ship and shielded SPS from the claims of cruelty and injustice that had unsettled their previous working consensus. The prison system itself was more accountable and publicly opposed to cruelty, but ultimately the power of the prison administration was expanded and prison order was more firmly re-established.

Scottish prison discipline became more cultivated, control became more subtle. These civilising reforms successfully renewed the prisons' institutional purpose: to confine *efficiently and effectively*. Civilising imprisonment as intensification of control has quite clear shades of Foucault's (1977) astute and sceptical interpretation about punishing better. However, the concept of civilising imprisonment goes further – it was not only a newly calculated approach to power and control. Civilised penal transformations do not transform punishment in fundamental ways (e.g. moving from the scaffold to the prison), but distil what is felt to be vulgar (e.g. moving from the electric chair to the lethal injection), improving the image of the penal state. Thus, they are dependent on and redeploy the inescapably contingent cultural mores, emotional sensibilities and anxieties that coalesce at precise moments in history – in this case, Scotland's nationalist aspirations and penal anxieties, neither of which provided the ideational resources for humanitarian prison reforms.

In this way, the prison was remade as a social institution. It was reconfigured as part of a new emerging cultural landscape, signalling a new Scottish identity, distinct within the UK. By 1998 Scotland had gained a devolved parliament, a momentous political change and separation of Scottish policy powers. The reinvention of Scottish penality was part of this regeneration, giving new symbolic power, moral authority and practical effect to this view that Scotland was different. These civilised prison policies, even if their practical implications were less progressive, helped produce new social meanings that enforced the image of liberal Scotland.

Those new performance management techniques and declarations of civilised penal sensibilities had other sociological impacts, entrenching the prison as the terminus for deadbeats and the dangerous. Philip reflected on the early 1990s 'sensible and humane' penal reform, but wondered why the use of the prison continued to expand. The demand for the prison was still driven by the fault of the prisoners:

> The thing is, bringing down the prison population is so difficult. I think it probably shouldn't be thought of, thinking back on it, as an end in itself. You do need some people in prison, very dangerous ones, and therefore it's making sure you're using it sparingly, and we didn't manage to solve that. I think that's a pity, but a lot of people were interested in doing that, trying to have less use of prison, and that in a sense is a failure. But the whole system, but it's not as if we had a little dial we could turn...the very difficult problem, the continuing offender, which drives quite a lot of it.

SPS never lost their faith in the use of or justification for confinement, nor challenged the sociological forces that caused crime. The prison remained extensive, because it had to; the prison still had to deal with those people who were dangerous. After *Opportunity and Responsibility* leaders in SPS felt they themselves had changed, but they accepted that the prisoner remained the same. SPS were still dealing with 'non-rehabilitable [people] in the first place given where the majority of the prison population are drawn from' (Douglas).

Scottish imprisonment regimes continued to perpetuate the social distance between society and the prisoner. Without the tenets of social justice, the transformation that took place by 1995 in Scotland was that the exclusionary prison was rendered rhetorically progressive, evidence-led. But it was riven with a neoliberal rationality and emboldened by a new nationalistic confidence. Thus, its forms of pain became more deniable. The prison was redeemed, appearing civilised rather than punitive, communicating an impression of Scottish penal superiority. The historical and mythopoeic narrative of Scottish prisons and pre-devolution penal welfarism, which has helped classify Scotland's more virtuous place in the Anglophone penological imagination, has as its source the institutional strategies, prison techniques and decisions made at this time in history.

Notes

i In the early 1990s there were reports published on HIV/AIDS in prison; physically disabled prisoners; psychological and mental disturbance among prisoners; research into vulnerable prisoners; a relational audit; a review of regimes and drug use in prison; evaluations of special handling units, drug reduction programmes and parole procedures; two research bulletins; and two prison surveys

ii Civic nationalism has a more collective and inclusive view of citizenship based on shared values, as opposed to ethnic nationalism which has the common grounds of race and ancestry (Keating 1996; Brubacker 1999).

9 Conclusion

Comparing the politics of punishment

Why do we punish as we do? Comparative study can help us answer this question as it can illuminate the general forces and specific factors that support penal arrangements. This study has focused on Ireland and Scotland, showing the effects of political culture and social order on the comparative differences in their imprisonment regimes.

Like other English-speaking nations, both the Irish and Scottish penal systems had undergone remarkable transformations by the 1990s. Across this period, Ireland's and Scotland's respective prison systems endured broadly similar events, confronted at different times by both prison violence, overcrowding, public opprobrium and rapid economic changes. While the governing administrations responded in ways that made immediate sense to the respective policymakers, these would have undoubtedly been startling, even incomprehensible, to their Scottish or Irish counterparts. This seemed to be borne out after many interviews, wherein participants were curious about what had happened in the other nation at the same time that they had been working in prison policy. People often exhibited genuinely visceral responses upon hearing the comparative differences. Many Scottish interviewees could not believe their Irish counterparts relied not on meticulously compiled data and regulated parole, but moral and social intuition, when releasing prisoners – and then to release prisoners with such frequency in the light of it. Correspondingly, the accounts of Scotland's deep, and deepening, segregation stunned many of Ireland's former prison policymakers, who found it hard to fathom how such responses could be justified and widely accepted. These responses readily demonstrate that looking at prisons cross-nationally, even for prison experts, can leave us feeling baffled, perplexed and surprised. How exactly do we explain these vivid differences in how these two neighbouring nations imprisoned?

The comparison has thus been orientated towards historical investigation, reassembling the systems in which people were imprisoned and reconstructing the political cultures that informed those penal strategies, tracing how both the political and the carceral changed from 1970. This has provided two fine-grained and small-n studies of the politics of punishment. In undertaking this endeavour, this book has also been equally intent upon improving comparative penality's interpretive power and expanding its explanatory field of vision.

While the preceding chapters have provided deep and detailed penal histories of Ireland and Scotland, what is required now is to lift our gaze from the empirical particulars to the broader analytical framework. What follows in this chapter is a synopsis of the findings and a setting out of the key comparative contributions and wider implications for comparative sociology of punishment. In summarising the comparative cases below we see that imprisonment regimes display the distinctive hallmarks of the prevailing political culture, which itself reflects structural biases and cultural norms. Political culture thus links large-scale social phenomena to actual penal outcomes. Therefore, the framework offered here reconnects the aims of sociology of punishment with the comparative penology project, providing the interpretive tools to empirically research and comparatively analyse the prison as a social institution, and showing how it comes to condense and contribute to a nation's array of social, political and cultural relations.

Comparative summary

In this book I have sought to recover and explain why the politics of punishment differ in the Irish and Scottish cases. Their differences present a curious comparative puzzle, and one that cannot be resolved or explained by using the existing frameworks of analysis that predominate in comparative sociology of punishment. These analyses tend to look at imprisonment on an abstract level, emphasising divergences or similarities in prisoner numbers – an undoubtedly effective summation of the stark comparative contrasts in levels of prison use, but lacking in its ability to convey important internal variations in how each prison estate is organised.

Much comparative work has also shown important patterns that connect either the political or the cultural to the penal. This is not scholarship I disagree with nor wish to disregard; these remain powerful analytical tools, but I seek to advance upon the sometimes broad sweep and grand narratives of punitiveness and exceptionalism that frame much of this work. It would also not be wise to neglect political economy, historical patterns or large-scale structural forces in our explanatory models. Yet we need to find a means not just to show cross-national correlations between macro forces and levels of punishment, but also to comparatively demonstrate the myriad social forces that shape penality and the mechanisms that translate them into divergent uses of imprisonment.

In seeking to achieve this theoretical and empirical agenda, this study departs from conventional forms of international penal comparison in three important ways. First, it begins from a belief that much of what makes politics and imprisonment different from one nation to the next reflects how these matters are bound up in more complex social, cultural and political contexts. Secondly, I developed a new comparative conception of imprisonment, as well as an alternative way to compare and contrast penal politics. *Imprisonment regimes* give us a means to compare the diverse strategies, routines, practices of movement, prisoner categories and rehabilitation programmes that constitute a prison system. *Political culture* allows us to explain these prison practices by capturing the ideas, sentiments and emotional dimensions (and how they relate to each other) that shaped decision making. Unlike the dominant frameworks in comparative penality, which tend to operate from a single analytical plane, the concepts of imprisonment regimes and political culture are both pluralistic and fluid. Third, and following on from this, to show the practical implications of the political rationalities and cultural meanings we need to investigate the thinking behind actual policymaking. Taking a grounded approach to comparison allows us to demonstrate how the varieties of conditioning social circumstances come to give cross-national imprisonment regimes their distinctive order. As a result, we can develop more subtle histories and nuanced understandings of the comparative differences in cross-national penality.

Ireland and Scotland: Divergent penal cultures

In the 1970s, Ireland and Scotland each had to meet the challenges of rising prisoner numbers and prison violence, but they responded to these problems in very different ways. Both administrations employed the techniques of authoritarian segregation, open prisons, prison expansion and rehabilitation. Yet what these policies meant differed between these two nations, resulting in very different prison styles and practical implications. As noted in Chapter 3, in Ireland during the 1970s the prison estate expanded. However, when we look at the imprisonment regime, we see that the prisons were being modernised and intentionally rendered more lenient. Temporary release was expanded, open prisons were established and mobility was thus concerned with moving prisoners out of the prison. Subversive prisoners were certainly subject to a form of segregation in light of their violent and dissident acts inside and outside the prison. Yet they were also given temporary release and a system of concessions was, albeit surreptitiously, part of their regime. Additionally, supportive professionals were employed – though rather than being motivated to purge prisoners of their criminal mentalities, their remit was intended to aid prisoners as they coped with imprisonment. New training schemes were implemented to provide a runway for prisoners into the new modern industries emerging in Ireland.

At the same time, Scotland was also experiencing rising prisoner numbers and concerns over prison disorder (Chapter 6). However, instead of developing ways to reduce or moderate the prison population, the prison was initially expanded without question (while finances allowed). Release, while a relatively new mechanism and certainly something that could have, like Ireland, helped reduce the daily prisoner population, was instead cautiously controlled and tightly regulated. Their prison system was organised around diversified prisoner risk categories and a hierarchical system that arranged the prisons in descending severity. At the top was the open prison or a Training for Freedom unit. At the bottom of the prison stratum were sites of extreme segregation where a prisoner would be subject to inhumane and austere incarceration. In contrast to the Irish approach, the prison dynamic sought to move prisoners (mostly long-termers) around the estate in a purportedly logical system of incentives and punishments – a practice intent upon instilling the skills of individual responsibility in appropriate prisoners while disciplining and incapacitating others. While the Barlinnie Special Unit was an impressive and innovative form of removal and separation, and had no therapeutic equivalent in Ireland, it was a minor tendency in an otherwise disciplinary prison system. Otherwise, the daily routine of the prison consisted of mundane labour and prison medical care.

Scotland's disciplinary system sits in stark contrast to Ireland's more humane developments in the same period. This is due in part to the prison in Ireland being implicitly viewed with scepticism, and seen as detrimental to social cohesion. Ireland was modernising, but it was still a traditional Catholic culture that emphasised the need to reiterate and inscribe family and community values in social policy. Better to return male prisoners to their families where possible then to disintegrate social bonds of solidarity. In Scotland, the prison was understood as a vital instrument of social order, its practical object being those people and groups viewed as permanently incapable, morally defective or too difficult to possess either freedom or welfare. The high levels of reliance upon incapacitation were likely self-defeating, undermining Scottish community cohesion and contributing to the very social problems which it sought to address. These costs paled in comparison to the prison's complex objectives. The Scottish prison emphasised exclusion in order to protect social harmony and the new welfare system from the disorder of Scotland's deep social schisms.

Ireland's conservative culture, simmering nationalism, and Catholic heritage were the ideas that assembled to inform its political culture and give its prison system a sense of acceptability during this era. While in Scotland, its political culture, imbued with a liberal and an oppressive paternal outlook, and rooted in othering class prejudices, shaped what were felt to be appropriate uses of imprisonment. The differences in the prison systems reflect Ireland's and Scotland's contrasting social landscape, cultural norms and political styles of reasoning, and, fundamentally, how these ideas informed the routine choices made by prison administrators in response to actual social and penal problems.

The comparison also exemplified the fact that prison systems are fluid, and the expansion and modifications to both Ireland's and Scotland's imprisonment regimes reveal the impact of various practical and social pressures during the 1980s. As we saw in Chapter 7, Scotland's prisons were engulfed in a period of unprecedented and systemwide protest and violence. This caused a doubling down of their security logic and an extension of their segregation mechanisms. More prisons and more separation units were devised to address the feeling that the prison population had become progressively and uncontrollably insubordinate. This drew prison policy into public disrepute, with new criticisms being raised about the heavy-handed nature of Scottish imprisonment. In Ireland in the 1980s, rising prisoner numbers, increasing crime and a crumbling economy meant that their political culture too morphed to adapt to the sense of imminent crisis (Chapter 4). In Ireland, more prisoners were released, though in an increasingly ad hoc manner, as they sought to keep the prisoners moving out and in turn minimise overcrowding. But the Irish prisoner was also coming to be seen as a social problem: images of drug addicts, gangland stooges and violent predators came to inflect prison discourse. The challenges the respective prison systems faced differed enormously, but both Irish and Scottish prison administrations were left reeling and panic-stricken by the end of the 1980s. Both prison administrations entered a contentious moment, with groups and individuals questioning the logic of their respective penal cultures. In Scotland in the period during and immediately following the disturbances, the question prison administrators confronted was whether the prison system was indeed too punitive, while in Ireland it was felt by some that mutiny was afoot inside the Prison Division as people began to ask the opposite question: had the logic of Irish imprisonment, and its propensity for release, been too permissive?

Such internal questions and contestations came to inform penal transformations in both Ireland and Scotland as the wider social and political circumstances in both countries changed, creating windows of opportunity for new ideas in the 1990s. These changes were not just in the organisation of the imprisonment regime, but in the very ethos and techniques of the political culture. As such, both penal politics and the imprisonment regimes were realigned in Ireland and Scotland at the end of the twentieth century. As we saw in Chapter 5, Ireland's political apparatus and prison regimes were both significantly expanded. The Irish Prison Service was created to give more power and authority to how the prisons were managed, organised via a new crime control sensibility. The prisons were made more incapacitating, and new programmes emerged, intent upon reducing crime by tackling prisoners' criminal proclivities. In stark contrast, the Scottish prison system and political culture were renewed along progressive lines (Chapter 8). Like in Ireland, the Scottish Prison Service was formed. However, it contrasted in its organisational outlook: SPS was a powerful independent state bureaucracy intent on deploying an evidence-based and business-like approach to prison and prisoner management. Prisons were reorganised using technocratic strategies and were harmonised around a revised system of incentives known as 'opportunity and responsibility'.

Each of these penal shifts was broadly intended by the respective architects and sponsors of Irish and Scottish transformation. However, Irish and Scottish penal transformations were not merely the product of those cadres campaigning internally for change, but were adaptions to the shifting social circumstances and problem contexts, in which the very idea of government and state had altered significantly. In Scotland, nationalism and neoliberal managerialism provided the basic materials with which prisons and prison administration could be remade. In Ireland, meanwhile, the arrival of late modernity and the atrophy of the Church gave the government the impetus to expand and augment its penal power and aims, fundamentally altering what problems it imagined the prison was addressing. In Ireland in the 1990s, this meant using the prison as a crime control technique to assuage public anxieties and political outrage. Ostensibly, this was done also for the purpose of protecting that still vaunted image of Irish social life: the community. Yet, increasing the use of the prison would have only deepened community divisions and enhanced inequality. These were collateral consequences accepted in order to achieve the wider objectives of incapacitation, exclusion and expressing Ireland's newly emboldened state authority. In Scotland the image of government also changed, but in contrast to Ireland the aims of Scottish incarceration never shifted: social failure remained the prison's practical focus. Instead, the politics of Scottish imprisonment were given a veneer of progressive-mindedness. From this stage of the comparison we see that the full weight of global social and political phenomena of late modernity during the 1990s were experienced in both nations. However, they clearly produced very different penal effects. We see that common challenges across similar nations provoke very different responses. These were dependent upon how they were received, resisted and translated into the logic of government, and adapted to address specific problems of penality and challenges of a shifting social order.

Describing and interpreting both imprisonment practices and political thinking and actions in Ireland and Scotland required an analysis that illuminates the complex conjuncture of social forces, cultural meanings, political factors and events. This kind of analysis saves us from explanations that become dense historical accounts, that emphasise specific actors and explicit scenarios or unduly privilege happenstance. It also means we avoid some of the typological theoretical variations common in comparative penality. When the social field shifted it only impacted upon imprisonment regimes once those changes reshaped the political culture – namely, augmenting what were considered appropriate, acceptable and desirable uses of imprisonment. How those ideas materialised in the outlook of those in charge of prisons was not automatic or obvious, but was dependent on the context, the events that were occurring inside government as well as in social life. Therefore, it is not enough to say that causality rests in the structural social field, in the conditioning forces of political economy, or to suggest alternatively that comparative difference is always a product of the relative local features of social life or deep history (Nelken 2009).

By divorcing the ideological from the expressive, and the embedded from the contemporary, we obstruct our ability to explain the comparative differences within and between penal systems. Hence, insisting on a single theoretical stance blocks us from explaining why these ideas give rise to precise uses of imprisonment, and why these systems of punishment and government change. The views, feelings and values that make up a nation's political culture are rooted in the organising social motifs, but they are not merely the attitudinal by-products of economic or cultural structures. These sensibilities and rationalities are determinative and generative, but also practical. They shape and inform differences in how the prison is used, how prisoners are seen, what the government imagines its problems are and how it conceives the appropriate role of government in addressing those problems. Seeing the comparative variation in Irish and Scottish penal culture, and exposing the sources of these differences, forces us to return to some of the logic of what constitutes the politics of punishment and the meanings of imprisonment.

Comparing the politics of punishment

Though the findings here reveal the inescapably complex convergence of cultural and social currents that underpin the politics of imprisonment. I want to suggest that (1) *the cultural meanings* as well as (2) *the governmental dynamics* of prison policymaking would help to reorient the comparative focus of punishment and society scholarship towards a more fulsome socio-political analysis of penality. By understanding the comparative differences in the political cultures that undergird the politics of punishment we can better comprehend national distinction in uses of imprisonment, who it is for and what various aims it seeks to achieve.

The political cultural meanings of imprisonment

Divergent penal cultures reflect variations in crime concerns. The moderate use of the prison in Ireland in the earlier period was woven together with a narrative about crime not being serious, or dissident acts being perceived to be founded upon a broadly legitimate nationalist movement. In Scotland, the prisons' unquestioning necessity speaks to what was the abiding belief that there were levels of social despair and violence that required coercive exclusion. As is accepted maxim now, there is little relationship between crime rates and imprisonment rates. But throughout we have seen that the uses of the prison are rested upon the authoritative analyses of the crime problem by those charged with the power to imprison.

Incarceration is not uniformly deployed against lawbreakers, however. And what the prison is for, and the social meanings that shaped the uses of imprisonment, are equally informed by who the prisoner is believed to be, their personhood. What is the boundary between prisoners and mainstream 'law-abiding' society? What sorts of affiliations shape those sensibilities? Answering these questions helps unlock our understanding of cross-national divergences in confinement. No matter where they are, prisons by and large tend to share the dismaying characteristic of disproportionally confining minorities and the socially marginalised. To think about that comparatively requires a precise understanding of who the prisoner is understood to be in each context. What is the social frequency of their otherness?

So, for example, in Ireland we observed in close detail that the 1970s imprisonment regimes emphasised decarceration and the integrity of collective efficacy, underpinned by a conservative Catholic culture. But this same broad social outlook had also supported Ireland's carceral archipelago (Fischer 2016). As such, the same general values were morphed by divergent perceptions of the respective institutions' charges: sexually, and thus morally, deviant women confined en masse in Magdalene Laundries, as opposed to fundamentally decent men who had merely transgressed the law. To think of the prisoner in the 1970s into the 1980s in Ireland was to think of a person, a human with problems, and to summon images of families and communities to which that person was seen to belong. During the 1990s, the punitive carceral developments that took place reflected Irish society's growing estrangement from the prisoner and the annulment of his social belonging. Meanwhile, in Scotland the prisoner was analogous to disease and the embodiment of danger. Images of morally unworthy, incapable and ultimately ineligible citizens were how the use of incapacitation, rather than progressive social welfare and social work, were justified – even for the lowest level of petty offenders. The Scottish prison was a measure of last resort; the welfare system was for those who could learn through social education how to conduct themselves in mainstream Scottish life. Thus, rather than saying there is a master political culture that shapes all aspects of social policy with equal weighting and consequence, each social institution works with particular images of who they are working with and upon, providing 'a regulatory and normative framework for human conduct *in that area*' (Garland 1990a:282; emphasis added).

Perceptions of the prisoner help justify imprisonment and legitimise its intensity, therefore. It is why the punishment might outweigh the seriousness of the crime, or why a group of prisoners might experience lenience in spite of their transgressions. It is how the prisoners' biography and inequality are questioned or affirmed that allows socially acceptable uses of imprisonment, despite what might be perceived from the outside or later in time as their peculiar lenience or excessive harshness. The socio-political 'knowledge' of the prisoner (Melossi 2000), elucidating the degrees of their dehumanisation, is an important part of the comparative puzzle. Grasping this exposes the ideas that inform the exclusionary or inclusionary tenor of a prison system, but also allows us to account for the kinds of regimes that prisoner populations were designated or denied. As such, understanding who policymakers believe the prisoner to be explains how and why prisoners were categorised and housed as they were, and why that diverges between nations.

Due to imprisonment always being entangled in the vagaries and instability of everyday social life, the choices behind these decisions were often emotionally charged by the challenges thrown up by the policymaking process. It should be evident from the comparative case studies that policy is not entirely the logical product of culturally adept political actors responding to the world around them to produce meaningful and socially functional prisons. As Fassin writes, '[r]ationality does not exhaust the reasons people punish as they do' (2018:81). Indeed, actors' responses were equally informed by emotional impulses. Crime offends and punishment pleases, provoking unreflective and irrational reactions. There is pleasure and satisfaction in remaking the prison system so that is gives practical expression to these emotional excesses. This view is broadly in line with arguments put forward by sociological theorists of punishment (Durkheim 1984; Garland 1990a; Fassin 2018). That there is a perverse satisfaction for those who hold the power to imprison, a solidifying sense of us-versus-them, when they mete out humiliation, pain and degradation must be part of our analysis (and as is broadly shown in comparative studies, e.g. Cavadino and Dignan 2006; Pratt 2008).

In light of the governmental focus of the comparison that has been conducted, however, I want to advance this crucial point by suggesting a fuller account of the emotional currents that give imprisonment its cultural charge, beyond penal punitiveness and tolerance. The prison reflects what policymakers feel is desirable, essential and appropriate. The prison is a social institution; because of this, the emotions that come to inform its logic are not restricted to feelings derived from or generated by the act of punishing. We saw in Ireland that the imprisonment regime in the 1970s was shaped by sympathy for what was imagined to be the prisoners' background and social biography. It certainly doesn't seem rational or politically opportune to increase the permissiveness of parole when crime is rising. But in Ireland those in charge at the Division displayed a sense of pride in demonstrating continued penal restraint, indulging their distaste for imprisonment and tolerant sympathies while avoiding what was felt to be inappropriate uses of confinement. Of course, later changes saw these feelings marginalised, as new senior officials were motivated by a deep indignation and anger at the permissive use of Ireland's political power. In Scotland, at the beginning of the 1990s a clamorous nationalist politics drove a sincere enthusiasm to display magnanimity in Scottish social policy where possible. This deep desire to be reformist and hence distinctive on the UK stage was part of the prison's civilising transformation. In both Ireland and Scotland in the 1990s, their respective penal transformations certainly tapped into the disdain that was felt towards the socially condemned. However, it is impossible to comprehend their contrastive penal changes without also grasping that they were underpinned by fear, anxiety and a pronounced sense of fragility in light of the contentious circumstances that engulfed their working lives.

These brief examples demonstrate that the sensibilities involved in punishment are not exclusively tied to the act of punishing. What we see is that the cultural imperatives of imprisonment tends to have a varied set of sources. And those feelings provoked by, and embedded in, the deployment of carceral power are not only those dubious thrills and pleasures of inflicting pain. This is why prison policy often appears to defy expectations, diverge so drastically from what is taken-for-granted as the settled penal culture or produce self-defeating social consequences. These passions, in all their variety, permit certain policy choices while ruling out others and are central to what makes punishment meaningful and socially resonant in its particular place.

While it is clear that Ireland and Scotland imprisoned differently, a recovery of the values and ideas of those who make, manage and administer prison systems reveals equally important political dynamics. How prisoners and imprisonment were understood and managed also embodied ideas of government. When we compare punishment, we should ask: how do those who organise and maintain prison systems think about the work of government? How do they understand its role? How do they envision the ideal citizen? How do governments rationalise their power? The politics of imprisonment is always governed through these governmental styles of reasoning. In making sense of the differences between Irish and Scottish imprisonment it was essential to expose their respective variants of conservativism and liberalism. We saw this particularly in how the Irish and Scottish imprisonment regimes had a productive nature, intent upon remaking citizens who displayed socially and politically unacceptable traits. In 1970–1980s Ireland, prison policy pivoted upon the conservative ideas of community, nation and family, goals they sought to instil in prisoners through lenient release. In this political position, government does not rule by reason and abstract ideas, but based on common sense, willing to use the authoritarian power of the state but also seeking 'penal prudence' (Loader 2020). Even in the later period, when the prison became more punitive, ideas of the community and nation dominated the security discourse. In Scotland, essential to working out how to best imprison were the operative features of liberalism, namely individual responsibility and encouraging rational subjectivities in their citizens. Within a liberal remit, the government's task is to maintain a civilised order. In both Ireland and Scotland, contrasting responses to penal and social problems were also conditioned by the prevailing political rationalities in both contexts.

Across these histories I have been concerned with using comparative reflection to excavate the social meanings of imprisonment in Ireland and Scotland as key to understanding how and why their prison systems differed. And in turn, employ the benefits of the comparative research terrain to make more general claims about how we might explain cross-national penal divergences. By identifying the ensemble of ideas that policymakers employ to justify their differential uses of prison, we see that political culture is the working practical logic behind prison choices, which links social forces to actual penal practices. This framework is clearly not like most mainstream models for comparative penological research. Perhaps it is not even right to suggest this is a framework in the proper sense of a fully set system of typological social patterns with anticipated punitive outcomes. Instead, the approach outlined might be better described as a toolkit, intended to support grounded and inductive cross-national comparisons. Certainly, this is a more laborious approach to comparison, but it seems to me that it may leave us better equipped to understand how and why penality diverges cross-nationally. Combined, the cultural sensibilities and political forces that buttress comparative differences in penal cultures reveal that imprisonment regimes are best understood and compared as complex social institutions.

Punishment as a social institution

The predominant cross-national comparative accounts of imprisonment in the sociology of punishment tend to be singular in their analysis and operate at the level of grand narrative, situating punishment as a punitive or lenient instrument of political ideology, or as a lingering cultural legacy. The image of the prison tends to have a fixed and monolithic quality, as something that is compared via contrasts in severity. The sociological study of punishment can be hampered by looking at it via a single penological purpose and analytical perspective (Garland 1990a). In setting out the analysis here, I have suggested we need to move beyond these conventional frameworks, instead, comparing penality as a multidimensional toolkit, we see that why prison differs reflects its configuration as a working social institution that *embodies and reinforces* visions of political authority, society's moral regulation, collective identity and social narratives. Following this, future comparative work thus might examine what kind of social institution the prison is presupposed to be by those charged with administering imprisonment regimes. What sort of wider moral sentiments and community values do policymakers seek to reinforce with their penal strategies? How is the prison linked to wider welfare, social control and political mechanisms? In asking these questions, we see that the comparative meanings of punishment, its social significance and its cultural effects stretch well beyond the prison, bolstering and remaking social order. We need to illuminate how, by parlaying political positions, cultural imagery and social anxieties into the prison system, the prison comes to reflect and fortify a wider 'sense of place' (Girling et al. 2000:170). And by advancing the analysis in this direction, we better understand what kind of institution the prison is and why it differs from one jurisdiction to the next.

Across both cases we see empirical support for the importance of this claim. In both Ireland and Scotland, prison policymakers relied on interpretations of prison as an institution with perceived social costs and benefits, beyond crime control, which then shaped the imprisonment regime's divergent parameters of use. We see this in particular in the opposing views of suspicion of the prison held in each nation, and as it changed across the period studied. From 1970 to 1995 in Scotland the prison was treated as a necessary and central strategy deployed against the nation's chronic social problems. While it underwent two periods of reform in quick succession, despite their differences in tone and aspiration – the segregative and then the civilising – these both resulted in penal expansion and an emphasis on security, and changes in rehabilitation meant refinement of the prison's controlling techniques. Similarly, by the end of the 1990s in Ireland the prison's meaning as a social institution took on a new positive and productive semblance. The prison was embraced as a useful tool to prevent threats to Ireland's community cohesion from newly marginalised communities and express new political authority. The prison was thus expanded and augmented accordingly in terms of size and security focus. These three examples highlight the expansion of the prison and carceral power, driven, respectively, by alarmist, progressive and punitive ideas. Despite their differences, each episode of transformation was informed by an underlying belief in the prison as making some effective impact on society and/or prisoners. Thus, when penal change is informed by a belief in the prison as something that contributes positively to supporting or protecting society's basic moral values, it leads to an expansion of the prison's capacity and its control mechanisms (Carlen 1983;

Barker 2017; Armstrong 2018). By contrast, in 1970s Ireland the consequences of imprisonment were viewed with overt misgivings, seen as indi-
vidually destructive and thus socially disruptive – the prison was perceived
as weakening Ireland's communitarian moral economy and social system.
This is an important moment to have recovered and adds to the comparative
perspective; we see that when it is accepted that social misery results from
imprisonment, it delegitimises excess use of confinement. This drove a policy
bias towards moderating mechanisms and using professional interventions as
support against the degradations of imprisonment.

These comparative penal changes further confirm that punishment is also
a social enactment that helps fix in place new political standards of conduct
and revised images of blameworthiness and dangerousness (Carlen 1983;
Garland 1990a). We saw throughout the findings that both Irish and Scottish imprisonment regimes were designed (and redesigned) with anxieties
about national change, government impotence and moral decline in mind.
Though the uses of imprisonment and penal transformations in both Ireland
and Scotland differed significantly, the longitudinal and grounded comparative approach allows us to observe a general pattern: policymakers were
(though often implicitly) aware of the prison's didactic effects. Prison policy
changes were not merely the product of internal battles and conflicts; they
were not just the end point of structural and economic forces. Penal policies
also resulted from the sense that the prison could meet and should support
transforming social demands, moral standards and cultural expectations. The
prison, through policymaking, thus regulates the preferred national image
and aspires to reinforce moral order and social conduct. As we saw, during
periods of respective penal transformation officials often tried to advocate for
various policy responses in light of an understanding (though rarely deliv-
ered in these sociological terms) of the kind of society they will become if
they continued down their respective alternative routes, emphasising how
the prison will be drawn into disrepute (and thus will fail as a social institution) if its aims and practices become detached from, or slavishly follow, the
prevailing social currents. They understood that changes in prison policy
could confirm new social, political and cultural scripts. In these contrasting
moments of combat and conflict we saw what was at stake in organising
imprisonment regimes: the constitution of society itself. A sociological study
of penal culture 'tells us how we react to disorderly persons and threats to
social order – but also, and more importantly, it can reveal some of the ways
in which personal and social order comes to be constructed in the first place'
(Garland 1990a:22), insights that are deepened by the contrasting light of
comparative reflection.

This productive dynamic is part of the explanation for why we imprison
differently. The comparative contrast throws into stark relief that the prison
signifies, shapes and fortifies social life as much as it reflects social difference.
Viewed comparatively, we see that by changing the uses of prison and altering the ideas underpinning its function, policymakers and administrators are
helping to redraw the boundary lines between social insiders and outsiders,

shifting the relationship between government and society. Cross-national case studies of punishment thus need to attend to how policy actors interpret the situations within which they operate and how they perceive the social, political and penal problems in which their work interacts and becomes entangled. It is essential we compare what sort of place they envision their nation to be, and what sort of idealised world they are seeking to create, remake and maintain. By mapping the comparative routines of imprisonment and charting how they change, we see that the prison's significance is never limited to reflecting anxieties and meanings about crime and punishment alone: they are also part of the sociological architecture that enforces social order, political authority and cultural norms. As such, the divergent characteristics of penal cultures must be understood as also being rooted in its distinctive socially symbolic and instructive force, and that this cannot be fully illuminated or understood if reduced to either a single instrumental aim or unified set of cultural sensibilities.

Finally, comparing punishment as a social institution and situating it as a fully contextualised set of practices makes binary comparisons based on penal severity less illuminating. One of the concerns of this research has been how the comparative interest in punitiveness and lenience risks perpetuating theoretical deficits, whereby how people are punished, and why, has not been sufficiently addressed. We have seen lenience in both the Irish and Scottish penal systems: the BSU, the liberal use of temporary release, Shelton Abbey and the aims of mainstreaming. We also observed visceral enactments of punitiveness: the cages, express prison building and tightening of release. Analysis that moves between macro and micro empirical registers and analytical planes makes claims that either Irish or Scottish penal cultures represent some master dynamic of national temper impossible to uphold. As Nelken remarked about the correlation between penal and cultural punitiveness that appears in comparative penology, 'the harshness of treatment in a given penal system will not necessarily reflect the harshness of social sanctions in social life' (2006:272).

In Scotland during the 1970s the prisons were dismaying and often cruel places, all while a progressive youth justice system and supportive welfare state were being implemented. Certainly, Scotland's prison system was punitive, but it underwent a progressive metamorphosis in the 1990s. To read this transformation as such a clearly defined and sharply delineated event is to lose sight of the meanings and intentions embedded in those penal changes, as summarised above. This was a civilising penal transformation, whereby the more vulgar and overtly cruel aspects of Scotland's carceral practices and governing techniques were aesthetically reconfigured to appear progressive and orderly. But the prison and political culture were not transmuted to become more humane – the prison's social foundations were never questioned. By contrast, at the same time Ireland's prison system underwent a starkly punitive transformation. It was one that would have been impossible, however, if Ireland had not simultaneously been undergoing an unquestionably progressive and liberating social transformation of secularisation. Irish people were being liberated from the strictures of a Catholic social system, as the government took their place at the axis of social order, though this happened at a time when fear of crime and social anxieties about imprisonment were high, and offenders were increasingly demonised. Thus, Ireland's social liberation was also accompanied by a newly increased penal punitivity.

The complexity of penal culture mirrors the complexity of the society. When we reduce comparisons to binary categorisations we do 'violence to the past' (Loader and Sparks 2004:14), often producing narrow and one-dimensional comparative accounts of penality. We lose our ability to reconstruct the patterns of imprisonment, government and socio-cultural order of the nations in question. The prison should be seen as a varied and mutable set of practices, and is but one interconnected aspect of the wider social field. Only by understanding the prison as having some place within that social system of provision, regulation and control can we fully grasp something more meaningful about the socio-cultural conventions of the comparative nations in question.

Why we punish

How is the power to imprison exercised, and why does that differ? How do we best capture and explain cross-national differences in penality's forms, functions and meanings? As Garland writes, the central weakness of the comparative study of punishment is that it generally offers 'no coherent model of the ongoing processes whereby factors interact to produce their effects, and they tell us little about the choices and contingencies at work therein' (2013:491). It is precisely this gap this study has sought to fill by developing a new comparative framework for penality. This book has provided an account of political culture that connects the structural, political and cultural dimensions of society to the material routines of imprisonment, and thus illuminates and explicates comparative differences in punishment. Having undertaken this project, this study breaks new ground, comparatively and historically.

In this book I have argued that political culture is essential to explain cross-national penal differences. Taken together, these case studies demonstrate that both the political and the cultural are suffused into all aspects of incarceration: the prisons, their regimes, tools of control and technical character; as well as the thinking, organisational mechanisms and bureaucratic practices that inform policymaking. Imprisonment regimes are the result of recurring administration, routine policy choices and everyday decisions. These decisions are shaped by the prevailing political culture. We saw that a comparative analysis of punishment is at its most revealing when it takes seriously the cultural dispositions and political rationalities of ordinary penal policymaking. These are what help determine imprisonment regimes – which routinely go beyond the demands of macroeconomics and cultural traditions and often seek to do more than to either hurt or heal. By insisting that the comparative politics of punishment should be viewed as a social institution that condenses these myriad forces, we are better able to understand, explain and evaluate cross-national differences in imprisonment.

Comparing political culture and imprisonment regimes in this manner takes us inside the world of prison policy and government, while also situating this close-up perspective within the field of contingent social relations. As a result, we now have two detailed accounts of the different cultural meanings, social values, political goals, structural shifts and unanticipated events that defined the differences in Irish and Scottish penal politics and imprisonment. We saw how new ideas took hold, became embedded and resulted in the aims and meanings of imprisonment being reframed. As a result, this study provides compelling new contemporary histories of penal culture for both Ireland and Scotland, differentiating their punitivity and exposing the specific sources for their respective penal cultures. Understanding how Irish and Scottish imprisonment regimes came to take their characteristic form, and the ideas and sensibilities that motivated their penal politics, also provides sociological insight: we see the underlying fault-lines of both societies, and how the prison contributed to their respective social (re)organisation. This also challenges the sometimes implied assumption that comparative research must sacrifice sociological texture and historical depth if it is to have explanatory value.

Comparative study of punishment has the ability to better explicate not just cross-national divergences, therefore. It holds the potential to reveal the deeper social meanings and political resonances of punishment in each time and place, and show how the prison contributes to the constitution and transformation of society. It is evident that when comparative penality is an empirically rich and theoretically advanced enterprise, it has the capacity to shed new light upon the old query of why we punish.

References

Adler, F. (1983) *Nations Not Obsessed with Crime*, Littleton: Rothman.

Adler, M., and Longhurst, B. (1994) *Discourse, Power, and Justice: Towards a New Sociology of Imprisonment*, London: Routledge.

Alyward, S. (2002) The Irish Prison Service, Past, Present and Future – A Personal Perspective, in O'Mahony, P. (ed.) *Criminal Justice in Ireland*, Dublin: Institute of Public Administration.

Annison, H. (2015) *Dangerous Politics: Risk, Political Vulnerability, and Penal Policy*, Oxford: Clarendon.

Annison, H. (2018) Politics and Penal Change: Towards an Interpretive Political Analysis of Penal Policymaking, *Howard Journal of Crime and Justice*, 57(3): 302–320.

Armstrong, S. (2013) 'Using the future to predict the past: prison population forecasts and colonisation of the penal imagination', in Malloch, M. and Munro, W. (eds), *Crime, Critique and Utopia*, Basingstoke: Palgrave Macmillan.

Armstrong, S. (2015) The cell and the corridor: imprisonment as waiting, and waiting as mobile, in *Time & Society*. doi: 10.1177/0961463X15587835.

Armstrong, S. (2017) *Prison Leviathan: On the Monstrous Agency of Prison*, presentation at *Centre for Law and Society*, University of Edinburgh, 28 September 2017.

Armstrong, S. (2018) Securing Prison through Human Rights: Unanticipated Implications of Rights-Based Penal Governance, in *Howard Journal of Crime and Justice*, 57(3): 401–421.

Armstrong, G., and Wilson, M. (1973) 'City Politics and Deviance Amplification.' in Taylor, I., and Taylor, L. (eds), *Politics and Deviance: Papers from the National Deviance Conference*, Middlesex: Pelican.

Asquith, S., and Docherty, M. (1999) Preventing Offending by Children and Young People in Scotland, in Duff, P., and Hutton, N. (eds), *Criminal Justice in Scotland*, Aldershot: Ashgate.

Bacik, I. (2002) The Practice of Sentencing in the Irish Courts, in O'Mahony, P. (ed), *Criminal Justice in Ireland*, Dublin: Institute of Public Administration.

Barker, V, (2006) The Politics of Punishing: Building a State Governance Theory of American Imprisonment Variation, in *Punishment and Society*, 8(1): 5–32.

Barker, V. (2009) *The Politics of Imprisonment: How the Democratic Process Shapes the Way America Punishes Offenders*, New York: Oxford University Press.

Barker, V. (2013) Nordic Exceptionalism Revisited: Explaining the Paradox of a Janus-faced Penal Regime, in *Theoretical Criminology*, 17(1): 3–23.

Barker, V. (2017) *Nordic Nationalism and Penal Order: Walling the Welfare State*, Abingdon: Routledge.

Barrett, E. (2015) Liberal Conservatism, 'Boardization' and the Government of Civil Servants, in *Organization*, 22(1): 40–57.

Barry, C. (2020) 'You Can't Tell Anyone How You Really Feel': Exploring Emotion Management and Performance Among Prison Staff Who Have Experienced the Death of a Prisoner, in *International Journal of Law, Crime and Justice*, 61: 100364.

Barry, A., Osborne, T., and Rose, N. (1993) Liberalism, Neo-Liberalism and Governmentality: An Introduction, in *Economy and Society*, 22: 265–266.

Bartie, A. (2010) Moral Panics and Glasgow Gangs: Exploring 'the New Wave of Glasgow Hooliganism', 1965–1970, in *Contemporary British History*, 24(3): 385–408.

Beatty, A. (2013) Irish Modernity and the Politics of Contraception, 1979–1993, in *New Hibernia Review*, 17(3): 100–118.

Beckett, K., and Western, B. (2001) Governing Social Marginality: Welfare Incarceration and the Transformation of State Policy, in *Punishment and Society*, 3: 43–59.

Begg, T. (1996) *Housing Policy in Scotland*, Edinburgh: John Donald.

Behan, C. (2018) "We Are All Convicted Criminals"? Prisoners, Protest and Penal Politics in the Republic of Ireland, in *Journal of Social History*, 52(2): 501–526.

Biber, K. (2019) *In Crime's Archive: The Cultural Afterlife of Evidence*, London: Routledge.

Biernacki, R. (1995) *The Fabrication of Labor: Germany and Britain, 1640-1914*, Berkeley: University of California Press.

Birkbeck, C. (2011) Imprisonment and internment: Comparing penal institutions North and South, *Punishment and Society*, 13(3): 307–332.

Black, L. (2016) Media, Public Attitudes and Crime, in Healy, D., Hamilton, C., Daly, Y., and Butler, M. (eds), *The Routledge Handbook of Irish Criminology*, London: Routledge.

Black, L. (2018) 'On the Other Hand the Accused is a Woman…': Women and the Death Penalty in Post-Independence Ireland, in *Law and History Review*, 36(1): 139–172.

Bonner, D. (1978) Ireland v United Kingdom, in *The International and Comparative Law Quarterly*, 27(4): 897-907.

Bottomley, A.K., Liebling, A., and Sparks, R. (1994) *The Barlinnie Special Unit and Shotts Unit: An Evaluation*, Edinburgh: Scottish Prison Service.

Bourdieu, P. (1990) *The Logic of Practice*, Cambridge: Polity.

Bourdieu, P. (1998) *Practical Reason: On the Theory of Action*. Cambridge: Polity.

Bourdieu, P. (2000) *Pascalian Meditations*, Cambridge: Polity Press.

Bowden, M. (2014) *Crime, Disorder and Symbolic Violence: Governing the Urban Periphery*, Basingstoke: Palgrave Macmillan.

Boyle, J. (1977) *A Sense of Freedom*, London: Pan Books.

Brady, C. (1974) *Guardians of the Police*, Dublin: Gill and Macmillan.

Brangan, L. (2019) Civilizing imprisonment: The limits of Scottish penal exceptionalism, *British Journal of Criminology*, 59(4): 780–799.

Brangan, L. (2020) Exceptional States: The Political Geography of Comparative Penology, in *Punishment and Society*, 22(5): 596–616. doi:10.1177/1462474520915995

Brangan, L. (2021) Pastoral penality in 1970s Ireland: Addressing the pains of imprisonment, *Theoretical Criminology*, 25(1): pp. 44–65.

Braun, V., and Clarke, V. (2006) Using Thematic Analysis in Psychology, in *Qualitative Research in Psychology*, 3(2): 77–101.

Brewer, J.D., Lockhart, B., and Rodgers, P. (1999) Crime in Ireland 1945-1995. in Heath, A., Breen, R., and Whelan, T.C. (eds), *Ireland North and South – Perspective from Social Science*, Oxford: Oxford University Press.

Brodie, I., Nottingham, C., and Plunkett, S. (2008) A Tale of Two Reports: Social Work in Scotland from Social Work and the Community (1966) to Changing Lives (2006), in *The British Journal of Social Work*, 38(4): 697–715.

Brubacker, R. (1999) Manichean Myth: Rethinking the Distinction between 'Civic' and 'Ethnic' Nationalism, in Kreisi, H., Armingeon, K., Siegrist, H., and Wimmer, A. (eds), *Nation and National Identity: The European Experience in Perspective*, Zurich: Verlag Rügger.

Bruce, M. (1982) Preface, in *The Journal of Association of Scottish Prison Governors*, 1: 3.

Buchan, J. (2020) The Struggle is Real: Theorising Community Justice Restructuring Agonistically, in *European Journal of Probation*, 12(2): 73–90. doi:10.1177/2066220320927353.

Butler, S. (2002) The Making of the Methadone Protocol: The Irish system? *Drugs: Education, Prevention and Policy*, 9(4): 311–324

Campbell, L. (2010) Responding to Gun Crime in Ireland, in *The British Journal of Criminology*, 21(1): 1–21.

Campbell, M., Ballas, D., Dorling, D., and Mitchell, R. (2013) Mortality inequalities: Scotland versus England and Wales, in *Health and Place*, 23: 179–186.

Canavan, J. (2012) Family and Family Change in Ireland – An Overview, in *Journal of Family Issues*, 33(1): 10–28.

Canton, R. (2015) Crime, punishment and the moral emotions: Righteous minds and their attitudes towards punishment, in *Punishment and Society*, 17(1): 54–72.

Carlen, P. (1983) *Women's Imprisonment: A Study in Social Control*, London: Routledge.

Carstairs, V., and Morris, R. (1989) Deprivation: Explaining Differences in Mortality Between Scotland and England and Wales, in *British Medical Journal*, 299(6704): 886-889.

Carvalho, H., and Chamberlen, A. (2017) Why Punishment Pleases: Punitive Feelings in a World Of Hostile Solidarity, in *Punishment in Society*, 20(2): 217–234.

Cavadino, M., and Dignan, J. (2006) *Penal Systems – A Comparative Approach*, London: Sage.

Central Statistics Office (2003) Population and Vital Statics http://www.cso.ie/en/media/csoie/releasespublications/documents/otherreleases/2003/population-andvitalstatistics.pdf [accessed July 20 2017].

Chubb, B. (1992) *The Government and Politics of Ireland* (3rd ed.), London: Longman.

Coakely, J. (1998) Religion, Ethnic Identity and Protestant Minority in the Republic, in Crotty, W., and Schmitt, D.E. (eds), *Ireland and the Politics of Change*, London: Routledge.

Coakely, J. (1999) Society and Political Culture, in Coakley, J., and Gallagher, M. (eds), *Politics in the Republic of Ireland* (3rd ed.), London: Routledge.

Cohen, S. (1972) *Folk Devils and Moral Panics: the creation of the Mods and Rockers*, London: MacGibbon and Kee.

Cohen, S. (1985) *Visions of Social Control: Crime, Punishment and Classification*, Cambridge: Polity.

Cohen, S., and Taylor, L. (1972) *Psychological Survival: The Experience of Long-Term Imprisonment*, Harmondsworth: Penguin.

Comfort, M. (2008) *Doing Time Together: Love and Family in the Shadow of the Prison*, Chicago; London: University of Chicago Press.

Committee of Inquiry into the Penal System (1985) *Report of the Inquiry into the Penal System*, Dublin: Stationary Office.

Condry, R. (2007) *Families Shamed: The Consequences of Crime for the Relatives of Serious Offenders*, Devon: Willan Publishing.

Connell, R. (2006) Northern Theory: The Political Geography of General Social Theory, in *Theory and Society*, 35(2): 237–264.

Cooke, D. (1989a) Containing Violent Prisoners – An Analysis of the Barlinnie Special Unit, in *The British Journal of Criminology*, 29(2): 129–143.

Cooke, D. (1989b) The Barlinnie Special Unit, in Scottish Prison Service, in Wozniak, D. (ed.) (1989) *Current Issue in Scottish Prisons: Systems of Accountability and Regimes for Difficult Prisoners – Proceedings of a Conference held at Stirling University 8th and 9th June 1988 and supported by the Criminology and Law Research Group and Scottish Prison Service*, Edinburgh: The Scottish Office

Cooke, D. (1994) *Psychological Disturbance in the Scottish Prison System: Prevalence*, Precipitants and Policy, Edinburgh: Scottish Prison Service.

Cooney, J. (1999) *John Charles McQuaid: Ruler of Catholic Ireland*, Dublin: O'Brien Press.

Coulter, C. (2003) The end of Irish history? An Introduction to the book, in Coulter, C., and Coleman, S. (eds), *The End of Irish History? Critical Reflections on the Celtic Tiger*, Manchester: Manchester University Press.

Cousins, M. (1995) *The Irish Social Welfare System: Law and Social Policy*, Dublin: Roundhall Press.

Coyle, A. (1987) The Management of Dangerous and Difficult Prisoners, in *The Howard Journal*, 26(2): 139–152.

Coyle, A. (1991) *Inside: Rethinking Scotland's Prisons*. Edinburgh: Scottish Child.

Coyle, A. (1992) The Responsible Prisoner: Rehabilitation Revisited, in *The Howard Journal of Crime and Justice*, 31(1): 1–7.

Coyle, A. (1994) *The Prisons We Deserve*, London: Harper Collins.

Crewe, B. (2009) *The Prisoner Society Power, Adaptation, and Social Life in an English Prison*, Oxford: Oxford University Press.

Crewe, B. (2011a) Soft Power in Prison: Implications for Staff – Prisoner Relationships, Liberty and Legitimacy, in *European Journal of Criminology*, 8(6): 455–468.

Crewe, B. (2011b) Depth, Weight, Tightness: Revisiting the Pains of Imprisonment, in *Punishment & Society*, 13(5): 509–529.

Crewe, B. (2020) The Depth of Imprisonment, in *Punishment and Society*, on-line first, doi: 10.1177/1462474520952153.

Croall, H. (2006) Criminal Justice in Post-Devolutionary Scotland, in *Critical Social Policy*, 26(3): 587–607.

Cunneen, C., Goldson, B., and Russell, S. (2018) Human Rights and Youth Justice Reform in England and Wales: A Systemic Analysis, in *Criminology and Criminal Justice*, 18(4): 405–430.

Damer, S. (1989) *From Moorepark to 'Wine Alley*, Edinburgh University Press: Edinburgh.

Damer, S. (1990) *Glasgow: Going for a Song*. London: Lawrence & Wishart.

Davies, A. (1998) Street Gangs, Crime and Policing in Glasgow during the 1930s: The Case of the Beehive Boys, in *Social History*, 23(3): 251–267.

Davies, A (2007a) Glasgow's 'Reign of Terror': Street Gangs, Racketeering and Intimidation in the 1920s and 1930s, in *Contemporary British History*, 21(4): 405–427.

Davies, A. (2007b) The Scottish Chicago? in *Cultural and Social History*, 4(4): 511–527. DOI:10.2752/147800407X243505.

De Sousa Santos, B. (2014) *Epistemologies of the South: Justice Against Epistemicide*, Boulder: Paradigm Publishers.

Dean, M. (2010) *Governmentality: Power and Rule in Modern Society* (2nd ed.), London: Sage.

Dean, G., O'Hare, A., O'Connor, A., Kelly, M., and Kelly, G. (1985) The opiate epidemic in Dublin 1979-1983, in *Irish Medical Journal*, 78: 107–110.

Delaney, E. (2000) *Demography, State and Society: Irish Migration to Britain, 1921-1971*, Montreal & Kingston: McGill-Queen's University Press.

Department of Justice (1973) Inquiry into Security, unpublished.

Department of Justice (1981a) Survey of Objectives, unpublished

Department of Justice (1981b) Effects of long term imprisonment, unpublished.

Department of Justice (1983) Draft Memo for Government, unpublished.

Department of Justice (1984a) Committee of Inquiry into the Penal System: Submission by the Department of Justice, unpublished.

Department of Justice (1984b) Notes on a Prison Board, unpublished.

Department of Justice (1984c) Staff/Management Relations – History and Implications, Draft Submission to Committee of Inquiry into the penal system, unpublished.

Department of Justice (1984d) Young Offenders Policy, Draft Submission to Committee of Inquiry into the penal system, unpublished.

Department of Justice (1984e) Capital Programme for Prisons and Places of Detention, unpublished.

Department of Justice (1984f) Major Developments in Prison Service Staffing Since 1970, Draft Submission to Committee of Inquiry into the penal system, unpublished.

Department of Justice (1984g), Prison Numbers and Shedding, Draft Submission to Committee of Inquiry into the penal system, unpublished.

Department of Justice (1986) Minister's Meeting with the Governors: The Whitaker Report, unpublished.

Department of Justice (1992) *Urban Crime and Disorder*, Dublin Stationary Office.

Department of Justice (1993) Report on the Advisory Committee on Communicable Diseases in Prisons Dublin: Stationary Office.

Department of Justice (1994) *Management of Offenders – A Five Year Plan*, Dublin: Stationary Office.

Department of Justice (1997a) *Tackling Crime*, Dublin: Stationary Office.

Department of Justice (1997b) *Strategic Management Imitative, appended in Tackling Crime*, Dublin: Stationary Office.

Department of Justice (1997c) *Towards an Independent Prison Agency*, Dublin: Stationary Office.

Department of Justice, Equality and Law Reform (1998) *Strategy Statement 1998-2000: Community Security and Equality*, Dublin: Department of Justice, Equality and Law Reform.

Department of Justice, Equality and Law Reform (1999) *Report on Probation and Welfare*, Dublin: Stationary Office.

Department of the Taoiseach (1984). *Building on Reality 1984-87 (National Economic Plan) Government Publications*, Ireland: Oireachtas

Dillon, M. (1998) Divorces and Cultural Rationality, in Peillon, M., and Slater, E. (eds), *Encounters with Modern Ireland – A Sociological Chronicle 1995-1996*, Dublin: Institute of Public Administration.

Donzelot, J. (1980) *The Policing of Families*, London: Hutchison University Press.

Dooley, E. (1995) *Homicide in Ireland 1972-1991*, Dublin: The Stationary Office.

Dooley, E. (2001) *Homicide in Ireland 1992-1996*, Dublin: The Stationary Office.

Douglas, M. (1992) *Risk and Blame – Essays in Cultural Theory*, London/New York: Routledge.

Downes, D. (1988) *Contrasts in Tolerance*, New York: Oxford University Press.

Downes, D., and Hansen, K. (2006) Welfare and Punishment in Comparative Perspective, in McAra, L., and Armstrong, S. (eds), *Perspectives on Punishment – The Contours of Control*, New York: Oxford University Press.

Downes, S., Holloway, D., and Randles, S. (eds.). (2018) *Feeling things: Objects and emotions through history*, Oxford: Oxford University Press.

Duff, P., and Hutton, N. (1999) Introduction, in Duff, P., and Hutton, N. (eds), *Criminal Justice in Scotland*, Aldershot: Ashgate.

Durkheim, É. (1984) *The Division of Labour in Society*, Basingstoke: Macmillan.

Elias, N. (1978) *The Civilizing Process / Vol. 1, The History of Manners*, translated by Edmund Jephcott. (Mole editions), Oxford: Blackwell.

Gateway Exchange (1987) *The Roof Comes Off-The Report of the Independent Committee of Inquiry into the Protests at Peterhead Prison*, Edinburgh: A Gateway Exchange Publication.

Fahey, T., and McLaughlin, E. (1999) Family and the State, in Heath, A., Breen, R., and Whelan, T.C. (eds), *Ireland North and South – Perspective from Social Science*, Oxford: Oxford University Press.

Fanning, B. (2007) *Immigration and Social Change in the Republic of Ireland*, Manchester: Manchester University Press.

Fassin, D. (2018) *The Will to Punish*, New York: Oxford University Press.

Feeley, M.M., and Simon, J. (1992) The New Penology: Notes on the Emerging Strategy of Corrections and its Implications, in *Criminology*, 30(4): 449–474.

Ferriter, D. (2012) *Ambiguous Republic: Ireland in the 1970s*, London: Profile Books.

Fianna Fáil (1997a) Fianna Fáil: 1997 General Election Manifesto, available at http://michaelpidgeon.com/manifestos/docs/ff/Fianna%20Fail%20GE%20 1997.pdf [accessed June 2017]

Fianna Fáil (1997b) Leading the Fight Against Crime – A Fianna Fáil Position Paper on Justice.

Fischer, C. (2016) Gender, Nation, and the Politics of Shame: Magdalen Laundries and the Institutionalization of Feminine Transgression in Modern Ireland, in *Signs: Journal of Women in Culture and Society*, 41(4): 821–843.

Fitzgerald, P., and Lambkin, B. (2008) *Migration in Irish History 1607-2007*, Basingstoke: Palgrave Macmillan.

Foucault, M. (1977) *Discipline and Punish: The Birth of the Prison*, New York: Pantheon.

Foucault, M. (1980) *Power/Knowledge: Selected Interviews and Other Writings, 1972-1977*, Brighton: Harvester Press.

Foucault, M. (1981) Omnes et singulatim/Towards a Criticism of Political Reason, in *Tanner Lectures on Human*, 2: 225–254.

Foucault, M. (1982) The Subject and Power, in *Critical Inquiry*, 8(4): 777–795.

Foucault, M. (1991a) Questions of Method, in Burchell, G., Gordon, C., and Miller, P. (eds), *The Foucault Effect*, Chicago: The University of Chicago.

Foucault, M. (1991b) Governmentality, in Burchell, G., Gordon, C., and Miller, P. (eds), *The Foucault Effect*, Chicago: The University of Chicago.

Franko Aas, K. (2004) From Narrative to Database: Technological Change and Penal Culture, in *Punishment & Society*, 6(4): 379–393.

Franko Aas, K. (2012) 'The Earth is One But the World Is Not': Criminological Theory and its Geopolitical Divisions, in *Theoretical Criminology*, 16(1): 5–20.

Fraser, A. (2015) *Urban Legends: Gang Identity in the Post-Industrial City*, Oxford: Oxford University Press.

Freeden, M. (1996) *Ideologies and Political Theory: A Conceptual Approach*, Oxford: Oxford University Press.

Freeden, M. (2003) *Ideology: A Very Short Introduction*, Oxford: Oxford University Press.

Freeman R., and Maybin, J. (2011) Documents, Practices and Policy, in *Evidence and Policy* 7(2): 155–170.

Frizzell, E. (1993) The Scottish Prison Service: Changing the Culture, in *Howard Journal of Criminal Justice*, 32(3): 203–214.

Gamble, A. (1994) *The Free Economy and the Strong State: The Politics of Thatcherism* (2nd ed.), Houndmills: Macmillan.

Ganiel, G. (2016) *Transforming Post-Catholic Ireland: Religious Practice in Late Modernity*, Oxford: Oxford University Press.

Garland, D. (1985) *Punishment and Welfare: A History of Penal Strategies*, London: Gower.

Garland, D. (1990a) *Punishment and Modern Society: A Study in Social Theory*, Oxford: Oxford University Press.

Garland, D. (1990b) Frameworks of Inquiry in the Sociology of Punishment, in *The British Journal of Sociology*, 41(1): 1–15.

Garland, D. (1991) Sociological Perspectives on Punishment, *Crime and Justice*, 14:115–165.

Garland, D. (1996) The Limits of the Sovereign State–Strategies of Crime Control in Contemporary Society, in *British Journal of Criminology*, 36(4): 445–471.

Garland, D. (1997) 'Governmentality' and the Problem of Crime, in *Theoretical Criminology*, 1: 173–214.

Garland, D. (2001) *The Culture of Control: Crime and Social Order in Contemporary Society*, Oxford: Oxford University Press.

Garland, D. (2010) *Peculiar Institution: America's Death Penalty in an Age of Abolition*, New York: Oxford University Press.

Garland, D. (2013) Penality and the Penal State, in *Criminology*, 51(3): 475–517.

Garland, D. (2017) Penal power in America: Forms, functions and foundations, in *Journal of the British Academy*, 5: 1–35.

Garland, D. (2018) Theoretical Advances and Problems in the Sociology of Punishment, in *Punishment and Society*, 20(1): 8–33.

Garland, D. (2020) Penal Controls and Social Controls: Toward a Theory of American Penal Exceptionalism, in *Punishment and Society*, 22(3): 321–352. doi:10.1177/1462474519881992

Garland, D., and Sparks, R. (2000) Criminology, social theory, and the challenge of our times, in *The British Journal of Criminology*, 40: 189–204.

Geertz, C. (1973) *The Interpretation of Cultures*, New York: Basic Books.

Geertz. C. (1983) *Local Knowledge: Further Essays in Interpretative Anthropology Further Essays in Interpretative Anthropology*, New York: Basic Books.

Genders, E., and Player, E. (1995) *Grendon: A Study of a Therapeutic Prison*, Oxford: Clarendon Press.

Gibson, J.S. (1985) *The Thistle and the Crown – A History of the Scottish Office*, Edinburgh: HMSO.

Girling, E., Loader, I., and Sparks, R. (2000) *Crime and Social Change in Middle England – Questions of Order in an English Town*, London: Routledge.

Girvin, B. (1986) Social Change and Moral Politics: The Irish Constitutional Referendum 1983, in *Political Studies*, 34(1): 61–81.

Godson, L. (2015) Charting the material culture of the 'Devotional Revolution': The Advertising Register of the Irish Catholic Directory, 1837-96, in *Proceedings of the Royal Irish Academy*, 116C: 1–30.

Goffman, E. (1963) *Stigma: Notes on the Management of Spoiled Identity*, Middlesex: Pneguin Books.

Goffman, A. (2015) *On the Run: Fugitive Life in an American City*, New York: Picador.

Golder, B. (2007) Foucault and the Genealogy of Pastoral Power, in *Radical Philosophy Review*, 10(2): 157–176.

Goodman, P. (2012) 'Another Second Chance': Rethinking Rehabilitation through the Lens of California's Prison Fire Camps, in *Social Problems*, 59(4): 437–458.

Goodman, P., Page, J., and Phelps, M. (2017) *Breaking the Pendulum – The Long Struggle Over Criminal Justice*, New York: Oxford University Press.

Gray, N., and Mooney, G. (2011) Glasgow's New Urban Frontier: 'Civilising' the Population of 'Glasgow East', in *City*, 15(1): 4–24.

Green, D. (2007) Comparing Penal Cultures: Child-on-Child Homicide in England and Norway, in Tonry, M. (ed), *Crime, Punishment and Politics in Comparative Perspective*, Chicago: University of Chicago.

Green, D. (2008) *When Children Kill Children*. New York: Oxford University Press.

Griffin, D. (2018) *Killing Time: Life Imprisonment and Parole in Ireland*, Palgrave Macmillan.

Griffin, D., and O'Donnell, I. (2012) The Life Sentence and Parole, in *The British Journal of Criminology*, 52: 611–629.

Guiney, T. (2018) *Getting Out*, Oxford: Oxford University Press.

Gunn, S. (2006) From Hegemony to Governmentality/Changing Conceptions of Power, in *Journal of Social History*, 39(3): 705–720.

Hall, S., Clarke, J., Critcher, C., Jefferson, T., and Roberts, B. [1978] (2013) *Policing the Crisis – 35th Anniversary Edition*, London: Palgrave Macmillan.

Halttunen, K. (1995) Humanitarianism and the Pornography of Pain in Anglo-American Culture, in *The American Historical Review*, 100(2): 303.

Hamilton, C. (2013) Punitiveness and Political Culture: Notes from Some Small Countries, in *European Journal of Criminology*, 10(2): 154–167.

Hamilton, C. (2014) *Reconceptualising Penality: A Comparative Perspective on Punitiveness in Ireland*, Scotland and New Zealand, Surrey: Routledge.

Hamilton, C. (2016) Penal Policy in Ireland: Notes from a Small Country, in Healy, D., Hamilton, C., Daly, Y., and Butler, M. (eds), *The Routledge Handbook of Irish Criminology*, London: Routledge.

Hannah-Moffat, K. (1997) From Christian maternalism to risk technologies: Penal powers and women's knowledges in the governance of female prisons, PhD dissertation, University of Toronto, Canada.

Hannah-Moffat, K. (2005) Criminality, need and the transformative risk subject: Hybridizations of risk/need in penality, in *Punishment and Society*, 7: 29–51.

Hannah-Moffat, K. (2014) '*Moving targets: Reputational risk, rights and accountability in punishment*', SCCJR 8th Annual Lecture, 19th May, Glasgow, Scotland, available online: http://www.sccjr.ac.uk/publications/moving-targets-reputational-risk-rights-and-accountability-in-punishment/ [accessed January 2016]

Hardiman, N., and Whelan, C. (1998) Changing Values, in Crotty, W., and Schmitt, D.E. (eds), *Ireland and the Politics of Change*, London: Routledge.

Hartnagel, T.F., and Templeton, L.J. (2012) Emotions about Crime and Attitudes to Punishment, in *Punishment & Society*, 14(4): 452–474.

Harvie, D. (1977) *Scotland and Nationalism: Scottish society and politics, 1707-1977*, London: Allen and Unwin.

Hay, C. (2002) *Political Analysis: A Critical Introduction*, Basingstoke: Palgrave.

Hazelkorn, E., and Patterson, H. (1994) The New Politics of the Irish Republic, in *New Left Review*, 207: 49–71.

Healy, D., and Kennifick, L. (2019) Hidden Voices: Practitioner Perspectives on the Early Histories of Probation in Ireland, in *Criminology and Criminal Justice*, 19(3): 346–363.

Heylin, G. (2001) *Evaluating Prisons, Prisoners, and Others*, Dublin: The Policy Institute/Department of Justice Equality and Law Reform.

Hirschle, J. (2010) From Religious to Consumption-Related Routine Activities? Analyzing Ireland's Economic Boom and the Decline in Church Attendance, *Journal for the Scientific Study of Religion*, 49(4): 673–687

Holland, K. (1997) City Problems: Where Is the Church? in *The Furrow*, 48(9): 461–466.

Holliday, I. (1992) Scottish Limits to Thatcherism, in *Political Quarterly*, 63(4), 448–459.

Hood, C. (1991) A Public Management for All Seasons? in *Public Administration*, 69(1), 3–19.

Houchin, R. (2005) Social Exclusion and Imprisonment in Scotland – A Report http://www.scotpho.org.uk/downloads/SocialExclusionandImprisonmentinScotland.pdf [accessed February 2014]

House of Commons (2017) UK Prison Population Statistics – Briefing Paper Number SN/SG/04334.

Hucklesby, A., Beyens, K., and Boone, M. (2020) Comparing Electronic Monitoring Regimes: Length, Breadth, Depth and Weight Equals Tightness, Punishment & Society, online first.

Hutchison, G.C.I. (1996) Government in the Union, 1945-95: The Changing Nature of the Union State, in Devine, T.M., and Finlay, R.J. (eds), *Scotland in the 20th Century*, Edinburgh: Edinburgh University Press.

Inglis, T. (1998) *Moral Monopoly – The Rise and Fall of the Catholic Church in Modern Ireland* (2nd ed.), Dublin: University College Dublin Press.

Inglis, T. (2003) *Truth, Power and Lies: Irish Society and the Case of the Kerry Babies*, Dublin: University College Dublin Press

Innes, M. (2004) Signal Crimes and Signal Disorders: Notes on Deviance as Communicative Action, in *The British Journal of Sociology*, 55(3): 335–354.

Irish Prison Service (2006) *Capital Expenditure Review*, Dublin: Fitzpatrick Associates

Jardine, C. (2020) *Families Imprisonment and Legitimacy The Cost of Custodial Penalties*, London: Routledge.

Johnston, R., and McIvor, A. (2004) Dangerous Work, Hard Men, and Broken Bodies: Masculinity in Clydeside Heavy Industries, 1930-1970s, in *Labour History Review*, 69(2): 135–151.

Johnstone, C. (1992) The tenants' movement and housing struggles in Glasgow, 1945-1990, unpublished PhD thesis.

Johnstone, J.G. (1996) *Medical Concepts and Penal Policy*, London: Cavendish.

Jones, T., and Newburn, T. (2005) Comparative Criminal Justice Policy-Making in the United States and the United Kingdom, *British Journal of Criminology*, 45(1): 58–80.

Jones, T., and Newburn, T. (2007) *Policy Transfer and Criminal Justice*. Berkshire: Open University Press.

Joyce, P. (2003) *The Rule of Freedom: Liberalism and the Modern City*, London, England; New York: Verso.

Keating, M. (1988) *The City that Refused to Die. Glasgow: The Politics of Urban Regeneration*, Aberdeen: Aberdeen University Press.

Keating, M. (1996) *Nations against the State: The New Politics of Nationalism in Quebec, Catalonia and Scotland*, New York: St, Martins Press.

Keating, M., and Midwinter A. (1983) *The Government of Scotland*, Edinburgh: Mainstream Publishing.

Kelleher, M., Keown, P., O'Gara, C., Keaney, F., Farrell, M., and Strang, J. (2005) Dying for Heroin: The Increasing Opioid-Related Mortality in the Republic of Ireland, 1980–1999, in *European Journal of Public Health*, 15(6): 589–592.

Keogh, D. (1994) *Twentieth-Century Ireland: Nation and State*, Dublin: Gill and Macmillan.

Kilbrandon, C. (1964) *The Kilbrandon Report: Children and Young Persons Scotland*, Edinburgh: Her Majesty's Stationary Office.

Kilcommins, S., O'Donnell, I., O'Sullivan, E., and Vaughan, B. (2004) *Crime, Punishment and the Search for Order in Ireland*, Dublin: Institute of Public Administration.

King, R.D., and McDermott, K. (1995) *The State of Our Prisons*, Oxford: Clarendon.

Kinsey, R. (1988) *The Politics and Ideology of the Prison Crisis, in Scottish Government reference: The Scottish Government Yearbook 1988*. Unit for the Study of Government in Scotland, University of Edinburgh.

Kirkwood, D. (1935) *My Life of Revolt*, London: George G. Harrap.

Lacey, N. (2008) *The Prisoners' Dilemma: Political Economy and Punishment in Contemporary Democracies*, Cambridge: Cambridge University Press.

Lamont, M. (1992) *Money, Morals, and Manners: The Culture of the French and American Upper-Middle Class*, Chicago: University of Chicago Press.

Lappi-Seppälä, T. (2008) Trust, Welfare and Political Culture: Explaining Differences in National Penal Policies, in M. Tonry (ed), *Crime and Justice, Volume 37*, Chicago: Chicago University Press.

Lappi-Seppälä, T. (2011) Explaining Imprisonment in Europe, in *European Journal of Criminology*, 8(4): 303–328.

Larkin, E. (1975) Church, State and Nation in Modern Ireland, in *American Historical Review*, 80(5): 1244–1276.

Latour, B. (2010) *The Making of Law: an ethnography of the Conseil d'Etat*, Cambridge: Polity.

Laursen, J., Mjåland, K., and Crewe, B. (2020) 'It's Like a Sentence Before the Sentence'—Exploring the Pains and Possibilities of Waiting for Imprisonment, in *British Journal of Criminology*, 60(2): 363–381.

Lawlor, P., and McDonald, E. (2001) *Story of a Success – Irish Prisons CONNECT Project 1998-2000*, Dublin: Irish Prison Service.

Lee, J., and O'Tuathaigh, G. (1982) *The Age of de Valera*, Dublin: Ward River Press.

Liebling, A. assisted by Arnold, H. (2004) *Prisons and Their Moral Performance: A Study of Values*, Quality and Prison Life, Oxford: Clarendon Press.

Lindblom, C.E. (1959) The Science of "Muddling Through", in *Public Administration Review*, 19(2): 79–88.

Loader, I. (2006) Fall of the 'Platonic Guardians' – Liberalism, Criminology and Political Responses to Crime in England and Wales, in *British Journal of Criminology*, 46(4): 561–586.

Loader, I. (2020) Crime, Order and the Two Faces of Conservatism: An Encounter with Criminology's other, in *British Journal of Criminology*, 60(5): 1181–1200.

Loader, I., and Mulcahy, A. (2003) *Policing and the Condition of England*, Oxford University Press.

Loader, I., and Sparks, R. (2004) For an Historical Sociology of Crime Policy in England and Wales since 1968, in *Critical Review of International Social and Political Philosophy*, 7(2): 5–32.

Loader, I., and Sparks, R. (2016) Ideologies and crime: political ideas and the dynamics of crime control, in *Global Crime*. doi:10.1080/17440572.2016.1169926

Lonergan, J. (2010) *The Governor – The life and times of the man who ran Mountjoy*, Dublin: Penguin.

Lynch, M. (2011) Mass imprisonment, legal change, and locale, in *Criminology and Public Policy*, 10(3): 673–698.

MacDonald, D., and Sim, J. (1978) *Scottish Prisons and the Special Unit*, Edinburgh: Scottish council for Civil Liberties.

MacGreil, M. (1996) *Prejudice in Ireland Revisited: Based on a National Survey of Intergroup Attitudes in the Republic of Ireland*. Dublin: Survey and Research Unit, St. Patrick's College, Maynooth.

Matthews, R. (2005) The Myth of Punitiveness, in *Theoretical Criminology*, 9: 175–201.

Matthews, R. (2009) *Doing Time: An Introduction to the Sociology of Imprisonment* (2nd ed.), Basingstoke: Palgrave Macmillan.

McAra, L. (1999) The Politics of Penality: An overview of the Development of Penal Policy in Scotland, in Duff, P., and Hutton, N. (eds), *Criminal Justice in Scotland*, Dartmouth: Ashgate.

McAra, L. (2005) Modelling Penal Transformation, in *Punishment and Society*, 7(3): 277–302.

McAra, L. (2008) Crime, Criminal Justice and Criminology in Scotland, in *European Journal of Criminology*, 5(4): 481–504.

McCartney G, Shipley M, Hart C, Davey-Smith G, Kivimäki M., Walsh, D., Watt, G., and Batty, G. (2012) Why Do Males in Scotland Die Younger than Those in England? Evidence from Three Prospective Cohort Studies, in *PLoS One*, 7(7): e38860. doi:10.1371/journal.pone.003886.

McCrone, D. (2001) *Understanding Scotland – A Sociology of a Nation* (2nd ed.), London: Routledge.

McCrone, D. (2006) The Same, but Different: Why Scotland? *Scottish Affairs*, 55(1): 11–22.

McCullagh, C. (2002) The Social Analysis of the Irish Prison System, in O'Mahony, P. (ed), *Criminal Justice in Ireland*, Dublin: Institute of Public Administration

McDonnell, O., and Allison, J. (2006) From Biopolitics to Bioethics: Church, State, Medicine and Assisted Reproductive Technology in Ireland, in *Sociology of Health and Illness*, 28(6): 817–837.

McEvoy, K. (1998) Prisoners, the Agreement, and the Political Character of the Northern Ireland Conflict, in *Fordham International Law Journal*, 22(4): 1539–1576.

McEvoy, K. (2001) *Paramilitary Imprisonment in Northern Ireland: Resistance, Management, and Release*, Oxford University Press.

McEwan, N. (2002) State Welfare Nationalism: The Territorial Impact of Welfare State Development in Scotland, in *Regional and Federal Studies*, 12(1): 66–90.

McGowan, D. (2016) Governed by marriage law, in *Social and Legal Studies*, 25(3): 311–331.

McKinlay, P. (1989) *Introduction*, in *Scottish Prison Service (edited by Ed Wozniak) Current Issue in Scottish Prisons: Systems of Accountability and Regimes for Difficult Prisoners*, held at Stirling University 8th and 9th June 1988 and supported by the Criminology and Law Research Group and Scottish Prison Service, Edinburgh: The Scottish Office

McLennan, G. (2006) Book Review: Living in Scotland: Social and Economic Change since 1980. *Sociology*, 40(3): 592–593

McManus, J.J. (1994) *Mentally Disturbed Prisoners: Issues in the Identification and Management of the Mentally Disturbed Within Penal Establishments*, Edinburgh: Scottish Prison Service.

McManus, J. (1999) Imprisonment and Other Custodial Sentences, in Duff, P., and Hutton, N. (eds), *Criminal Justice in Scotland*, Aldershot: Ashgate.

McNally, G. (2007) Probation in Ireland: A Brief History of the Early Years, in *Irish Probation Journal*, 4(1): 4–23.

McNeill, J. (1988) Classification Procedures in Scottish Prisons: 'Sweeties for the Good Boys?' in Backett, S., McNeil, J., and Yellowlees, A. (eds), *Imprisonment Today – Current Issues in the Prison Debate*, Basingstoke: Macmillan.

McNeill, F. (2005) Remembering Probation in Scotland, in *The Probation Journal*, 52(1): 23–38.

McNeill, F. (2019) *Pervasive Punishment: Making Sense of Mass Supervision*, UK: Emerald Publishing.

McVerry, P. (1985) *Spike Island – The Answer to What?* Dublin: Resource Publications.

Melossi, D. (1994) The "Economy" of Illegalities: Normal Crimes, Elites and Social Control in Comparative Analysis, in Nelken, D. (ed), *The Futures of Criminology*, London: Sage.

Melossi, D. (2000) Social Theory and Changing Representations of the Criminal, in *British Journal of Criminology*, 40(2): 296–320.

Melossi, D. (2001) The Cultural Embeddedness of Social Control: Reflections on the Comparison of Italian and North-American Cultures, in *Theoretical Criminology*, 5(4): 403–424.

Melossi, D. (2004) The Cultural Embeddedness of Social Control: Reflections on the Comparison of Italian and North-American Cultures Concerning Punishment, in Newburn, T., and Sparks, R. (eds), *Criminal Justice and Political Cultures*. Cullompton: Willan.

Merton, R.K. (1987) Three Fragments from a Sociologists Notebooks: Establishing the Phenomenon Specified Ignorance, and Strategic Research Materials, in *Sociology Annual Review*, 13: 1-28.

Midwinter, A. (1990) A Return to Ratepayer Democracy? The Reform of Local Government Finance in Historical Perspective, in *Scottish Economic and Social History*, 10(1): 61–69.

Midwinter, A., Keating, M., and Mitchell, J. (1991) *Politics and public Policy in Scotland*, London: MacMillan Education.

Miller, L. (2015) What's Violence Got to Do With It? Inequality, Punishment and State Failure in US Politics, in *Punishment and Society*, 17(2): 184–210.

Miller, L. (2016) *The Myth of Mob Rule: Violent Crime and Democratic Politics*, New York: Oxford University Press.

Mills, C.W. (1940a) Situated Actions and Vocabularies of Motive, in *American Sociological Review*, 5(6): 904–913.

Mills, C.W. (1940b) Situated Actions and Vocabularies of Motive, in *American Sociological Review*, 5(6): 904–913.

Mitchell, J., and Bennie, L. (1995) Thatcherism and the Scottish question, in *British Elections and Parties Yearbook*, 90–104.

Mohr, T. (2017) Embedding the Family in the Irish Constitution, in Howlin, N., and Costello, K. (eds), *Law and the Family in Ireland, 1800–1950*, Basingstoke: Palgrave Macmillan.

Mooney, G., Croall, H., Munro, M., and Scott, G. (2015) Scottish Criminal Justice: Devolution, Divergence and distinCtiveness, in *Criminology and Criminal Justice*, 2: 205–224.

Moore, G. (1978) Crisis in Scotland, in *Howard Journal of Criminal Justice*, 17(1): 32–40.

Morris, N. (1966) Impediments to Penal Reform, in *The University of Chicago Law Review*, 33(4): 627–656.

Mulcahy, A. (2002) The Impact of the Northern "Troubles" on Criminal Justice in the Irish Republic, in O'Mahony, P (ed), *Criminal Justice in Ireland*, Dublin: Institute of Public Administration.

Muncie, J. (1990) Failure Never Matters: Detention Centres and The Politics of Deterrence, in *Critical Social Policy*, 10(28): 53–66.

Munro, C.R. (1999) Scottish Devolution: Accommodating a Restless Nation, in *International Journal on Minority and Group Rights*, 6(1–2): 97–119.

Nelken, D. (2002) Comparing Criminal Justice, in Maguire, M., Morgan, R., and Reiner, R. (eds), *The Oxford Handbook of Criminology* (3rd ed.), Oxford: Clarendon Press.

Nelken, D. (2005) When is a Society Non-Punitive? The Italian Case, in Pratt, J., Brown, D., Brown, M., Hallsworth, S., and Morrison, W. (eds), *The New Punitiveness: Trends*, Theories, Perspectives, Willan: Cullompton.

Nelken, D. (2006) Patterns of Punitiveness, in *The Modern Law Review*, 69(2): 262–277.

Nelken, D. (2009) Comparative Criminal Justice: Beyond Ethnocentrism and Relativism, in *European Journal of Criminology*, 6(4): 291-311.

Nelken, D. (2010) *Comparative Criminal Justice*, London: Sage.

Nelken, D. (2011) Explaining Differences in European Prison Rates: A Comment on Lacey's The Prisoners' Dilemma, in *Punishment and Society*, 13(1): 104–114.

Nelken, D. (2017) Rethinking Comparative Criminal Justice, in Liebling, A., Maruna, S., and McAra, L. (eds), *The Oxford Handbook of Criminology* (6th ed.), Oxford: Oxford University Press.

Nellis, M. (2010) Creative Arts and the Cultural Politics of Penal Reform; the early years of the Barlinnie Special Unit 1973-1981, in *The Scottish Journal of Criminal Justice Studies*, 16: 47–73.

Newburn, T., and Sparks, R. (2004) Criminal Justice and Political Cultures, in Newburn, T., and Sparks, R. (eds), *Criminal Justice and Political Cultures: National and International Dimensions of Crime Control*, Devon: Willan Publishing.

Norris, G.M. (1983) Poverty in Scotland 1979-1983, in Brown, G., and Cook, R. (eds), *Scotland the Real Divide – Poverty and Deprivation in Scotland*, Edinburgh: Mainstream Publishing.

O'Connell, P.J. (1999) Sick Man or Tigress? The Labour Market in the Republic of Ireland, in *Proceedings in the British Academy*, 98: 215–249.

O'Donnell, I. (2004) Imprisonment and Penal Policy in Ireland, in *The Howard Journal*, 43(3): 253–266.

O'Donnell, I. (2005) Crime and Justice in the Republic of Ireland, in *The European Journal of Criminology*, 2(1): 121–133.

O'Donnell, I. (2008) Stagnation and Change in Irish Penal Policy, in *Howard Journal of Criminal Justice*, 47(2): 121–133.

O'Donnell, I., and Jewkes, Y. (2011) Going home for Christmas: Prisoners, a Taste of Freedom and the Press, in *Howard Journal of Criminal Justice*, 50(1): 75–91.

O'Donnell, I., and O'Sullivan, S. (2001) *Crime Control in Ireland: The Politics of Intolerance*, Cork: Cork University Press.

O'Donnell, I., and O'Sullivan, S. (2003) The Politics of Intolerance – Irish Style, in *British Journal of Criminology*, 43: 41–62.

O'Donnell, I., and O'Sullivan, E., (2012) *Coercive Confinement – Patients, Prisoners and Penitents*, Manchester: Manchester University Press.

O'Donnell, I., O'Sullivan, E., and Healy, E. (2005) *Crime and Punishment in Ireland, 1922 to 2003 – A Statistical Sourcebook*, Dublin: Institute of Public Administration.

O'Dowd, L. (1987) Town and Country in Irish Ideology, in *The Canadian Journal of Irish Studies*, 13(2): 43–53.

O'Mahony, P. (1996) *Criminal Chaos – Seven crises in Irish Criminal Justice*, Dublin: Round Hall.

O'Mahony, P. (1997) *Mountjoy Prisoners: A Sociological and Criminological Profile*, Dublin: Stationary Office.

O'Mahony, P (2000a) Crime in the republic of Ireland: A Suitable Case for Social Analysis, in *Irish Journal of Sociology*, 10: 3–26.

O'Mahony, P (2000b) *Prison Policy in Ireland – Criminal Justice Versus Social Justice*, Cork: Cork University Press.

O'Malley, P. (1992) Risk, Power and Crime Prevention, in *Economy and Society*, 21(3): 252–275.

O'Malley, P. (1999) Volatile and Contradictory Punishment, in *Theoretical Criminology*, 3(2): 175–196.

O'Malley, T. (2006) *Sentencing Law and Practice* (2nd ed.), Dublin: Thomson Round Hall.

O'Malley, P. (2010) *Crime and Risk*, London: SAGE.

O'Malley, P., and Valverdre, M. (2004) Pleasure, Freedom and Drugs: The Uses of 'Pleasure' in Liberal Governance of Drug and Alcohol Consumption, in *Sociology*, 38(1): 25–42.

O'Sullivan, E., and O'Donnell, I. (2007) Coercive Confinement in the Republic of Ireland – The Waning of a Culture of Control, in *Punishment and Society*, 9(1): 27–48.

O'Brien, J.A. (ed) (1953) *The Vanishing Irish*, London: W.H.Allen.

O'Donnell, I. (2001) Prison Matters, in *Irish Jurist*, 2001(36): 153–173.

O'Malley, P. (2010) Resilient Subjects: Uncertainty, Warfare and Liberalism, in *Economy and Society*, 39(4): 488–509.

O'Malley, P., Weir, L., and Shearing, C. (1997) Governmentality, Criticism, Politics, in *Economy and Society*, 26(4): 501–517.

Pacione, M. (1995) *Glasgow: The Socio-Spatial Development of the City*, Chichester: Wiley.

Page, J. (2011) *The Toughest Beat: Politics, Punishment and the Prison Officers Union in California*, New York: Oxford University Press.

Patterson, H. (2006) *Ireland since 1939: The Persistence of Conflict*, London: Penguin Books

Pease, K. (1994) Cross-National Imprisonment Rates: Limitations of Method and Possible Conclusions, in *British Journal of Criminology*, 34: 116–130.

Peillon, M. (1998a) Community of Distrust, in Peillon, M., and Slater, E. (eds), *Encounters with Modern Ireland – A Sociological Chronicle 1995-1996*, Dublin: Institute of Public Administration.

Peillon, M. (1998b) Rubbish, in Peillon, M., and Slater, E. (eds), *Encounters with Modern Ireland – A Sociological Chronicle 1995–1996*, Dublin: Institute of Public Administration.

Perchard, A. (2013) "Broken Men" and "Thatcher's Children": Memory and Legacy in Scotland's Coalfields, in *International Labor and Working-Class History*, 84: 78–98.

Phelps, M. (2017) Mass Probation: Towards a More Robust Theory of State Variation in Punishment, in *Punishment and Society*, 9(1): 53–73. doi:10.1177/1462474516649174

Phillips, R. et al. (1994) *Physically disabled prisoners in Scotland*, Edinburgh: Scottish Prison Service.

Pierson, P. (2004) *Politics in Time: History, Institutions and Social Analysis*, Princeton, NJ: Princeton University Press.

Power, K.G. (1997) *Evaluation of the Scottish Prison Service suicide prevention strategy*, Edinburgh: Scottish Prison Service.

Power, K.G., Markova, I., and Rowlands, A. (1994) *HIV/AIDS Knowledge, Attitudes and Personal Risk in the Scottish Prison Service: A Summary of Recent Research*, Edinburgh: Scottish Prison Service.

Pratt, J. (2008) Scandinavian Exceptionalism in an Era of Penal Excess, in *British Journal of Criminology*, 48(3): 275–292.

Pratt, J., and Eriksson, A. (2013) *Contrasts in Punishment – An Explanation of Anglophone Excess and Nordic Exceptionalism*, Oxon: Routledge.

Pratt, J., Brown, D., Brown, M., Hallsworth, S., and Morrison, W. (eds) (2005) *The New Punitiveness: Trends*, Theories, Perspectives, Willan: Cullompton.

Reid, J. (2009) Excess mortality in the Glasgow conurbation: exploring the existence of a 'Glasgow effect'. Unpublished PhD thesis.

Reiter, K., Sexton, L., and Sumner, J. (2018) Theoretical and Empirical Limits of Scandinavian Exceptionalism: Isolation and normalization in Danish prisons, in *Punishment and Society*, 20, 92–112.

Rhodes, R. (1994) The Hollowing Out of the State: The Changing Nature of the Public Service in Britain, in *Political Quarterly*, 65(2): 138–151.

Robinson, G. (2008) Late-Modern Rehabilitation, in *Punishment and Society*, 10(4): 429–445.

Robinson, G. (2016) The Cinderella Complex: Punishment, Society and Community Sanctions, in *Punishment and Society*, 18(1): 95–112.

Rogan, M. (2011) *Prison Policy in Ireland: Politics,* Penal-Welfarism and Political Imprisonment, Oxon: Routledge.

Rooney, L. (2020) Gendered Perceptions of Child Sexual Abusers: The Paradox of the "Vulnerable Other", in *Journal of Contemporary Criminal Justice,* online first, doi:10.1177/1043986220936099.

Rose, N. (1989) *Governing the Soul,* London: Routledge.

Rose, N. (1993) Government, Authority and Expertise in Advanced Liberalism, in *Economy and Society,* 22(3): 283–299.

Rose, N., and Miller, P. (2010) Political Power Beyond the State: Problematic of Government, in *The British Journal of Sociology,* 61(1): 271–303.

RTÉ (1972a) Bloody Sunday Taoiseach Gives Reaction, available at: http://www.rte.ie/archives/2017/0201/849359-british-embassy-burns/ {accessed March 2016]

RTÉ (1972b) Archives, Protestors Set Fire to Embassy, available at: http://www.rte.ie/archives/2017/0201/849359-british-embassy-burns/ [accessed March 2016]

RTÉ (1974) Archives Prisoners Escape Disguised as Prison Officers 1974, available at: http://www.rte.ie/archives/2014/0818/637799-ira-prisoners-escape-from-portlaoise-prison/ [accessed at March 2016].

Ruane, F. (2007) Foreword, in Fahey, T., Russell, H., and Whelan, C.T. (eds), *Best of Times? Social Impact of the Celtic Tiger,* Dublin: Institute of Public Policy.

Said, E.W. (2003) *Orientalism* (2nd ed.), London: Penguin Books.

Sampson, R.J., Raudenbush, S.W., and Earls, F. (1997) Neighborhoods and Violent Crime: A Multilevel Study of Collective Efficacy, in *Science,* 277: 918–924.

Sarat, A. (1995) Violence, Representation, and Responsibility in Capital Trials: The View from the Jury, in *Indiana Law Journal,* 70: 1103–1135.

Sauder M., and Espeland, W.N. (2009) The discipline of rankings: Tight coupling and organizational change, in *American Sociological Review,* 74: 63–82.

Savelsberg, J. (1994) Knowledge, Domination, and Criminal Punishment, in *American Journal of Sociology,* 99(4): 911–943.

Schalet, A. (2011) *Not Under My Roof: Parents, Teens, and the Culture of Sex,* Chicago: University of Chicago Press.

Scharff Smith, P. (2012) A Critical Look at Scandinavian Exceptionalism: Welfare State Theories, Penal Populism and Prison Conditions in Denmark and Scandinavia, in: Ugelvik, T. and Dullum, J. (eds), *Penal Exceptionalism? Nordic Prison Policy and Practice,* London: Routledge.

Scharff Smith, P. and Ugelvik, T. (2017). *Scandinavian Penal History, Culture and Prison Practice,* London: Palgrave.

Scottish Home and Health Department (1971) *Treatment of Certain Male Long Term Prisoners and Potentially Violent Prisoners,* Edinburgh: Scottish Home and Health Department.

Scottish Home and Health Department (1975) *Crime and the Prevention of Crime – A Memorandum by the Scottish Council on Crime,* Edinburgh: Her Majesty's Stationary Office.

Scottish Home and Health Department (1987) *HM Chief Inspectorate Report on the Disturbances at Peterhead HMSO,* Edinburgh: Scottish Home and Health Department

Scottish Prison Service (1988a) Assessment and control: The management of violent and disruptive prisoners; a Scottish Prison Service discussion paper. Part 1, Issues and proposals, Edinburgh: Her Majesty's Stationary Office.

Scottish Prison Service (1988b) *Custody and Care: Policy and plans for the Scottish Prison Service,* Edinburgh: Her Majesty's Stationary Office.

Scottish Prison Service (1989) *Business Plan 1989-1992*, Edinburgh: SPS Planning Unit.

Scottish Prison Service (1990a) *Organising for Excellence – Organisation Review of the Scottish prison Service Final Report*, Edinburgh: Scottish Prison Service.

Scottish Prison Service (1990b) *Opportunity and Responsibility – Developing new approaches to the Management of the Long Term Prison System in Scotland*, Edinburgh: Scottish Prison Service

Scottish Prison Service (1990c) *Shared Enterprise: Outline Corporate Strategy for the Scottish Prison Service*, Edinburgh: Scottish Prison Service.

Scottish Prison Service (1993) *Scottish Prison Service: Framework Document*, Edinburgh: Scottish Prison Service.

Scottish Prison Service (1994) *Small Units in the Scottish Prison System: The Report of the Working Party on the Barlinnie Special Unit*, Edinburgh: Scottish Prison Service.

Scottish Prison Service (1995a) *Report of a Relational Audit Pilot at Darroch Hall*, Edinburgh: Scottish Prison Service.

Scottish Prison Service (1995b) *Vulnerable Prisoners Report*, Edinburgh: Scottish Prison Service.

Scottish Prison Service (1995c) *A Review of Regimes*, Edinburgh: Scottish Prison Service.

Scottish Prison Service (1995d) *Research Bulletin*, Edinburgh: Scottish Prison Service.

Scottish Prison Service (1996) *Factsheet*, Edinburgh: Scottish Prison Service.

Scottish Prison Service (1998) *Factsheet*, Edinburgh: Scottish Prison Service.

Scraton, P., Sim, J., and Skidmore, P. (1988) Through the Barricades: Prisoner Protest and Penal Policy in Scotland, in *Journal of Law and Society*, 15(3): 247–262.

Sewell, W.H. (1996) Historical Events as Transformation of Structures: Inventing Revolution at the Bastille, in *Theory and Society*, 6(25): 841–881.

Shalev, S. (2007) The Power to Classify: Avenues into a Supermax Prison, in Downes, D., Rock, P., Chinkin, C., and Gearty, C. (eds), *Crime, Social Control and Human Rights: From moral panics to states of denial, Essays in Honour of Stanley Cohen*, Cullompton: Willan Publishing.

Shammas, V.L. (2014) The pains of freedom: Assessing the ambiguity of Scandinavian penal exceptionalism on Norway's Prison Island, in *Punishment and Society*, 16(1): 104–123.

Shewan, D., Gemmell, M., and Davies, J.B. (1994) *Drug use and Scottish Prisons: Summary Report*, Edinburgh: Scottish Prison Service.

Simon, J. (1993) *Poor Discipline: Parole and the Social Control of the Underclass, 1890-1990*, Chicago/London: University of Chicago Press.

Simon, J. (2007) *Governing Through Crime: How the War on Crime Transformed American Democracy and Created a Culture of Fear*, New York: Oxford University Press.

Skarbek, D., 2020. *The Puzzle of Prison Order: Why Life Behind Bars Varies Around the World*, New York: Oxford University Press.

Smith, P. (2008) *A Culturalist Theory of Punishment?* Punishment and Culture, Chicago: University of Chicago Press.

Smith, D.J., and Young, P. (1999) Crime Trends in Scotland Since 1950, in Duff, P., and Hutton, N. (eds), *Criminal Justice in Scotland*, Aldershot: Ashgate.

Smith, M., Sparks, R., and Girling, E. (2000) Educating Sensibilities – The Image of 'The Lesson' in Children's Talk about Punishment, in *Punishment and Society*, 2(4): 395–415.

Sparks, R. (2001) Degree of Estrangement: The Cultural Theory of Risk and Comparative Penology, in *Theoretical Criminology*, 5(2): 159–176.

Sparks, R. (2002) Out of the `Digger': The Warrior's Honour and the Guilty Observer, in *Ethnography*, 3: 556–581.

Sparks, R. (2006) Ordinary Anxieties and States of Emergency: Statecraft and Spectatorship in New Politics of Insecurity, in Armstrong, S., and McAra, L (eds), *Perspectives on Punishment – The Contours of Control*, Oxford: Oxford University Press.

Sparks, R., Bottoms, A., and Hay, W. (1996) *Prisons and the Problem of Order*, Oxford: Oxford University Press.

Sparks, R., Girling, E., and Loader, I. (2001) Fear and Everyday Urban Lives, in *Urban Studies*, 38(5–6): 885–898.

Spencer, A. (1983) The Age of Responsibility, in *The Journal of the Association of Scottish Prison Governors*, 2: 24–29.

Steele, J. (1992) *The Bird That Never Flew*, London: Sinclair-Stevenson.

Stephen, I. (1988) The Barlinnie Special Unit: A Penal Experiment, in Backett, S., McNeil, J., and Yellowlees, A. (eds), *Imprisonment Today – Current Issues in the Prison Debate*, Basingstoke: Macmillan.

Stewart, D. (2009) *The path to devolution and change: A political history of Scotland under Margaret Thatcher*, London: Tauris Academic Studies.

Stewart, J. (2004) *Taking Stock: Scottish Social Welfare after Devolution*, Bristol: Policy Press

Stoler, A.L. (2002) Colonial Archives and the Arts of Governance, in *Archival Science*, 2: 87–109.

Stoler, A.L. (2009) *Along the Archival Grain: Epistemic Anxieties and Colonial Common Sense*, Princeton University Press.

Story, B. (2016) The Prison in the City: Tracking the Neoliberal Life of the "Million Dollar Block", in *Theoretical Criminology*, 20(3): 257–276.

Super, G. (2011) 'Like Some Rough Beast Slouching towards Bethlehem to Be Born': A Historical Perspective on the Institution of the Prison in South Africa, 1976–2004, in *British Journal of Criminology*, 51(1): 201–221.

Sutton, J. (2004) The Political Economy of Imprisonment in Affluent Western Democracies, 1960–1990, in *American Sociological Review*, 69: 170–189.

Sweeney, P. (1999) *The Celtic Tiger: Ireland's Continuing Economic Miracle*, Dublin: Oak Tree Press.

Swidler, A. (1986) Culture in Action: Symbols and Strategies, in *American Sociological Review*, 51: 273–286.

Swidler, A. (2001) *Talk of Love: How Culture Matters*, Chicago: University of Chicago Press.

Tata, C. (2010) Sentencing and Penal Decision-Making in Scotland, in Croall, H., Mooney, G., and Munro, M. (eds), *Criminal justice in Scotland*, Cullompton: Willan.

Terry, P. (2012) Rambling Recollections, unpublished.

The Katherine Howard Foundation, Irish Penal Reform Trust (2007) *The Whitaker Committee Report 20 Years on: Lessons Learned or Lessons Forgotten*, Dublin: The Katherine Howard Foundation.

Thompson, P. (1988) *Voice of the Past – Oral History* (2nd ed.), Oxford: Oxford University Press.

Tonry, M. (2001a) Symbol, Substance and Severity in Western Penal Politics, in *Punishment and Society*, 3(4): 517–536.

Tonry M. (2001b) Unthought Thoughts: The Influence of Changing Sensibilities on Penal Policies, in *Punishment and Society*, 3(1): 167–181.

Tonry, M. (2007a) Determinants of Penal Policy, in Tonry, M. (ed), *Crime, Punishment, and Politics in Comparative Perspective*, Chicago: Chicago University Press.

Tonry, M. (ed.) (2007b) Crime, Punishment, and Politics in Comparative Perspective, in Tonry, M. (ed.), *Crime and Justice: A Review of Research*, Chicago: University of Chicago Press.

Tonry, M. (2009) Explanations of American Punishment Policies: A National History, in *Punishment and Society*, 11: 377–394.

Tonry, M. (2015) Is Cross-National Comparative Research on the Criminal Justice System Useful? in *European Journal of Criminology*, 12(4): 505–516.

Tovey, H., and Share, P. (2003) *A Sociology of Ireland* (2nd ed.), Dublin: Gill and Macmillan.

Ugelvik, T., and Dullum, J. (eds.) (2012) *Penal Exceptionalism? Nordic Prison Policy and Practice*, London: Routledge.

Valverde, M. (1998) *Diseases of the Will – Alcohol and the Dilemmas of Freedom*, Cambridge: Cambridge University Press.

Valverde, M. (2017) *Michel Foucault*, London: Routledge.

Vaughan, D. (1996) *The Challenger Launch Decision: Risky Technology, Culture, and Deviance at NASA*, Chicago: University of Chicago Press.

Vaughan, D. (2004) Theorizing Disaster – Analogy, Historical Ethnography, and the Challenger Accident, in *Ethnography*, 5(3): 315–347.

Wacquant, L. (2009a) *Punishing the Poor: The Neoliberal Government of Social Insecurity, Durham*; London: Duke University Press.

Wacquant, L. (2009b) *Prisons of Poverty*, Expanded., Minneapolis; London: University of Minnesota Press.

Wagner-Pacifici, R., and Schwartz, B. (1991) The Vietnam Veterans Memorial: Commemorating a Difficult Past, in *American Journal of Sociology*, 97: 376–420.

Walker, A. (1987) What does FMI mean to me as a Governor, in *The Journal of Association of Scottish Prison Governors*, 6: 60–67.

Walsh, D., Taulbut, M., and Hanlon, P. (2010) The Aftershock of Deindustrialization—Trends in Mortality in Scotland and Other Parts of Post-Industrial Europe, in *The European Journal of Public Health*, 20(1): 58–64.

Walsh, D., McCartney, G., Collins, C., Taulbut, M., and Batty, G.D. (2016) History, politics and vulnerability: explaining excess mortality: A report by the Glasgow Centrefor Population Health, NHS Health Scotland, the University of the West of Scotland and University College London available at http://www.gcph.co.uk/assets/0000/5988/Excess_mortality_final_report_with_appendices.pdf [accessed August 2017]

Warner, K. (2007) Against the Narrowing of Perspectives: How Do We See Learning, Prisons and Prisoners? in *The Journal of Correctional Education*, 58(2): 170–183.

Warr, J. (2015) Transformative Dialogues (re)privileging the Informal in Prison Education, in *The Prison Journal*, 225: 18–25.

West, K. (2020) Feeling Things: From Visual to Material Jurisprudence, in *Law and Critique*, 31(1): 113–126.

Whitman, J.Q. (2003) *Harsh Justice*, New York: Oxford University Press.

Whyte, J.H. (1980) *Church and State* (2nd ed.), Dublin: Gill & Macmillan.

Wilde, M.J. (2004) How Culture Mattered at Vatican II: Collegiality Trumps Authority in the Council's Social Movement Organizations, in *American Sociological Review*, 69(4): 576-602.

Williams, R. (1964) *The Long Revolution*, Harmondsworth: Penguin.

Williams, R. (1976) *Keywords: A Vocabulary of Culture and Society*. New York: Oxford University Press.

Withers, P. (1984–1985) Staff Training and the Scottish Prison Service – A Model Approach and a Few Thought on Current Developments, in *The Journal of Association of Scottish Prison Governors*, 4: 13–22.

Working Party on Alternative Regimes (1985) Report of Working Party on Alternative Regimes, unpublished.

Wozniak, E. (1987) Education in Prisons: an Examination of the Origins and Development of Education in Scottish Prisons, in *Journal of the Association of Scottish Prison Officers*, 6(Spring).

Wozniak, E. (1989) The Inverness Segregation Unit, in Scottish Prison Service, in Wozniak, E. (ed), *Current Issue in Scottish Prisons: Systems of Accountability and Regimes for Difficult Prisoners – Proceedings of a Conference held at Stirling University 8th and 9th June 1988 and supported by the Criminology and Law Research Group and Scottish Prison Service*, Edinburgh: The Scottish Office.

Wozniak, E., and McAllister, D. (1992) *The Prison Survey*, Edinburgh: Central Research Unit.

Wozniak, E., Gemmell, M., and Machin, D. (1994) *The Second Prison Survey*, Edinburgh: Scottish Prison Service.

Young, H. (2007) Hard Man, New Man: Re/Composing Masculinities in Glasgow, c.1950-2000, in *Oral History*, 35(1): 71–81.

Index